HODDER GIBSON

Model Papers

WITH ANSWERS

PLUS: Official SQA 2014 & 2015
Past Papers With Answers

National 5
History

Model Papers, 2014 & 2015 Exams

HODDER
GIBSON
AN HACHETTE UK COMPANY

This book contains the official SQA 2014 and 2015 Exams for National 5 History, with associated SQA approved answers modified from the official marking instructions that accompany the paper.

In addition the book contains model papers, together with answers, plus study skills advice. These papers, some of which may include a limited number of previously published SQA questions, have been specially commissioned by Hodder Gibson, and have been written by experienced senior teachers and examiners in line with the new National 5 syllabus and assessment outlines, Spring 2013. This is not SQA material but has been devised to provide further practice for National 5 examinations in 2014 and beyond.

Hodder Gibson is grateful to the copyright holders, as credited on the final page of the Answer Section, for permission to use their material. Every effort has been made to trace the copyright holders and to obtain their permission for the use of copyright material. Hodder Gibson will be happy to receive information allowing us to rectify any error or omission in future editions.

Hachette UK's policy is to use papers that are natural, renewable and recyclable products and made from wood grown in sustainable forests. The logging and manufacturing processes are expected to conform to the environmental regulations of the country of origin.

Orders: please contact Bookpoint Ltd, 130 Park Drive, Milton Park, Abingdon, Oxon OX14 4SE. Telephone: (44) 01235 827720. Fax: (44) 01235 400454. Lines are open 9.00–5.00, Monday to Saturday, with a 24-hour message answering service. Visit our website at www.hoddereducation.co.uk. Hodder Gibson can be contacted direct on: Tel: 0141 848 1609; Fax: 0141 889 6315; email: hoddergibson@hodder.co.uk

This collection first published in 2015 by
Hodder Gibson, an imprint of Hodder Education,
An Hachette UK Company
2a Christie Street
Paisley PA1 1NB

Typeset by Aptara, Inc.

Printed in the UK

A catalogue record for this title is available from the British Library

ISBN: 978-1-4718-6062-1

3 2 1

2016 2015

Introduction

Study Skills – what you need to know to pass exams!

Pause for thought

Many students might skip quickly through a page like this. After all, we all know how to revise. Do you really though?

Think about this:

"IF YOU ALWAYS DO WHAT YOU ALWAYS DO, YOU WILL ALWAYS GET WHAT YOU HAVE ALWAYS GOT."

Do you like the grades you get? Do you want to do better? If you get full marks in your assessment, then that's great! Change nothing! This section is just to help you get that little bit better than you already are.

There are two main parts to the advice on offer here. The first part highlights fairly obvious things but which are also very important. The second part makes suggestions about revision that you might not have thought about but which WILL help you.

Part 1

DOH! It's so obvious but …

Start revising in good time

Don't leave it until the last minute – this will make you panic.

Make a revision timetable that sets out work time AND play time.

Sleep and eat!

Obvious really, and very helpful. Avoid arguments or stressful things too – even games that wind you up. You need to be fit, awake and focused!

Know your place!

Make sure you know exactly **WHEN and WHERE** your exams are.

Know your enemy!

Make sure you know what to expect in the exam.

How is the paper structured?

How much time is there for each question?

What types of question are involved?

Which topics seem to come up time and time again?

Which topics are your strongest and which are your weakest?

Are all topics compulsory or are there choices?

Learn by DOING!

There is no substitute for past papers and practice papers – they are simply essential! Tackling this collection of papers and answers is exactly the right thing to be doing as your exams approach.

Part 2

People learn in different ways. Some like low light, some bright. Some like early morning, some like evening / night. Some prefer warm, some prefer cold. But everyone uses their BRAIN and the brain works when it is active. Passive learning – sitting gazing at notes – is the most INEFFICIENT way to learn anything. Below you will find tips and ideas for making your revision more effective and maybe even more enjoyable. What follows gets your brain active, and active learning works!

Activity 1 – Stop and review

Step 1

When you have done no more than 5 minutes of revision reading STOP!

Step 2

Write a heading in your own words which sums up the topic you have been revising.

Step 3

Write a summary of what you have revised in no more than two sentences. Don't fool yourself by saying, "I know it, but I cannot put it into words". That just means you don't know it well enough. If you cannot write your summary, revise that section again, knowing that you must write a summary at the end of it. Many of you will have notebooks full of blue/black ink writing. Many of the pages will not be especially attractive or memorable so try to liven them up a bit with colour as you are reviewing and rewriting. **This is a great memory aid, and memory is the most important thing.**

Activity 2 – Use technology!

Why should everything be written down? Have you thought about "mental" maps, diagrams, cartoons and colour to help you learn? And rather than write down notes, why not record your revision material?

What about having a text message revision session with friends? Keep in touch with them to find out how and what they are revising and share ideas and questions.

Why not make a video diary where you tell the camera what you are doing, what you think you have learned and what you still have to do? No one has to see or hear it, but the process of having to organise your thoughts in a formal way to explain something is a very important learning practice.

Be sure to make use of electronic files. You could begin to summarise your class notes. Your typing might be slow, but it will get faster and the typed notes will be easier to read than the scribbles in your class notes. Try to add different fonts and colours to make your work stand out. You can easily Google relevant pictures, cartoons and diagrams which you can copy and paste to make your work more attractive and **MEMORABLE**.

Activity 3 – This is it. Do this and you will know lots!

Step 1

In this task you must be very honest with yourself! Find the SQA syllabus for your subject (www.sqa.org.uk). Look at how it is broken down into main topics called MANDATORY knowledge. That means stuff you MUST know.

Step 2

BEFORE you do ANY revision on this topic, write a list of everything that you already know about the subject. It might be quite a long list but you only need to write it once. It shows you all the information that is already in your long-term memory so you know what parts you do not need to revise!

Step 3

Pick a chapter or section from your book or revision notes. Choose a fairly large section or a whole chapter to get the most out of this activity.

With a buddy, use Skype, Facetime, Twitter or any other communication you have, to play the game "If this is the answer, what is the question?". For example, if you are revising Geography and the answer you provide is "meander", your buddy would have to make up a question like "What is the word that describes a feature of a river where it flows slowly and bends often from side to side?".

Make up 10 "answers" based on the content of the chapter or section you are using. Give this to your buddy to solve while you solve theirs.

Step 4

Construct a wordsearch of at least 10 × 10 squares. You can make it as big as you like but keep it realistic. Work together with a group of friends. Many apps allow you to make wordsearch puzzles online. The words and phrases can go in any direction and phrases can be split. Your puzzle must only contain facts linked to the topic you are revising. Your task is to find 10 bits of information to hide in your puzzle, but you must not repeat information that you used in Step 3. DO NOT show where the words are. Fill up empty squares with random letters. Remember to keep a note of where your answers are hidden but do not show your friends. When you have a complete puzzle, exchange it with a friend to solve each other's puzzle.

Step 5

Now make up 10 questions (not "answers" this time) based on the same chapter used in the previous two tasks. Again, you must find NEW information that you have not yet used. Now it's getting hard to find that new information! Again, give your questions to a friend to answer.

Step 6

As you have been doing the puzzles, your brain has been actively searching for new information. Now write a NEW LIST that contains only the new information you have discovered when doing the puzzles. Your new list is the one to look at repeatedly for short bursts over the next few days. Try to remember more and more of it without looking at it. After a few days, you should be able to add words from your second list to your first list as you increase the information in your long-term memory.

FINALLY! Be inspired...

Make a list of different revision ideas and beside each one write **THINGS I HAVE** tried, **THINGS I WILL** try and **THINGS I MIGHT** try. Don't be scared of trying something new.

And remember – "FAIL TO PREPARE AND PREPARE TO FAIL!"

National 5 History

The course requirements

The Assignment – how to be successful

The Assignment is an essay written under exam conditions and then sent to the SQA to be marked.

The Assignment counts for 20 marks out of a total of 80 so doing well in it can provide you with a very useful launch pad for future success.

How long does my essay have to be?

There are NO word limits in the Assignment – it is whatever you can write in one hour!

What should I write about?

First, it makes sense to choose a question from the syllabus you are studying, which you can check at: www.sqa.org.uk/sqa/47447.html.

Second, your essay title should be based on a question that allows you to use your evidence to answer the question. You must avoid titles that are just statements such as "The Slave Trade" or "Appeasement". They do not allow you to use information to provide an overall answer to your title question.

Finally, try NOT to make up questions that are too complicated or that ask two questions within the same title.

What is the Resource Sheet?

Your Resource Sheet provides a framework and notes for your essay.

It shows the marker

- that you have researched, selected and organised your information
- that you have thought about your work and reached a decision about the question in your title
- which sources you have used and demonstrates how you have used them.

Your Resource Sheet MUST be sent to the SQA with your finished essay.

Your Resource Sheet should NOT be just a collection of facts, figures and quotes. It should outline the main parts of your essay and remind you what to write.

The Exam Paper

The question paper is made up of three **sections**:

Section 1 – Historical Study: Scottish
Section 2 – Historical Study: British
Section 3 – Historical Study: European and World.

In each **section** you will select **one** part to answer questions on:

Section 1: Historical Study: Scottish

Part A: The Wars of Independence, 1286–1328 ✓
Part B: Mary Queen of Scots and the Scottish Reformation, 1542–1587 ✓
Part C: The Treaty of Union, 1689–1715 ✓
Part D: Migration and Empire, 1830–1939 ✓
Part E: The Era of the Great War, 1910–1928 ✓

Section 2: Historical Study: British

Part A: The Creation of the Medieval Kingdoms, 1066–1406
Part B: War of the Three Kingdoms, 1603–1651
Part C: The Atlantic Slave Trade, 1770–1807 ✓
Part D: Changing Britain, 1760–1900 ✓
Part E: The Making of Modern Britain, 1880–1951 ✓

Section 3: Historical Study: European and World

Part A: The Cross and the Crescent, the Crusades, 1071–1192
Part B: 'Tea and Freedom': the American Revolution, 1774–83 ✓
Part C: USA 1850–1880 ✓
Part D: Hitler and Nazi Germany, 1919–1939 ✓
Part E: Red Flag: Lenin and the Russian Revolution, 1894–1921 ✓
Part F: Mussolini and Fascist Italy, 1919–1939
Part G: Free at Last? Civil Rights in the USA, 1918–1968 ✓
Part H: Appeasement and the Road to War, 1918–1939 ✓
Part I: World War II, 1939–1945 ✓
Part J: The Cold War 1945–1989 ✓

The titles with the tick after them are all included in the model papers.

Answering the Exam Questions

The first rule is simple and is the most important thing that will get you marks:

Answer the question that you are asked, NOT what you would like it to ask.

The Exam paper has 6 types of questions.

TYPE 1 – the **"Describe"** question, worth **5 or 6 marks**.

In this type of question you must describe what happened by using five or six pieces of your own knowledge, known as **recall**. There is no source to help you with information so your answer will be based on your own recall.

TYPE 2 – the **"Explain"** question, worth **5 or 6 marks**.

To be successful with this type of question you must give 5 or 6 reasons why something happened. Once again, there is no source to help you. Use recall that is correct and accurate.

TYPE 3 – the **"To what extent…"** question, worth **8 marks**.

To be successful with this type of question you must write a balanced answer. That means you must decide how important a particular factor was in explaining why something happened. Include at least five pieces of relevant information and give a short conclusion which sums up your answer to the question.

TYPE 4 – the **"How useful…"** question, worth **5 or 6 marks**. This question will ask "Evaluate the usefulness of a source as evidence of …."

Evaluate means **to judge** how good a source is as evidence for finding out about something. The short answer is that it will always be partly useful but it will never be entirely useful in giving all the information you need.

In this type of question it is never enough just to **describe** what is in a source. It might be helpful to base your answer around the following guide questions.

WHO produced the source? Why is the AUTHORSHIP of the source relevant and therefore useful in assessing the value of a source?

WHEN was the source produced and how might that help in the evaluation of the source?

WHY was the source produced? What did the person who produced the source want the readers to think or do or feel because of the information in the source?

WHAT information is in the source and how relevant is that to the question?

WHAT'S NOT THERE? What important information is missing from the source that makes you think the source was not as useful as it could be?

TYPE 5 – the **"Compare"** question, worth **4 marks**

You will always get one question that asks you to compare two sources in your exam. To be successful with this type of question you must make clear connections between sources but do not just describe the two sources.

These questions are easy to spot because they are the only ones that will refer to TWO sources. For this type of question you must say whether you think the sources agree or not and then support your decision by making two comparisons using evidence from the sources.

TYPE 6 – the **"How fully…"** question, worth **5 or 6 marks**.

To be successful with this type of question you must select information from the source which is relevant to the question – usually there will be three points of information in the source for you to use. Use recall that is accurate and relevant to make your answer more balanced. You will never get a source that gives the full story so it is up to you to say that the source PARTLY explains or describes something but there is more information needed to give the full story. That's where you show off your recalled extra knowledge.

Good luck!

Remember that the rewards for passing National 5 History are well worth it! Your pass will help you get the future you want for yourself. In the exam, be confident in your own ability. If you're not sure how to answer a question, trust your instincts and just give it a go anyway. Keep calm and don't panic! GOOD LUCK!

Model Paper 1

Whilst this Model Paper has been specially commissioned by Hodder Gibson for use as practice for the National 5 exams, the key reference documents remain the SQA Specimen Paper 2013 and the SQA Past Papers 2014 and 2015.

National Qualifications MODEL PAPER 1

SQ23/N5/01

History

Duration — 1 hour and 30 minutes

Total marks — 60

SECTION 1 — SCOTTISH CONTEXTS — 20 marks

Attempt ONE part.

SECTION 2 — BRITISH CONTEXTS — 20 marks

Attempt ONE part.

SECTION 3 — EUROPEAN AND WORLD CONTEXTS — 20 marks

Attempt ONE part.

Before attempting the questions you must check that your answer booklet is for the same subject and level as this question paper.

On the answer booklet, you must clearly identify the question number you are attempting.

Use **blue** or **black** ink.

Before leaving the examination room you must give your answer booklet to the Invigilator. If you do not, you may lose all the marks for this paper.

SECTION 1 — SCOTTISH CONTEXTS

PARTS

SECTION 2 — BRITISH CONTEXTS

PARTS

SECTION 3 — EUROPEAN AND WORLD CONTEXTS

PARTS

SECTION 1 — SCOTTISH CONTEXTS — 20 marks

Attempt ONE part

Part A – The Wars of Independence, 1286–1328

Attempt the following questions using recalled knowledge and information from the sources where appropriate.

1. Describe the events between 1286 and 1292 that led to Edward I becoming overlord of Scotland.

    5

Source A explains King Edward's decision to attack Scotland.

Source A

> In 1296 the Scots organised a rebellion against Edward. They rejected his claim to be overlord of Scotland. This was a very dangerous step for Scotland which was less powerful than England. However, Scotland had made an alliance with France to fight against Edward. Angered by these actions, King Edward invaded Scotland and attacked Berwick.

2. How fully does **Source A** explain King Edward's decision to attack Scotland?
    (Use **Source A** and recall.)

    5

3. Explain the reasons why the leadership of William Wallace was important during the Wars of Independence?

    5

Source B is a description of a Scots raid on Northern England in 1322, written by an English monk.

Source B

> Now after 6th January 1322, when the truce between the kingdoms lapsed, the Scottish army invaded England and marched to Durham and the Scots went forward plundering the country in all directions. One of them raided towards the town of Richmond. The people of Richmond had no defenders and bought off the invaders with a great sum of money.

4. Evaluate the usefulness of **Source B** as evidence showing the tactics used by Robert I to persuade the English to accept him as King of Scots.

    5

    (You may want to comment on who wrote it, when they wrote it, why they wrote it, what they say or what has been missed out.)

SECTION 1 — SCOTTISH CONTEXTS

Part B – Mary Queen of Scots and the Scottish Reformation, 1542–1587

Attempt the following questions using recalled knowledge and information from the sources where appropriate.

1. Explain the reasons why Henry VIII of England ordered the invasions of Scotland after 1544.   **5**

Source A is from a contemporary *History of the Reformation in Scotland* by John Knox.

Source A

> That cruel man, falsely called Archbishop of St Andrews, arrested Walter Myln, a man of old age, and cruelly put him to death by fire in St. Andrews, on 28th April, 1558. That made so many people angry that a new strength of purpose developed amongst the whole people.
>
> On 2nd of May 1559, arrived John Knox from France, who went to Dundee, where he preached the reformed faith amongst them.

2. Evaluate the usefulness of **Source A** as evidence of the growth of Protestantism in Scotland before the Reformation of 1560?

   (You may want to comment on who wrote it, when they wrote it, why they wrote it, what they say or what has been missed out.)   **5**

Source B is a comment on how well Mary ruled Scotland.

Source B

> Until Mary allowed her heart to rule her head by marrying Darnley, she had been a successful ruler in Scotland. She had defeated the nobles who challenged her authority and had established a successful government under her half-brother Moray. As a Roman Catholic, her tolerant treatment of Scotland's new Protestant church was ahead of its time.

3. How fully does **Source B** explain how well Mary, Queen of Scots ruled Scotland? (Use **Source B** and recall.)   **5**

4. Describe the problems caused by Mary when she was in England.   **5**

SECTION 1 — SCOTTISH CONTEXTS

Part C – The Treaty of Union, 1689–1715

Attempt the following questions using recalled knowledge and information from the sources where appropriate.

1. Describe what happened during the Worcester affair.   5

Source A is from *History of the Union* (1709) by Daniel Defoe.

Source A

> The people cried out that they were Scotsmen and they would remain Scotsmen. They condemned the word "British" as fit only for the Welsh, who had already been made the subjects of the English. Scotland had always had a famous name in foreign courts, and had enjoyed privileges and honours there for many years. The common people went about the streets crying "no union", and called those negotiators traitors, and threatened them to their faces.

2. Evaluate the usefulness of **Source A** as evidence of the arguments for and against the Treaty of Union?

   (You may want to comment on who wrote it, when they wrote it, why they wrote it, what they say or what has been missed out.)   5

Source B is about the worries that some Scots had about the effects of the Union.

Source B

> Scots feared that, once they lost their independence, they would have little influence over government decisions. Others worried that businesses in Scotland would suffer from competition from English imports. They also thought the money paid to Scotland was a bribe to rich and powerful men—the only way that a Union could be passed.

3. How fully does **Source B** explain the opposition arguments used in the debate over the Union?
   (Use **Source B** and recall.)   5

4. Explain the reasons why many Scots were disappointed by the Act of Union by 1715.   5

SECTION 1 — SCOTTISH CONTEXTS

Part D – Migration and Empire, 1830–1939

Attempt the following questions using recalled knowledge and information from the sources where appropriate.

1. Explain the reasons why Irish immigrants were attracted to Scotland between 1830 and 1930.

    5

Source A is from a newspaper called *The Glasgow Reporter*, 4 March 1846.

Source A

> A mass attack of 300 Irish navvies working near Edinburgh to free two of their companions who had been imprisoned by the police, led to disastrous consequences for themselves and their families. One of the policemen died of his injuries received in the scuffle. A squad of police from Edinburgh then marched to where the Irish navvies were working, set fire to row after row of the Irishmen's huts and beat men, women and children out of the district.

2. Evaluate the usefulness of **Source A** as evidence of the impact of Irish immigration on law and order in Scotland.

    (You may want to comment on who wrote it, when they wrote it, why they wrote it, what they say or what has been missed out.)

    5

Source B explains why poor Scots were able to emigrate in the 19th century.

Source B

> Some landlords saw it as in their own interests to encourage poor tenants to seek their fortunes elsewhere. The landlords were willing to pay the full travelling costs, especially to Canada. Landlords often wrote off rent arrears so that the tenants would have some money for their new life and some even bought their cattle which provided the emigrant with some extra help. Glasgow and Edinburgh feared a massive influx of Highlanders and the city authorities made a contribution towards their expenses in emigrating.

3. How fully does **Source B** explain the reasons why so many Scots emigrated during the 19th century?
   (Use **Source B** and recall.)

    5

4. Describe ways in which Scots helped to improve the lands to which they emigrated.

    5

SECTION 1 — SCOTTISH CONTEXTS

Part E – The Era of the Great War, 1910–1928

Attempt the following questions using recalled knowledge and information from the sources where appropriate.

Source A is from Colonel Swinton, an officer who helped develop the tank during the First World War.

Source A

> The immediate purpose of the tank was the destruction of the machine gun which, until the tank appeared, was responsible for more deaths than any other weapon. The tank was the one completely British invention in the war and a great one. It was a great life-saver of infantry. The tank took the place of the artillery bombardment, with more certain results. It also reintroduced the element of surprise in an attack which the artillery bombardment had lost.

1. Evaluate the usefulness of **Source A** as evidence of the use of new technology during the First World War.

    (You may want to comment on who wrote it, when they wrote it, why they wrote it, what they say or what has been missed out.)   5

Source B is about women during World War One.

Source B

> During World War One, many things changed. As men left their jobs to go and fight, their places in industry were increasingly taken by women. Women's most vital work was in munitions factories where they produced weapons and shells. This work was both dirty and dangerous. Women worked on trams and buses to keep the transport system going. With so many men away fighting, women had to take the responsibility of being head of the family.

2. How fully does **Source B** describe the changing role of women during the First World War?
    (Use **Source B** and recall.)   5

3. Describe the economic difficulties faced by Scotland after 1918.   5

4. Explain the reasons why the actions of the militant Suffragettes harmed the campaign for votes for women.   5

SECTION 2 — BRITISH CONTEXTS — 20 marks

Attempt ONE part

Part C – The Atlantic Slave Trade, 1770–1807

Attempt the following questions using recalled knowledge and information from the sources where appropriate.

Source A is from a description in 1789 by a former slave, Olaudah Equiano, of his experiences during the Middle Passage.

Source A

> I can now tell of the hardships which cannot be separated from this accursed trade. The wretched conditions below decks were made worse by the chains. The shrieks of women, and the groans of the dying, rendered the whole scene one of unimaginable horror.

1. Evaluate the usefulness of **Source A** as evidence of the treatment of slaves during the Middle Passage.

   (You may want to comment on who wrote it, when they wrote it why they wrote it what they say or what has been missed out.)

   6

2. Describe the effects of the slave trade on African societies.

   5

3. Explain the concerns that people had about the treatment of slaves in the Caribbean.

   5

Sources B and **C** are about the importance of the slave trade for Britain.

Source B

> There were many reasons why it took so long to abolish the slave trade. One reason was that the slave trade had many powerful supporters. Plantation owners and merchants in British ports which relied on the slave trade were well organised and had political influence. They had enough wealth to bribe MPs to support them. They also had the support of King George III. Many people believed that the trade had helped them to make Britain wealthy and prosperous.

Source C

> The Abolitionists faced powerful opposition. The plantation owners allied themselves with important groups to promote the case for slavery and the slave trade. Their case seemed overwhelming. Dozens of British ports and surrounding areas relied on the slave trade. British consumers had become addicted to the products of the slave trade, most notably sugar. The Atlantic slave trade represented a large amount of British trade and seemed vital to the continuing prosperity of Britain and the Caribbean Islands.

4. Compare the views in **Sources B** and **C** about the reasons why the slave trade continued in Britain throughout the 18th century.
   (Compare the sources overall and/or in detail.)

   4

SECTION 2 — BRITISH CONTEXTS

Part D – Changing Britain, 1760–1900

Attempt the following questions using recalled knowledge and information from the sources where appropriate.

1. Explain the reasons why the health of the British population improved in the 19th century.

    5

Source A was written by a visitor to a cotton mill in Bolton, Lancashire in 1847.

Source A

> The factory people are better clothed and fed than many other working class people. I found the mill to be a large building and very clean. The working rooms were spacious and well ventilated. There were many windows in each room. This left me wondering if there was a window tax to pay. I observed that great care had been taken to put guards on dangerous machinery. I was told accidents in the factory were very rare and were caused by stupidity or negligence by the worker. However, accidents did occur.

2. Evaluate the usefulness of **Source A** as evidence about working conditions in cotton mills in the 19th century.

    (You may want to comment on who wrote it, when they wrote it, why they wrote it, what they say or what has been missed out.)

    6

3. Describe the impact of new technology on coal mining in the 19th century.

    5

Sources **B** and **C** explain the rise of the Chartist movement.

Source B

> Many working people had supported the 1832 Reform Act in the belief that this would be a first step towards wider democracy. They were angry at the Whig government's failure to deliver. Also, these were hard times; trade was poor, wages were low and faced further cuts and there was fury over the new Poor Law which established the workhouse system. This led to an increased demand for revolutionary change in society which found an outlet in Chartism. This was also a time when, following the repeal of the anti-trade union Combination Acts, working people were becoming more confident in forming their own organisations.

Source C

> The Great Reform Act of 1832 gave the vote to male householders who owned property which meant that more middle class men benefited. Only one man in every five had the vote in England this caused fury among many members of the working class who had expected to be given the vote. Two years later parliament passed the Poor Law Amendment Act which introduced the hated workhouses. This combined with the case of the Tolpuddle Martyrs created a working class backlash which gave rise to the Chartist movement.

4. Compare the views in **Sources B** and **C** on the reasons for the rise of the Chartist movement.
    (Compare the sources overall and/or in detail.)

    4

SECTION 2 — BRITISH CONTEXTS

MARKS

Part E – The Making of Modern Britain, 1880–1951

Attempt the following questions using recalled knowledge and information from the sources where appropriate.

Source A is from a speech by Lloyd George, a leading Liberal MP in 1906.

Source A

> What are some of the causes of poverty? There is the fact that a man's earnings are not enough to maintain himself and his family. There is the inability to obtain employment for economic reasons. There is the inability of men to work owing to sickness, old age or lack of physical stamina or vitality. Then there is the most fertile cause of all – a man's own habits such as drinking and gambling.

1. Evaluate the usefulness of **Source A** as evidence about the causes of poverty in the early 20th century.

   (You may want to comment on who wrote it, when they wrote it, why they wrote it, what they say or what has been missed out.)

   6

Sources B and **C** describe the impact of the Liberal social reforms.

Source B

> The Liberal social reforms were in no sense a welfare state. They were not intended as a comprehensive system of welfare provision. Rather, they involved targeting certain small areas of the problem of poverty. Those not included continued to need a safety net. The poor law was less important but still necessary.

Source C

> All the Liberal reforms offered levels of support that were only designed to support the poor, not free them from poverty. They helped to insure certain types of workers against sickness and unemployment. Some people were freed from having to seek poor relief but living on 5 shillings a week in old age was almost impossible.

2. Compare the views in **Sources B** and **C** as evidence about the impact of the Liberal reforms.
   (Compare the sources overall and/or in detail.)

   4

3. Describe the impact of the Blitz on people's attitude towards poverty.

   5

4. Explain the reasons why the Beveridge Report was popular with so many people.

   5

SECTION 3 — EUROPEAN AND WORLD CONTEXTS — 20 marks

Attempt ONE part

Part B – "Tea and Freedom": the American Revolution, 1774–1783

Attempt the following questions using recalled knowledge and information from the sources where appropriate.

1. Describe the Boston Tea Party and the British government's response to it.   **6**

Source A is from a letter written by the leaders of the 13 colonies when they met in May 1775.

Source A

> On the 19th day of April, General Gage sent out a large detachment of his army who made an unprovoked attack on the inhabitants of the town of Lexington. They murdered eight of the inhabitants and wounded many others. The troops then proceeded to the town of Concord, where they cruelly slaughtered several people and wounded many more, until they were forced to retreat by a group of brave colonists suddenly assembled to repel this cruel aggression.

2. Evaluate the usefulness of **Source A** as evidence about what happened at Lexington and Concord in April 1775.   **6**

   (You may want to comment on who wrote it, when they wrote it, why they wrote it, what they say or what has been missed out.)

3. To what extent did the involvement of foreign countries cause difficulties for Britain in the War of Independence?   **8**

SECTION 3 — EUROPEAN AND WORLD CONTEXTS

Part C – USA, 1850–1880

Attempt the following questions using recalled knowledge and information from the sources where appropriate.

1. Explain the reasons why tensions existed between Native Americans and white settlers.

   6

Source A is from George Ogden's diary in which he describes the impact of Reconstruction on black Americans in the South.

Source A

> My first impression of the South was shock at the shabby conditions of the living quarters that many black Americans still lived in. I was dismayed their life had shown no improvement. Initially I was puzzled why so many black Americans remained in the South, still working for their old masters, when they could move freely. Congress passed many laws. However, it always struck me as worrying that some white Americans felt justified in lynching and using violence against a black American. At first I found it strange that the white and black Americans did not work together in the field or elsewhere.

2. Evaluate the usefulness of **Source A** as attitudes towards Reconstruction in the South.

   (You may want to comment on who wrote it, when they wrote it, why they wrote it, what they say or what has been missed out.)

   6

3. To what extent did differing attitudes to the union bring about the Civil War?   **8**

SECTION 3 — EUROPEAN AND WORLD CONTEXTS

Part D – Hitler and Nazi Germany, 1919–1939

Attempt the following questions using recalled knowledge and information from the sources where appropriate.

1. Explain the reasons why the Spartacist Revolt failed.   6

Source A is from the memories of Sebastian Haffner who lived in Germany in 1918. They were published in 2002.

Source A

> Although November 1918 meant the end of the war, I recall no sense of joy. There was only confusion as men returned from the Front. On Saturday the papers announced the Kaiser's abdication. On Sunday, I heard shots fired in the streets of Berlin. During the whole war I hadn't heard a single shot, yet now the war was over they began shooting. I felt uneasy. On November 11th, I saw the newspaper headline "Armistice Signed". I turned to stone. I felt my whole world had collapsed.

2. Evaluate the usefulness of **Source A** as evidence about Germany at the end of the First World War.   6

   (You may want to comment on who wrote it, when they wrote, it why they wrote it, what they say or what has been missed out.)

3. To what extent was Hitler's success in 1933 due to violence and intimidation?   8

SECTION 3 — EUROPEAN AND WORLD CONTEXTS

Part E – Red Flag: Lenin and the Russian Revolution, 1894–1921

Attempt the following questions using recalled knowledge and information from the sources where appropriate.

1. Explain the reasons why the Orthodox Church was important in Tsarist Russia.

   6

2. To what extent was defeat in the Russo-Japanese war the main cause of the 1905 Revolution?

   8

Source A is from a letter by the leader of the Provisional Government to his parents on 3 July 1917.

Source A

> Without doubt, the country is heading for chaos. We are facing famine, defeat at the front and the collapse of law and order in the cities. There will be wars in the countryside as desperate refugees from the cities fight each other for food and land.

3. Evaluate the usefulness of **Source A** as evidence of the problems facing the Provisional Government.

   (You may want to comment on who wrote it, when they wrote it, why they wrote it, what they say or what has been missed.)

   6

SECTION 3 — EUROPEAN AND WORLD CONTEXTS

MARKS

Part G – Free at Last? Civil Rights in the USA, 1918–1968

Attempt the following questions using recalled knowledge and information from the sources where appropriate.

1. Describe the problems facing European immigrants to the USA in the 1920s.   **6**

Source A is from a speech made in 1954 by the Grand Dragon of the Federated Klans of Alabama.

Source A

> The Klan don't hate nobody! In fact, the Klan is the black man's best friend. He should behave himself and not allow himself to be fooled by the lies of Northerners. Then he will reap the rewards of hard work, instead of the disappointments of chasing unrealistic dreams!

2. Evaluate the usefulness of **Source A** as evidence of attitudes towards black Americans in the Southern states at the time of the Civil Rights Movement.   **6**

   (You may want to comment on who wrote it, when they wrote it, why they wrote it, what they say or what has been missed out.)

3. To what extent was the growth of the Civil Rights Movement due to the experience of black Americans in the Second World War?   **8**

SECTION 3 — EUROPEAN AND WORLD CONTEXTS

Part H – Appeasement and the Road to War, 1918–1939

Attempt the following questions using recalled knowledge and information from the sources where appropriate.

1. Describe the ways in which Britain appeased Germany between 1933 and 1936.   **6**

Source A is from a report by the British ambassador to Germany, August 1938.

Source A

> No matter how badly the Germans behave, we must also condemn Czechoslovakia. No one has much faith in the Czech government's honesty or even their ability to do the right thing over the Sudetenland. We must not blame the Germans for preparing their army because they are convinced that the Czechs want to start a war as soon as possible so they can drag Britain and France into it.

2. Evaluate the usefulness of **Source A** as evidence of Britain's attitude to Czechoslovakia in 1938.   **6**

    (You may want to comment on who wrote it, when they wrote it, why they wrote it, what they say or what has been missed out.)

3. To what extent was fear of bombing the main reason why the people of Europe wanted to avoid war during the 1930s?   **8**

SECTION 3 — EUROPEAN AND WORLD CONTEXTS

Part I – World War II, 1939–1945

Attempt the following questions using recalled knowledge and information from the sources where appropriate.

1. To what extent was sea power the main reason for American success in the war with Japan 1941–1945?

   8

Source A was written by a member of US President Truman's government in 1945.

Source A

> Using the atomic bomb was a mistake. Conventional bombing was increasingly effective. Using this barbarous weapon on Hiroshima and Nagasaki was of no real help in our war against Japan. The Japanese were already defeated and ready to surrender. The effectiveness of our sea blockade had brought them to their knees. It was all a dreadful waste of life.

2. Evaluate the usefulness of **Source A** as evidence of attitudes towards the atomic bombing of Japan.

   (You may want to comment on who wrote it, when they wrote it, why they wrote it, what they say or what has been missed out.)

   6

3. Explain the reasons why Germany was finally defeated in 1945.

   6

SECTION 3 — EUROPEAN AND WORLD CONTEXTS

Part J – The Cold War, 1945–1989

Attempt the following questions using recalled knowledge and information from the sources where appropriate.

1. To what extent was the Cold War caused by mutual suspicion between the USA and the USSR?   **8**

2. Describe the ways in which people showed their opposition to the war in Vietnam.   **6**

Source A is from a speech by President Leonid Brezhnev in 1976.

Source A

> We are attempting to follow the path of peaceful co-existence. We are trying to bring about lasting peace to reduce, and in the longer term to eliminate, the danger of another world war. This is the main element of our policy towards the capitalist states. It may be noticed that considerable progress in this area has been achieved in the last five years.

3. Evaluate the usefulness of **Source A** as evidence of the Soviet attitude towards détente.

    (You may want to comment on who wrote it, when they wrote it, why they wrote it, what they say or what has been missed out.)   **6**

[END OF MODEL PAPER]

Model Paper 2

Whilst this Model Paper has been specially commissioned by Hodder Gibson for use as practice for the National 5 exams, the key reference documents remain the SQA Specimen Paper 2013 and the SQA Past Papers 2014 and 2015.

**National
Qualifications
MODEL PAPER 2**

SQ23/N5/01

History

Duration — 1 hour and 30 minutes

Total marks — 60

SECTION 1 — SCOTTISH CONTEXTS — 20 marks

Attempt ONE part.

SECTION 2 — BRITISH CONTEXTS — 20 marks

Attempt ONE part.

SECTION 3 — EUROPEAN AND WORLD CONTEXTS — 20 marks

Attempt ONE part.

Before attempting the questions you must check that your answer booklet is for the same subject and level as this question paper.

On the answer booklet, you must clearly identify the question number you are attempting.

Use **blue** or **black** ink.

Before leaving the examination room you must give your answer booklet to the Invigilator. If you do not, you may lose all the marks for this paper.

SECTION 1 — SCOTTISH CONTEXTS
PARTS

SECTION 2 — BRITISH CONTEXTS
PARTS

SECTION 3 — EUROPEAN AND WORLD CONTEXTS
PARTS

SECTION 1 — SCOTTISH CONTEXTS – 20 marks

Attempt ONE part

MARKS

Part A – The Wars of Independence, 1286–1328

Attempt the following questions using recalled knowledge and information from the sources where appropriate.

1. Explain the reasons why the Scots asked King Edward of England to help them after the death of King Alexander III.   **5**

2. Describe the events that led to the defeat and capture of King John Balliol.   **5**

Source A was written by the English chronicler, Walter of Guisborough in 1298.

Source A

> On one side of a little hill close to Falkirk, the Scots placed their soldiers in four round circles with their pikes held outwards at an angle. Between these circles, which are called schiltrons, were the archers and behind them was the cavalry. When our men attacked, the Scots horsemen fled without striking a sword's blow.

3. Evaluate the usefulness of **Source A** as evidence of what happened at the Battle of Falkirk.   **5**

    (You may want to comment on who wrote it, when they wrote it, why they wrote it, what they say or what has been missed out.)

Source B explains why Bruce was not fully accepted as King of Scots until 1328.

Source B

> It took almost twenty-two years of fighting before Bruce was accepted as King of Scots. He had to force many Scots to abandon King John Balliol, and others to reject the claims of Edward II as overlord. Bruce emphasised his own royal blood to justify his claim and his victory at Bannockburn as a sign of God's approval. However, he was unable to change the mind of Edward II.

4. How fully does **Source B** explain the reasons why it took so long for Robert the Bruce to be accepted as King of Scots?   **5**
    (Use **Source B** and recall.)

SECTION 1 — SCOTTISH CONTEXTS

Part B – Mary Queen of Scots and the Scottish Reformation, 1542–1587

Attempt the following questions using recalled knowledge and information from the sources where appropriate.

1. Describe the events which led to the assassination of Cardinal Beaton at St Andrews in 1546.   **5**

Source A is from a book by F. Mignet called *The History of Mary, Queen of Scots,* published in 1851.

Source A

> Mary's actions before and after the murder are quite sufficient to convince us that she was involved in the murder plot. Her journey to Glasgow took place at a time when she was openly expressing her distrust and hatred of Darnley. She persuaded him to come with her to Edinburgh. Kirk o' Field was selected as the most convenient place to commit the crime. On the evening before the murder she removed from the house all the furniture of any value that it contained.

2. Evaluate the usefulness of **Source A** as evidence of the involvement of Mary, Queen of Scots, in the death of Darnley.

    (You may want to comment on who wrote it, when they wrote it, why they wrote it, what they say or what has been missed out.)   **5**

3. Explain the reasons why events surrounding Queen Mary's marriage to Bothwell led to her downfall.   **5**

Source B describes Mary's involvement in the Babington Plot in 1585.

Source B

> Mary enjoyed the excitement of plotting and sending coded letters hidden in a beer keg to Babington. Elizabeth's men knew about the plot from the beginning because they had a spy in Mary's household. The end came when Mary sent a letter enthusiastically approving the assassination of Elizabeth. When the letter was decoded, the spy drew a gallows on the letter.

4. How fully does **Source B** explain Mary's involvement in the Babington Plot in 1585? (Compare the sources overall and/or in detail.)   **5**

SECTION 1 — SCOTTISH CONTEXTS

Part C – The Treaty of Union, 1689–1715

Attempt the following questions using recalled knowledge and information from the sources where appropriate.

1. Explain the reasons why there was bad feeling between Scotland and England over the Worcester incident.   **5**

Source A is from a report by Daniel Defoe, an English spy sent to Scotland in 1706.

Source A

> I had not been in Edinburgh for long when I heard a great noise and, looking out, I saw a terrible mob coming up the High Street led by a drummer. They were shouting and swearing and crying out "all Scotland will stand together!", "No Union! No Union!", "English dogs" and things like that.

2. Evaluate the usefulness of **Source A** as evidence about Scottish attitudes to the Union.

   (You may want to comment on who wrote it, when they wrote it, why they wrote it, what they say or what has been missed out.)   **5**

3. Describe how the passing of the Act of Union helped the Jacobite Cause.   **5**

Source B was written about the effects of the Union on Scotland.

Source B

> Now that their Parliament is gone, the Scottish nobles and gentlemen spend their time and consequently their money in England. The Union has opened the door to English manufacturers and ruined Scottish ones. Their cattle are sent to England, but money is spent there too. The troops raised in Scotland are in English service and Scotland receives no money from them either.

4. How fully does **Source B** explain the effects of the Union on Scotland?
   (Use **Source B** and recall.)   **5**

SECTION 1 — SCOTTISH CONTEXTS

Part D – Migration and Empire, 1830–1939

Attempt the following questions using recalled knowledge and information from the sources where appropriate.

1. Describe the "pull" factors, which led many Irish people to leave for Scotland after 1830.

5

2. Explain the reasons why so many Scots disliked Irish immigrants.

5

Source A is from Angus Nicholson, Canada's Special Immigration Agent in the Highlands of Scotland. It was written in 1875.

Source A

> All the competing Emigration Agencies are still at work as actively as ever. The New Zealand and Australian authorities are particularly alert, the streets of every town and village being always well covered with their posters offering free passages to emigrants. It is extremely difficult for us to attract emigrants when these territories are offering free passages while we expect the emigrants to pay their own fares to Canada.

3. Evaluate the usefulness of **Source A** as evidence about the reasons for Scottish emigration.

   (You may want to comment on who wrote it, when they wrote it, why they wrote it, what they say or what has been missed out.)

5

Source B is about the impact of the Scots on the British Empire.

Source B

> Two countries more than any other have been moulded by the Scots: Canada and Australia. Though numbering only one fifteenth of the population, Scots dominated the government and controlled the fur trade, the educational institutions and the banks. Australia saw similar manipulation by Scots, John Macarthur introducing the Merino sheep and considered to be the founder of Australia's sheep industry.

4. How fully does **Source B** illustrate the impact of Scots emigrants on the British Empire?
   (Use **Source B** and recall.)

5

SECTION 1 — SCOTTISH CONTEXTS

Part E – The Era of the Great War, 1910–1928

Attempt the following questions using recalled knowledge and information from the sources where appropriate.

1. Explain the reasons why large numbers of Scots volunteered to fight during the war.   **5**

2. Describe how conscientious objectors were treated during the First World War.   **5**

Source A was written by a modern historian.

Source A

> By 1923, 14.3 percent of workers in Scotland were out of work compared with 11.6 per cent in the United Kingdom as a whole. It was also a different kind of unemployment from the short, irregular lay-offs which had marked the years before 1914. After the war it was long-term unemployment and it affected the skilled more than the unskilled. The huge demand for labour in wartime manufacturing had gone.

3. How fully does **Source A** show the effect of the war on the Scottish economy between 1914 and 1928?
   (Use **Source A** and recall.)

Source B is an extract from *Women's Suffrage*, written by a Suffragist, Milicent Fawcett, in 1912.

Source B

> The Women's Social and Political Union had not attracted any public notice until 1905. By adopting new and startling methods they succeeded in drawing a large amount of public attention to the cause of votes for women. However many campaigners viewed these methods with disgust. They believed the lawful and peaceful action would prove more effective in the long run as a way of converting the public and government to believe in women's suffrage.

4. Evaluate the usefulness of **Source B** as evidence of the contribution of the Suffragettes to the extension of female suffrage.

   (You may want to comment on who wrote it, when they wrote it, why they wrote it, what they say or what has been missed out.)   **5**

SECTION 2 — BRITISH CONTEXTS — 20 marks

Attempt ONE part

MARKS

Part C – The Atlantic Slave Trade, 1770–1807

Attempt the following questions using recalled knowledge and information from the sources where appropriate.

Source A was written by a modern historian in 1997.

Source A

> Most slaves in the West Indies were involved in the production of sugar which was hard, heavy work. The life of the slave on the plantation was controlled by strict slave laws, or codes. Some slaves, however, refused to accept their circumstances and attempted to escape or plotted revolt. Those who escaped would be hunted down. Slave owners lived in constant fear of a revolt by their slaves. Slave risings took place throughout the colonies but very few had effective leadership and they were soon crushed by the better armed and organised whites.

1. Evaluate the usefulness of **Source A** as evidence about why resistance was difficult for slaves on the plantations.

   (You may want to comment on who wrote it, when they wrote it, why they wrote it, what they say or what has been missed out.)   **6**

2. To what extent was the abolitionist movement important in bringing about the end of the slave trade?   **8**

3. Explain the reasons why the need for the slave trade declined in Britain by the late 18th century.   **6**

SECTION 2 — BRITISH CONTEXTS

MARKS

Part D – Changing Britain, 1760–1900

Attempt the following questions using recalled knowledge and information from the sources where appropriate.

1. To what extent were improvements in health in Britain's towns due to better sanitation?

   8

2. Describe the impact of the growth of the railway network on the British economy.

   6

Source A is from a Police spy's report of a Chartist meeting in November 1839.

Source A

> One man shouted that they should petition the Queen to ask for universal suffrage. Many answered him saying that they would rather fight and die for it. The man then said that if the Queen would not give them universal suffrage then he would be willing to fight. Mr Parks than addressed the meeting. He asked how many in the room were ready to fight. About half raised their hands.

3. Evaluate the usefulness of **Source A** as evidence of the aims of the Chartists.

   (You may want to comment on who wrote it, when they wrote it, why they wrote it, what they say or what has been missed out.)

   6

SECTION 2 — BRITISH CONTEXTS

Part E – The Making of Modern Britain, 1880–1951

Attempt the following questions using recalled knowledge and information from the sources where appropriate.

Source A is by the Aberdeen association for Improving the Conditions of the Poor. It was written in the late 19th century.

Source A

> Our aims are to encourage, in every available way, the efforts of the poor to live sober lives and to discourage idleness. In general, we want to help those who are sober and hardworking but who through illness or accident are in danger of being plunged into poverty. These are the only people who deserve our help.

1. Evaluate the usefulness of **Source A** as evidence of attitudes to the poor at the end of the 19th century.

   (You may want to comment on who wrote it, when they wrote it, why they wrote it, what they say or what has been missed out.)   **6**

2. Explain the reasons why the Second World War changed people's attitudes towards welfare reform.   **6**

3. To what extent was free health care the main reason why people welcomed the Labour reforms?   **8**

SECTION 3 — EUROPEAN AND WORLD CONTEXTS — 20 marks

Attempt ONE part

Part B – "Tea and Freedom": the American Revolution, 1774–1783

Attempt the following questions using recalled knowledge and information from the sources where appropriate.

1. Describe what happened during the Gaspée incident in 1772. **5**

Source A describes the Battle of Bunker Hill

Source A

> In June 1775, General Howe was ordered to re-capture the high ground known as Bunker Hill which had been occupied by the colonists. On the morning of 17th June, the British navy opened fire on the colonists' positions, but their shells fell short. They then charged the hill on three occasions in order to drive the American forces away.

2. How fully does **Source A** describe what happened at the Battle of Bunker Hill? **5**
   (Use **Source A** and recall.)

Sources B and **C** are about the defeat of British forces, led by General Cornwallis, at Yorktown.

Source B

> In 1781, Cornwallis moved into Virginia and began to build a base at Yorktown. By late summer, Cornwallis's position at Yorktown was deteriorating fast. While American forces prevented him from moving inland, a large French fleet carrying 3,000 troops had sailed up from the West Indies to join the siege. The fate of Cornwallis was sealed when the French defeated the British fleet in Chesapeake Bay. On October 19 Cornwallis surrendered his entire army of 7,000 men.

Source C

> To launch his campaign in Virginia, Cornwallis's army carried out raids, harassing the Americans wherever he could. In August 1781, Cornwallis set up camp at Yorktown but this turned out to be a poor position. American troops moved quickly to surround him and keep him there. The British could not help Cornwallis's army to escape or bring in reinforcements. In September, the French defeated the British fleet in a naval battle near Yorktown, giving the allies control over the sea in the area.

3. Compare the views in **Sources B** and **C** about the reasons for the defeat of the forces led by Cornwallis at Yorktown. **4**
   (Compare the sources overall and/or in detail.)

4. Explain the reasons why the colonists were able to achieve victory in their war against the British by 1783. **6**

SECTION 3 — EUROPEAN AND WORLD CONTEXTS

Part C – USA, 1850–1880

Attempt the following questions using recalled knowledge and information from the sources where appropriate.

1. Describe the effects of the westward expansion of Mormons.   **5**

Source A is about the events at Fort Sumter in April, 1861.

Source A

> Lincoln sent a naval expedition to supply Fort Sumter with food. Unwilling to permit this, the Confederates opened fire on the fort on April 12th, before the ships arrived. After holding out for 34 hours, Major Robert Anderson and his men surrendered. The attack started an outburst of patriotic fever in the North. America's civil war had begun.

2. How fully does **Source A** explain the outbreak of the Civil War?   **6**
   (Use **Source A** and recall.)

3. Explain how important a problem the restrictions of the Black Codes were for Black Americans in the South after 1865.   **5**

Source B is from George Ogden's diary in which he describes the impact of Reconstruction.

Source B

> My first impression of the South was shock at the shabby conditions of the living quarters that many Black Americans still lived in. I was dismayed their life had shown no improvement. Initially I was puzzled why so many Black Americans remained in the South, still working for their old masters, when they could move freely. Congress passed many laws. However, it always struck me as worrying that some White Americans felt justified in lynching and using violence against a Black American. At first I found it strange that the White and Black Americans did not work together in the field or elsewhere.

Source C is from a history textbook and describes life during Reconstruction.

Source C

> Freed black slaves had gained their freedom but because they were too poor, many stayed in the South. The 1875 Civil Rights Act was the last government attempt to improve conditions for black people, but it had little effect in the South. Black churches and Freedmen's Bureaus made education more available for black Americans so the percentage of illiteracy went down. In effect, black people came nowhere near attaining social acceptance, with many white Americans remaining fearful and hostile, encouraging little interaction. Secret organisations were set up to terrorise black people.

4. Compare the views in **Sources B** and **C** about the effects of Reconstruction in the South.   **4**
   (Compare the sources overall and/or in detail.)

SECTION 3 — EUROPEAN AND WORLD CONTEXTS

Part D – Hitler and Nazi Germany, 1919–1939

Attempt the following questions using recalled knowledge and information from the sources where appropriate.

1. Describe the effects of the Paris Peace Settlement on Germany.   5

2. Explain the reasons why Hitler was able to increase his control over Germany in 1933/34.   5

Source A explains the reasons why Germans supported the Nazis.

Source A

> The most important thing for me was that I had personally to choose between a future Communist Germany or a future National Socialist Germany. My mother saw an SA parade on the streets of Heidelburg. The sight of their discipline in a time of chaos won her over even though she had never read a Nazi pamphlet.

3. How fully does **Source A** explain the reasons why Germans supported the Nazi Party in the 1930s?
   (Use **Source A** and recall.)   6

Source B was written by a member of the League of German Maidens.

Source B

> We had to be present for meetings with local leaders and businessmen. We had to attend events relating to health and well-being. Our week-ends were crammed full with camps and sporting activities. It was fun in a way. We certainly had a lot of exercise, but it had a bad effect on my school work. None of this was going to help me to get a good career in the future.

Source C is by a modern historian.

Source C

> Many young Germans enjoyed the emphasis on activity and sport. However, those who had wanted to achieve academic success were frustrated and resentful at the amount of time spent on outdoor activities. Girls in particular felt that their education was being downgraded and their future prospects were being limited.

4. Compare the views in **Sources B** and **C** on the effects of Nazi policies on young people.
   (Compare the sources overall and/or in detail.)   4

SECTION 3 — EUROPEAN AND WORLD CONTEXTS

MARKS

Part E – Red Flag: Lenin and the Russian Revolution, 1894–1921

Attempt the following questions using recalled knowledge and information from the sources where appropriate.

Source A explains the treatment of national minorities in the Russian Empire.

Source A

> The diversity of the Empire made it difficult to govern. Many minorities resented the policy of Russification. It made non-Russians use the Russian language instead of their own. Russian style clothes were to be worn and Russian customs were to be adopted. Russian officials were put in to run regional government in non-Russian parts of the Empire like Poland, Latvia and Finland. When Poles complained they were treated as second class citizens, they were told to change and become Russian citizens.

1. How fully does **Source A** explain the reasons why national minorities disliked the policy of Russification?
   (Use **Source A** and recall.)   **6**

2. Explain the reasons why the Tsar was able to remain in power following the 1905 revolution.   **5**

3. Describe Lenin's return to Russia in April 1917.   **5**

Sources B and **C** discuss the reasons for the success of the October Revolution.

Source B

> The Bolsheviks were a small group of extremists who were able to seize power for themselves. They did not have the support of Russian people. There was nothing inevitable about this. The Bolsheviks simply took advantage of the chaos brought about by the First World War. The revolution was a skillfully led military operation with little popular involvement resulting in a dictatorship being imposed on the Russian people

Source C

> In the months leading up to the revolution Bolshevik demands for Peace, Bread and Land won them massive support from workers and peasants. Lenin succeeded because he spoke for the ordinary people. The October revolution was a popular rising which was guided by the Bolsheviks. The events of October 1917 were the next stage of an inevitable process driven by a desire for greater justice for the downtrodden people of the world.

4. Compare the views in **Sources B** and **C** as evidence about the reasons for the Bolshevik success in October 1917.
   (Compare the sources overall and/or in detail.)   **4**

SECTION 3 — EUROPEAN AND WORLD CONTEXTS

Part G – Free at Last? Civil Rights in the USA, 1918–1968

Attempt the following questions using recalled knowledge and information from the sources where appropriate.

1. Describe the activities of the Ku Klux Klan in the 1920s and 1930s.

    5

2. Explain the reasons for the growth of the Civil Rights Movement after World War II.

    5

Sources A and **B** describe the results of the Montgomery Bus Boycott.

Source A

> Throughout the boycott a young black preacher inspired the black population of Montgomery. His name was Martin Luther King and this was to be his first step towards becoming the leading figure in the Civil Rights Movement. The boycott lasted over a year until eventually the courts decided that segregation on Montgomery's buses was illegal. On its own the bus boycott only had limited success. Montgomery remained a segregated town. There were still white-only theatres, pool rooms and restaurants.

Source B

> The bus company's services were boycotted by 99% of Montgomery's African Americans for over a year. As a result of the protest, the US Supreme Court announced that Alabama's bus segregation laws were illegal. However, most other facilities and services in Montgomery remained segregated for many years to come. As a result of the boycott, Martin Luther King became involved in the Civil Rights Movement. He went on to become an African American leader who was famous throughout the world.

3. Compare the views in **Sources A** and **B** about the results of the Montgomery Bus Boycott.
    (Compare the sources overall and/or in detail.)

    4

Source C explains why Malcolm X opposed non-violent protest.

Source C

> Malcolm X was mistreated in his youth and this gave him a different set of attitudes to Martin Luther King. Later, while in jail, he was influenced by the ideas of Elijah Muhammad who preached hatred of the white race. In his speeches he criticised non-violence. He believed that the support of non-violence was a sign that black people were still living in mental slavery. However, Malcolm X never undertook violent action himself and sometimes prevented it. Instead he often used violent language and threats to frighten the government into action

4. How fully does **Source C** explain the reasons why Malcolm X opposed non-violent protest?
    (Use **Source C** and recall.)

    6

SECTION 3 — EUROPEAN AND WORLD CONTEXTS

MARKS

Part H – Appeasement and the Road to War, 1918–1939

Attempt the following questions using recalled knowledge and information from the sources where appropriate.

Source A explains why Britain and France were worried about Germany's actions.

Source A

> From 1933 onwards it looked as if Germany's policies were beginning to change. As soon as he could, Hitler removed the German representatives from the Disarmament Conference in Geneva. Hitler was working hard to create an image of strong leadership among his own people and most of them supported him when Germany gave up her membership of the League of Nations. Germany's non-aggression treaty with Poland meant that France lost a valuable ally in Eastern Europe. In 1935 Germany announced the creation of an air force and navy.

1. How fully does **Source A** describe the worries Britain and France had about Germany's actions by 1936?
   (Use **Source A** and recall.)   6

2. Explain the reasons why Germany wanted to expand its territories between 1933 and 1938.   5

Sources B and **C** are about the Germans in the Sudetenland, Czechoslovakia.

Source B

> Germany's justification for interfering in Czechoslovakia was that the Sudetenland wanted to return to the German Fatherland. Ever since 1919 the Sudeten Germans had resented being part of the new state of Czechoslovakia which was based on the medieval kingdom of Bohemia. The German government claimed that the Germans in Czechoslovakia had suffered constant persecution because they were an ethnic minority.

Source C

> Sudeten German unrest grew only after the economic depression began in the early 1930s. Germany seemed to be the only country whose economy was improving. Although they shared the same language and culture, the Sudetenland had never been part of Germany. Since 1919, the Sudeten Germans had been treated with respect in Czechoslovakia because they had contributed greatly to the nation's wealth.

3. Compare the views of **Sources B** and **C** about the Germans living in Czechoslovakia.
   (Compare the sources overall and/or in detail.)   4

4. Describe the events in 1939 that led to the outbreak of war between Britain and Germany.

SECTION 3 — EUROPEAN AND WORLD CONTEXTS

MARKS

Part I – World War II, 1939–1945

Attempt the following questions using recalled knowledge and information from the sources where appropriate.

1. Explain the reasons why German forces were so successful in the early years of the war.

   5

Source A is about the activities of the French Resistance.

Source A

> For two years the resistance movements of Europe had found it hard to make much of an impression on the might of the German military. However, they had been useful in gathering intelligence for the Allies. The devastating attacks of 1939 to 1941 had given little time for each country to prepare any kind of a secret army to undermine the invaders. Resistance members organised themselves in secret to discover French collaborators, kill many ranking Nazi officials, and destroy trains, convoys, and ships used by the German army.

2. How fully does **Source A** explain how effective resistance groups were in Nazi occupied Europe?
   (Use **Source A** and recall.)

   6

3. Describe the difficulties faced by the allies in planning and carrying out the Normandy landings.

   5

Source B was written by a member of US President Truman's government in 1945.

Source B

> Using the atomic bomb was a mistake. Conventional bombing was increasingly effective. Using this barbarous weapon on Hiroshima and Nagasaki was of no real help in our war against Japan. The Japanese were already defeated and ready to surrender. The effectiveness of our sea blockade had brought them to their knees. It was all a dreadful waste of life.

Source C was written by an Allied prisoner of the Japanese after the Second World War.

Source C

> There is no doubt in my mind or the other prisoners' that using the atomic bomb was justified. The bomb saved the lives of thousands of prisoners as well as the Allied servicemen who would have had to invade Japan. Make no mistake, the Japanese government had decided to fight on to the last man. Listen to the emperor's speeches if you don't believe me. I have no doubt Hiroshima and Nagasaki made them surrender sooner.

4. Compare the views of **Source B** and **C** about the use of the atomic bomb on Japan.
   (Compare the sources overall and/or in detail.)

   4

SECTION 3 — EUROPEAN AND WORLD CONTEXTS

MARKS

Part J – The Cold War, 1945–1989

Attempt the following questions using recalled knowledge and information from the sources where appropriate.

1. Describe the events which led to the formation of the Warsaw Pact in 1955.   5

Sources **A** and **B** are about the Cuban Missile Crisis.

Source A

> Under Fidel Castro, Cuba was a proud example of a Communist country and was a role model to other countries. Khrushchev had the idea of installing a small number of nuclear missiles on Cuba without letting the USA know until it was too late to stop them. Khrushchev said they only wanted to keep the Americans from invading Cuba. He stated they had no desire to start a war.

Source B

> To the American government, placing missiles on Cuba was a warlike act by the Soviets. They believed that the Soviet Union intended to supply a large number of powerful nuclear weapons. Spy photographs proved the offensive purpose of the missiles which were pointed directly at major American cities. It was estimated that within a few minutes of them being fired, 80 million Americans would be dead.

2. Compare the views in **Sources A** and **B** about the Soviet Union's actions during the Cuban Missile Crisis.
   (Compare the sources overall and/or in detail.)   4

Source **C** explains why the United States became involved in a war in Vietnam.

Source C

> In its early stages, the war in Vietnam had nothing to do with the USA. American involvement began when it was asked by its ally, France, for assistance. France was fighting to regain control over its former colony. The Americans agreed. They disapproved of French colonialism, but feared Communism more. They believed that they could establish a friendly government in South Vietnam, under the leadership of President Diem. By the early 1960s an increase in Vietcong attacks in South Vietnam led to a fear that a civil war was developing.

3. How fully does **Source C** explain the reasons why America became involved in a full scale war in Vietnam by 1964?
   (Use **Source C** and recall.)   6

4. Explain the reasons why a crisis developed in Berlin in 1961.   5

[END OF MODEL PAPER]

Model Paper 3

Whilst this Model Paper has been specially commissioned by Hodder Gibson for use as practice for the National 5 exams, the key reference documents remain the SQA Specimen Paper 2013 and the SQA Past Papers 2014 and 2015.

National Qualifications
MODEL PAPER 3

SQ23/N5/01 — History

Duration — 1 hour and 30 minutes

Total marks — 60

SECTION 1 — SCOTTISH CONTEXTS — 20 marks

Attempt ONE part.

SECTION 2 — BRITISH CONTEXTS — 20 marks

Attempt ONE part.

SECTION 3 — EUROPEAN AND WORLD CONTEXTS — 20 marks

Attempt ONE part.

Before attempting the questions you must check that your answer booklet is for the same subject and level as this question paper.

On the answer booklet, you must clearly identify the question number you are attempting.

Use **blue** or **black** ink.

Before leaving the examination room you must give your answer booklet to the Invigilator. If you do not, you may lose all the marks for this paper.

SECTION 1 — SCOTTISH CONTEXTS

PARTS

SECTION 2 — BRITISH CONTEXTS

PARTS

SECTION 3 — EUROPEAN AND WORLD CONTEXTS

PARTS

SECTION 1 — SCOTTISH CONTEXTS — 20 marks

Attempt ONE part

Part A – The Wars of Independence, 1286–1328

Attempt the following questions using recalled knowledge and information from the sources where appropriate.

Sources **A** and **B** are about who should be the next King of Scots.

Source A

> John Balliol said he had the strongest right to be King of Scots. He argued this was because he was descended from the eldest daughter in the family of David, Earl of Huntingdon, the brother of King William the Lion. Balliol said it did not matter that he was a generation younger than Bruce because the feudal law of primogeniture always supported the eldest line of a family.

Source B

> Robert Bruce was determined that he was to be the next King of Scots. He said that Imperial Law supported him because he was one generation closer to the Earl of Huntingdon's family than Balliol. Bruce argued that the feudal law of primogeniture did not apply to kingdoms. He argued that it did not matter that Balliol was descended from the eldest of Earl David's daughters.

1. Compare the views in **Sources A** and **B** about who should be the next King of Scots. (Compare the sources overall and/or in detail.)   **4**

2. Explain the reasons why Balliol was a failure as King of Scots.   **5**

Source C describes the Battle of Stirling Bridge.

Source C

> The Scots allowed as many of the English to cross the bridge as they could hope to defeat, and then, having blocked the bridge, they slaughtered all who had crossed over. Among those who perished was Cressingham. De Warenne escaped with difficulty and with a small following.

3. How fully does **Source C** explain what happened at the Battle of Stirling Bridge? (Use **Source C** and recall.)   **6**

4. Describe how Robert Bruce made all the Scots accept him as King.   **5**

SECTION 1 — SCOTTISH CONTEXTS

Part B – Mary Queen of Scots and the Scottish Reformation, 1542–1587

Attempt the following questions using recalled knowledge and information from the sources where appropriate.

Source A explains why King Henry VIII interfered in Scotland after 1542.

Source A

> King James V of Scots died in 1542, only eight days after the birth of his daughter Mary. King Henry VIII of England immediately realised the benefits of marrying the young Queen Mary to his son. It would also end French influence in Scotland and bring about an end to centuries of warfare between Scotland and England. The most recent war had contributed to the early death of James V. Henry VIII also saw an opportunity to spread Protestantism north of the border.

1. How fully does **Source A** explain the reasons why King Henry VIII interfered in Scotland after 1542?
   (Use **Source A** and recall.)

   6

2. Describe the problems that Mary, Queen of Scots faced when she arrived in Scotland in 1561.

   5

Sources B and **C** describe what happened in Scotland after Mary, Queen of Scots, fled to England.

Source B

> Queen Mary's supporters fought for several years after she fled to England. They hoped that the tribunal Elizabeth held in England would lead to their Queen's return. When this failed, one of Mary's supporters assassinated the Regent Moray. A year later, his replacement, the Earl of Lennox, was killed in a skirmish. The capture of Edinburgh Castle in 1573 removed Mary's last power base in Scotland.

Source C

> Mary's support in Scotland was undermined in 1569 when her Governor, Châtelherault and his deputy, the Earl of Argyll, changed sides. Nevertheless, her supporters killed both the Regent Moray and his successor. In 1573, after a few years of fighting, the Regent Morton finally persuaded most of Mary's supporters to recognise his authority. A few months later, Edinburgh Castle was forced to surrender.

3. Compare the views in **Sources B** and **C** about what happened in Scotland after Mary, Queen of Scots, fled to England.
   (Compare the sources overall and/or in detail.)

   4

4. Explain the reasons why Queen Elizabeth kept Mary, Queen of Scots, in prison for so long.

   5

SECTION 1 — SCOTTISH CONTEXTS

MARKS

Part C – The Treaty of Union, 1689–1715

Attempt the following questions using recalled knowledge and information from the sources where appropriate.

Source A explains why so many Scots decided to invest in the Darien Scheme.

Source A

> After the Union of the Crowns, the Scots became aware that the prosperity of their country depended on farming which suffered from bad weather and poor soil. In fact, very little was done to improve Scottish farming for another fifty years. Scottish overseas trade was limited and it did not make huge amounts of money for the country. The Scots thought that England's prosperity came from its overseas trade with its colonies. William Paterson promised them a colony where "trade will increase and money will make money".

1. How fully does **Source A** show why the Scots invested in the Darien Scheme?   6
    (Use **Source A** and recall.)

Sources B and **C** are about why some Scots suggested a Union.

Source B

> Queen Anne had always wanted a union between her two kingdoms. A number of Scots supported the idea believing that trading with England's colonies would make Scotland a wealthier country. Many English people worried that a union would make England poorer. England's frequent wars with France annoyed the Scots because Scotland's trade with France was badly affected. The Scottish "Act of Security" offered England a shared monarch in return for access to its colonies.

Source C

> Bad feelings between Scotland and England erupted into a crisis when Anne became Queen in 1702. The Scots were angry because the ban from trading with England's colonies stopped them from increasing their wealth, especially since they blamed England for the failure of Darien. In 1703, they demanded access to England's colonies in return for sharing a monarch. Then they passed the Wine Act to reduce the bad effects of England's wars against France on Scotland's trade.

2. Compare the views in **Sources B** and **C** about why some Scots suggested a Union.   4
    (Compare the sources overall and/or in detail.)

3. Describe how Queen Anne's government won support for the Act of Union.   5

4. Explain the reasons why support for the Jacobites grew between 1707 and 1715.   5

SECTION 1 — SCOTTISH CONTEXTS

MARKS

Part D – Migration and Empire, 1830–1939

Attempt the following questions using recalled knowledge and information from the sources where appropriate.

1. Describe the "push" factors, which led many Irish to emigrate after 1830. **5**

Source A explains why the Catholic Church was important for many Irish immigrants in the 19th century.

Source A

> The Irish immigrants were not very well-off and the native Scots often did not welcome them. The church gave them a place to worship and a sense of security. Immigrants knew that they could be baptised, married and buried according to their religion. The priests usually spoke Irish so there was someone to whom they could explain their problems. Over time a number of Catholic churches were established in the west of Scotland. The church became a centre of social life and gave the immigrants an opportunity to meet their fellow countrymen.

2. How fully does **Source A** explain the importance of the Catholic Church to many Irish immigrants in the 19th century?
    (Use **Source A** and recall.) **6**

3. Explain the reasons why so many Scots emigrated between 1830 and 1900. **5**

Sources B and **C** are about the experiences of Scottish emigrants.

Source B

> I feel that everything the agent told me about this country has turned out to be false and I dearly wish to return home. I am very much dissatisfied with the poor quality of the land which will never be of much use. The nearest town is two days' journey away and my daughter and I suffer a great deal from loneliness.

Source C

> I have already prepared 14 acres of good land and, if I am spared, I shall have 40 ready next year. I got a splendid horse and a good cow and a calf, plenty milk and butter, plenty to eat of everything. Our wee community is doing well and our fellow immigrants have already built a church and a school-house. There is not a better place in the whole world.

4. Compare the views in **Sources B** and **C** about the experiences of Scottish emigrants.
    (Compare the sources overall and/or in detail.) **4**

SECTION 1 — SCOTTISH CONTEXTS

Part E – The Era of the Great War, 1910–1928

Attempt the following questions using recalled knowledge and information from the sources where appropriate.

Source A is about the recruitment campaign to the armed forces in 1914.

Source A

> At first the outbreak of war was exciting. The opportunity to go on an adventure with your pals in a kilted uniform was too good to miss. There were more Scots volunteers in proportion to the size of the population than any other area of the UK. The possibilities of facing serious injury or death were put aside. War hysteria also played a part. The War Propaganda Bureau told stories of Belgian babies being bayoneted and nurses and nuns being raped by German soldiers.

1. How fully does **Source A** explain why so many Scots volunteered for the armed forces in 1914?   6
    (Use **Source A** and recall.)

2. Describe the impact of war on the lives of women in Scotland.   5

3. Explain the reasons for the decline of heavy industry after World War I.   5

Source B was written by William Gallacher, a Glasgow Trade Union leader in 1919.

Source B

> A socialist rising was expected and it should have taken place. The workers were ready and able to carry it out. The mistake we made on Friday 31st January was marching to the centre of Glasgow. If we had gone to the barracks at Maryhill we could easily have persuaded the soldiers to support us and Clydeside would have been in our hands.

Source C was written by a modern historian.

Source C

> The government was worried about the loyalty of the police and armed forces in Glasgow. Had the government understood the situation better they could have saved themselves and the country a lot of bother. The leaders of the movement had no real support for their plans. The day after their protest in George Square the strikers went to the football just as they always did.

4. Compare the views in **Sources B** and **C** about what happened on Clydeside in 1919.   4
    (Compare the sources overall and/or in detail.)

SECTION 2 — BRITISH CONTEXTS — 20 marks
Attempt ONE part

Part C – The Atlantic Slave Trade, 1770–1807

Attempt the following questions using recalled knowledge and information from the sources where appropriate.

Source A was written by a modern historian, describing the treatment of slaves on the middle passage.

Source A

> Troublesome slaves were kept in chains and only let on the deck a few at a time for exercise. To keep the slaves as healthy as possible the crew would whip them to make them dance during exercise time. In desperation some slaves tried to jump overboard. Many slaves died during the middle passage from harsh treatment, poor food and disease. So did many of the crew.

1. Evaluate the usefulness of **Source A** as evidence of how slaves were treated on the middle passage.

   (You may want to comment on who wrote it, when they wrote it, why they wrote it, what they say or what has been missed out.)   **6**

2. Explain the reasons for the success of British ports involved in the slave trade.   **6**

3. To what extent was the case of the Zong important to the growth of the abolitionist campaign?   **8**

SECTION 2 — BRITISH CONTEXTS

MARKS

Part D – Changing Britain, 1760–1900

Attempt the following questions using recalled knowledge and information from the sources where appropriate.

1. Explain the reasons for poor health in British cities at the start of the 19th century.   6

Source A is from the *New Statistical Account* for the parish of Lochwinnoch, 1846.

Source A

> The population has increased rapidly since 1791. The chief reason for this was the building of cotton mills and the boost this gave to every other kind of business. The cotton mill employees can afford to live and dress well. A new mill stands on the banks of the River Calder. It employs 345 workers. Those employed in the mills work twelve hours a day, five days a week, and nine hours on Saturdays. The high temperatures in the mills weaken the body and damage the workers' health.

2. Evaluate the usefulness of **Source A** for investigating how improvements in technology in the textile industry affected the Scottish people.

   (You may want to comment on who wrote it, when they wrote it, why they wrote it, what they say or what has been missed out.)   6

3. To what extent was Britain a democratic country by 1914?   8

SECTION 2 — BRITISH CONTEXTS

Part E – The Making of Modern Britain, 1880–1951

Attempt the following questions using recalled knowledge and information from the sources where appropriate.

1. Explain the reasons why Liberals introduced reforms to support children and the elderly.

    6

Source A is taken from a speech made by Winston Churchill before the 1945 election.

Source A

> Here in old England we do not like to have every aspect of our lives organized for us. Let us leave Labour's welfare reformers to their unrealistic dreams. Let us make sure that the home to which the soldiers return is blessed with modest but solid prosperity but that Britons remain free to plan their lives for themselves and for those they love

2. Evaluate the usefulness of **Source A** as evidence of attitudes towards welfare reform after the Second World War.

    (You may want to comment on who wrote it, when they wrote it, why they wrote it, what they say or what has been missed out.)

    6

3. To what extent was the experience of rationing important in changing attitudes to poverty by 1945?

    8

SECTION 3 — EUROPEAN AND WORLD CONTEXTS — 20 marks

Attempt ONE part

Part B – "Tea and Freedom": the American Revolution, 1774–1783

Attempt the following questions using recalled knowledge and information from the sources where appropriate.

Source A explains why many colonists were unhappy with British rule by 1774.

Source A

> The writer Thomas Paine was firmly opposed to British rule. In January 1776, he published a cleverly written pamphlet called "Common Sense". In it, he argued that the British government was abusing the rights of the American people and many colonists were persuaded by his arguments. The answer, Paine believed, was independence. Paine's ideas were very popular and 150,000 pamphlets were sold. The King's rejection of the Olive Branch Petition also moved many colonists towards independence, as did news that the British were hiring mercenary soldiers from Germany to help them control the colonies.

1. How fully does **Source A** explain the reasons why many colonists had turned against British rule by 1776?
   (Use **Source A** and recall.)   **5**

Source B is from the trial of a British officer which followed the Boston Massacre in 1770.

Source B

> One of my soldiers received a severe blow with a stick, which caused him to fire his weapon accidentally. There followed a general attack on my men by a great number of heavy clubs. At this point our lives were in imminent danger and three or four of my soldiers fired, claiming that they heard an order to shoot. I can assure you that I gave no such order.

2. Evaluate the usefulness of **Source B** as evidence of why the Boston Massacre took place?   **5**

   (You may want to comment on who wrote it, when they wrote it, why they wrote it, what they say or what has been missed out.)

3. Describe the ways in which foreign countries helped the colonists in the war against the British.   **5**

4. Explain the reasons why some colonists remained loyal to Britain during the War of Independence.   **5**

SECTION 3 — EUROPEAN AND WORLD CONTEXTS

Part C – USA, 1850–1880

Attempt the following questions using recalled knowledge and information from the sources where appropriate.

Source A explains why there was tension between the whites and Native Americans.

Source A

> Professional hunters like "Buffalo Bill" were hired to shoot the buffalo to provide meat for settlers and railway workers. They crossed the sacred land of the Native Americans to do this. The white settlers also shot the buffalo for sport which offended the Sioux. Relations between the whites and Native Americans grew more and more tense.

1. How fully does **Source A** explain the causes of tension between whites and Native Americans?
    (Use **Source A** and recall.)

    5

2. Explain the reasons why many people in the North were opposed to slavery.

    5

3. Describe the aims of the Republican Party in 1860.

    5

Source B was written by the historian Janet Riehecky in her book *The Abolition of Slavery*, published in 2002.

Source B

> A secret terrorist organisation called the Ku Klux Klan was formed in 1866. Their main objective was to maintain white supremacy. They did this by taking steps to prevent black Americans from voting. The Klan wore hooded robes to maintain their anonymity and intimidate their victims. They used burning crosses to frighten victims. Most importantly they attacked and murdered black Americans, sometimes by lynching. They burned down their homes and churches. Schools were a particular target to prevent black Americans from becoming literate.

4. Evaluate the usefulness of **Source B** as evidence about the effects of the Ku Klux Klan's tactics on black Americans.

    (You may want to comment on who wrote it, when they wrote it, why they wrote it, what they say or what has been missed out.)

    5

SECTION 3 — EUROPEAN AND WORLD CONTEXTS

MARKS

Part D – Hitler and Nazi Germany, 1919–1939

Attempt the following questions using recalled knowledge and information from the sources where appropriate.

1. Describe the events of the Beer Hall Putsch.   5

Source A explains why many Germans disliked the Weimar Republic by the mid 1920s.

Source A

> The system of elections for the Reichstag meant no one party ever won a majority of seats. Germany, therefore, had a series of coalition governments which some people believed made the government weak. Many Germans felt the parties were too busy arguing amongst each other to solve the country's problems. Any success the government achieved was quickly forgotten.

2. How fully does **Source A** explain the reasons why the Weimar government was so unpopular by the mid 1920s?
   (Use **Source A** and recall.)   5

3. Explain the reasons why it was so difficult to oppose the Nazi government after 1933.   5

Source B was written by historians J. F. Corkery and R. C. F. Stone in *Weimar Germany and the Third Reich*, published in 1980.

Source B

> Government organisation of the workers gave opportunity for brainwashing them. In 1935 the Labour Service was established. This meant that every male between the ages of 18 and 25 had to do six months in public work camps. Camp discipline was semi-military. Camp leaders were given ranks. Men drilled with spades instead of rifles. The Labour Service was an opportunity to spread Nazi propaganda, building upon that already provided by the schools and Hitler Youth. Workers were urged to regard themselves as 'soldiers of work'.

4. Evaluate the usefulness of **Source B** as evidence about militarism in Nazi Germany.   5

   (You may want to comment on who wrote it, when they wrote it, why they wrote it, what they say or what has been missed out.)

SECTION 3 — EUROPEAN AND WORLD CONTEXTS

MARKS

Part E – Red Flag: Lenin and the Russian Revolution, 1894–1921

Attempt the following questions using recalled knowledge and information from the sources where appropriate.

Source A is from *History of the Russian Revolution* by Leon Trotsky, written in 1932.

Source A

> Nicholas II was unreliable and not to be trusted. He kept his gentlest smiles and kindest words for officials whom he planned to dismiss. He drew back with distaste from anyone gifted or capable. He only felt relaxed among very average and unimaginative people such as so-called holy men— people who could not show up his stupidity.

1. Evaluate the usefulness of **Source A** as evidence about Nicholas II.

    (You may want to comment on who wrote it, when they wrote it, why they wrote it, what they say or what has been missed out.)   **5**

2. Describe the events of Bloody Sunday in January 1905.   **5**

3. Explain the reasons why the Russian people were so discontented by February 1917.   **5**

Source B explains why the Bolsheviks were able to stay in power in Russia in 1917–1918.

Source B

> The successful seizure of power in Petrograd was only a beginning. Almost immediately the Congress of Soviets pleased the peasants by declaring that landlords' rights to property were abolished so that the land could be redistributed. A new Bolshevik Cabinet, Sovnarkom, was set up and given authority to pass new laws. In November, the Bolsheviks allowed the long-awaited elections to the Constitutional Assembly to be held; over 47 million Russians, including many peasants, voted. In December, Sovnarkom created a new secret police, the Cheka, to wipe out any counter-revolutionary activity.

4. How fully does **Source B** explain why the Bolsheviks were able to stay in power in Russia in 1917–1918?
    (Use **Source B** and recall.)   **5**

SECTION 3 — EUROPEAN AND WORLD CONTEXTS

MARKS

Part G – Free at Last? Civil Rights in the USA, 1918–1968

Attempt the following questions using recalled knowledge and information from the sources where appropriate.

1. Describe the impact of the Jim Crow laws on the lives of black Americans.   5

Source A is from a statement made by President Kennedy in May 1963.

Source A

> I think that the situation in Birmingham will be peacefully settled in the next 24 hours. Quite obviously the situation was damaging the reputation of Birmingham and the United States. It seems to me that the best way to prevent that kind of serious damage is to take steps to provide equal treatment for all of our citizens. That is the best remedy in this case and other cases.

2. Evaluate the usefulness of **Source A** as evidence of the effects of the Civil Rights protest in Birmingham.

    (You may want to comment on who wrote it, when they wrote it, why they wrote it, what they say or what has been missed out.)   5

Source B is about the march on Washington in 1963.

Source B

> More than thirty Freedom Trains and 2000 Freedom Buses were hired to take marchers to the capital city. Marchers assembled in front of the Lincoln Memorial in the capital city of the USA. Many of the marchers were African Americans, but about 20 per cent of the crowd was made up of white marchers who were demonstrating their support for the Civil Rights Movement. The demonstration was peaceful and orderly.

3. How fully does **Source B** explain the reasons why the march on Washington was important for the Civil Rights Movement?
    (Use **Source B** and recall.)   5

4. Explain the reasons for the riots by black Americans in northern cities in the late 1960s.   5

SECTION 3 — EUROPEAN AND WORLD CONTEXTS

MARKS

Part H – Appeasement and the Road to War, 1918–1939

Attempt the following questions using recalled knowledge and information from the sources where appropriate.

Source A is from one of the school textbooks introduced by the Nazis in 1934.

Source A

> For many centuries the Germans have protected Europe from the dangers of the east. It was German blood that defended Europe from Slav invaders and proved the superiority of our race. It is important that the Aryan race remains pure to fulfill its historic sacred mission to dominate inferior peoples and spread German culture and civilisation wherever possible.

1. Evaluate the usefulness of **Source A** as evidence of Nazi ideas on race.

    (You may want to comment on who wrote it, when they wrote it, why they wrote it, what they say or what has been missed out.)   **5**

Source B explains why Hitler wanted to rearm Germany in the 1930s.

Source B

> Hitler claimed that Germany alone was forced to leave herself defenceless as part of the punishment dictated by her enemies in 1919. He never missed an opportunity to attack the Treaty of Versailles. Hitler further stated that Germany was surrounded by hostile countries whose main purpose was to keep her in a weakened position and this could no longer be tolerated. A strong Germany would not only restore the balance of power in Europe but was also necessary to safeguard European civilisation against the threat from the east.

2. How fully does **Source B** explain the reasons why Hitler wanted to rearm Germany in the 1930s?   **5**
    (Use **Source B** and recall.)

3. Explain the reasons by Britain followed a policy of appeasement in the 1930s.   **5**

4. Describe the events that led to the takeover of Czechoslovakia.   **5**

SECTION 3 — EUROPEAN AND WORLD CONTEXTS

Part I – World War II, 1939–1945

Attempt the following questions using recalled knowledge and information from the sources where appropriate.

Source A is from a diary journal kept by General Erwin Rommel, leader of the 7th Panzer Division. In this excerpt, he describes the action on May 14 as he leads a tank attack against French forces.

Source A

> The tanks now rolled in a long column through the line of fortifications and on towards the first houses, which had been set alight by our fire. Our artillery was dropping heavy harassing fire on villages and the road far ahead of the regiment. Gradually the speed increased. We crossed the railway line and then swung north to the main road which was soon reached. Civilians and French troops, their faces distorted with terror, lay huddled in the ditches. We passed refugee columns, the carts abandoned by their owners, who had fled in panic into the fields. On we went, at a steady speed, towards our objective. We were through the Maginot Line!

1. Evaluate the usefulness of **Source A** as evidence of Blitzkreig tactics used by Germany in 1940.

   (You may want to comment on who wrote it, when they wrote it, why they wrote it, what they say or what has been missed out.)   **5**

2. Describe the problems facing ordinary people living in occupied Europe.   **5**

Source B is about the activities of the Dutch underground resistance groups in Nazi occupied Europe.

Source B

> Underground resistance groups were organized to serve a variety of functions including the rescue and sheltering of Jews and other persecuted individuals. Underground cells were involved in the manufacture of false papers or acted as couriers of secret documents to countries outside of the Netherlands to assist Allied war efforts. It is estimated that over fifty to sixty thousand individuals were directly involved in underground activities with hundreds of thousands more offering assistance.

3. How fully does **Source B** describe the activities of resistance groups in Nazi occupied Europe?
   (Use **Source B** and recall.)   **5**

4. Explain the reasons why America was able to defeat Japan by 1945.   **5**

SECTION 3 — EUROPEAN AND WORLD CONTEXTS

MARKS

Part J – The Cold War, 1945–1989

Attempt the following questions using recalled knowledge and information from the sources where appropriate.

Source A explains why there was a crisis in Berlin in 1961.

Source A

> By 1960 the situation in East Berlin was very dangerous. A new East German labour law, which stopped workers from going on strike, had led to growing unrest in the factories. The East German government's reforms of agriculture had led to shortages of food and higher prices. All of this led to a massive increase in the numbers of refugees fleeing to the West. At a meeting of the Warsaw Pact states, Khrushchev had been informed about the situation. In the six months up to June 1961, 103,000 East Germans had fled through Berlin. The decision to act was taken.

1. How fully does **Source A** explain the reasons why there was a crisis in Berlin in 1961? (Use **Source A** and recall.) 5

2. Describe the part played by the USSR in the Cuban Missile Crisis. 5

3. Explain the reasons why most Americans were opposed to the war in Vietnam by 1970. 5

Source B is from a speech to the American people by President Reagan in March 1983.

Source B

> Our efforts to rebuild America's forces began two years ago. For twenty years the Soviet Union has been accumulating enormous military might. They didn't stop building their forces, even when they had more than enough to defend themselves. They haven't stopped now. I know that all of you want peace, and so do I. However, the freeze on building nuclear weapons would make us less, not more, secure and would increase the risk of war.

4. Evaluate the usefulness of **Source B** as evidence of why the process of détente had come to a halt by the early 1980s.

    (You may want to comment on who wrote it, when they wrote it, why they wrote it, what they say or what has been missed out.) 5

[END OF MODEL PAPER]

NATIONAL 5

2014

National Qualifications 2014

X737/75/01

History

WEDNESDAY, 7 MAY

9:00 AM – 10:30 AM

Total marks — 60

SECTION 1 — SCOTTISH CONTEXTS — 20 marks

Attempt ONE part.

SECTION 2 — BRITISH CONTEXTS — 20 marks

Attempt ONE part.

SECTION 3 — EUROPEAN AND WORLD CONTEXTS — 20 marks

Attempt ONE part.

Write your answers clearly in the answer booklet provided. In the answer booklet, you must clearly identify the question number you are attempting.

Use **blue** or **black** ink.

Before leaving the examination room you must give your answer booklet to the Invigilator; if you do not, you may lose all the marks for this paper.

SECTION 1 — SCOTTISH CONTEXTS

PARTS

SECTION 2 — BRITISH CONTEXTS

PARTS

SECTION 3 — EUROPEAN AND WORLD CONTEXTS

PARTS

SECTION 1 — SCOTTISH CONTEXTS — 20 marks

MARKS

Part A — The Wars of Independence, 1286–1328

Attempt the following questions using recalled knowledge and information from the sources where appropriate.

1. Explain the reasons why Edward I was able to become involved in Scottish affairs between 1286 and 1292.

   5

2. Describe what happened at the Battle of Stirling Bridge in 1297.

   5

Source A is from the chronicle of Walter of Guisborough, written in 1306.

Source A

> Robert the Bruce wanted to be king of Scotland but feared Lord John Comyn would stop him. He lured him to a meeting in Greyfriars Church in Dumfries to deal with business concerning them both. Comyn suspected nothing and they greeted each other in a friendly way. Suddenly Bruce accused Comyn of telling lies about him to the king of England. He struck him with his sword and marched out.

3. Evaluate the usefulness of **Source A** as evidence of Bruce's actions in 1306.

   (You may want to comment on who wrote it, when they wrote it, why they wrote it, what they say or what has been missed out.)

   5

Source B describes how Bruce established himself as king of an independent Scotland.

Source B

> After Bannockburn, Bruce's parliament agreed that Scots nobles who had not made peace with him would lose their lands in Scotland. Bruce gave this forfeited land to his own supporters. The Douglases benefited greatly from this. Scots nobles would no longer be allowed to have English estates so their loyalties would not be divided. Bruce also backed his brother's campaign in Ireland to continue to challenge English rule. He continued to raid the north of England to put pressure on Edward to recognise him as king of an independent nation.

4. How fully does **Source B** describe how Bruce established himself as king of an independent Scotland after the Battle of Bannockburn? (Use **Source B** and recall.)

   5

[Now go to SECTION 2 starting on *Page eight*]

SECTION 1 — SCOTTISH CONTEXTS — 20 marks

Part B — Mary Queen of Scots and the Scottish Reformation, 1542–1587

Attempt the following questions using recalled knowledge and information from the sources where appropriate.

1. Describe the events which led Mary, Queen of Scots, to move to France in 1548.

5

Source A is about the growth of Protestantism in Scotland.

Source A

> The Protestant form of worship meant that people could participate much more in services. The Bible was available in English, not Latin; therefore people who could not read Latin could still understand it. Only churchmen and a few others could understand Latin. A conflict between Catholics and Protestants was developing in Scotland for various reasons. Some people began to criticise the Catholic Church because of its great wealth. Local priests were resented for charging people for christening their children. This was a ceremony people would not dare go without.

2. How fully does **Source A** explain the reasons for the growth in the Protestant religion in Scotland? (Use **Source A** and recall.)

5

Source B is from a sermon written in the 1560s by John Knox.

Source B

> In 1563 there was a great famine in Scotland. But in the north of the country, where Mary had travelled before harvest time, the famine was hardest with great suffering. Many people died. Thus did God punish the many sins of our wicked Queen and her followers. The excessive celebrations and huge feasts in the palace and in the country provoked God into this action.

3. Evaluate the usefulness of **Source B** as evidence of Protestant attitudes towards Mary, Queen of Scots, during her reign in Scotland.

   (You may want to comment on who wrote it, when they wrote it, why they wrote it, what they say or what has been missed out.)

5

4. Explain the reasons why Riccio became unpopular with Darnley and the Scottish nobles.

5

[Now go to SECTION 2 starting on *Page eight*]

SECTION 1 — SCOTTISH CONTEXTS — 20 marks

MARKS

Part C — The Treaty of Union, 1689–1715

Attempt the following questions using recalled knowledge and information from the sources where appropriate.

1. Describe the worsening relations between Scotland and England between 1689 and 1705.

5

Source A is from a leaflet written by Andrew Fletcher in 1706.

Source A

> Let me explain my opposition to Union. Scotland needs to keep its own separate law and church. They cannot be governed and supported by a Parliament in London. If the Scots agree to these interests being controlled by a single Parliament they will surrender control to the English. The Scots deserve no pity if they surrender their interests to a Parliament where the English will have a vast majority.

2. Evaluate the usefulness of Source A as evidence of the arguments used by Scots against the Union.

   (You may want to comment on who wrote it, when they wrote it, why they wrote it, what they say or what has been missed out.)

5

Source B is about the Treaty of Union.

Source B

> I could give you some account of the many advantages we will obtain by a union with England. By this union we will all have access to all the advantages of trade that the English enjoy at the moment. We will be able to improve our wealth which will be for the benefit of the whole island. We will have our liberty, our property and our religion secured. Scotland will be under the protection of one sovereign and one Parliament of Great Britain.

3. How fully does Source B explain the arguments used by Scots in favour of the Union? (Use Source B and recall.)

5

4. Explain the reasons why many Scots participated in the Jacobite rebellion of 1715.

5

[Now go to SECTION 2 starting on *Page eight*]

SECTION 1 — SCOTTISH CONTEXTS — 20 marks   MARKS

Part D — Migration and Empire, 1830–1939

Attempt the following questions using recalled knowledge and information from the sources where appropriate.

1. Explain the reasons why many Scots resented immigrants between 1830 and 1939.   5

2. Describe the assistance given to Scots to help them to emigrate to the Empire.   5

Source **A** describes the career of a Scots emigrant to Australia in the 19th century.

Source A

> Alexander Spark left Elgin for lack of local opportunities. With a good education and some inherited money he applied for a land grant in Australia. He settled in Sydney. Within three years he was a leading member of the business community, prominent in banking and by 1840 owned £40,000 of land. He became the local agent for a variety of companies including shipping, banks and the Australian Gas company. Scottish Agents in Australia handled the interests of many Scots who invested money in Australian businesses without ever leaving Scotland.

3. How fully does **Source A** describe the contribution of Scots to their new countries? (Use **Source A** and recall.)   5

Source **B** is from a memoir by Mary Contini, about her Italian grandparents who emigrated to Scotland in the early 20th century.

Source B

> When my grandparents visited other Italian families, invariably the conversation turned to the price of potatoes. The price they paid was important because so many of them made their living selling fish and chips. The unfamiliar ideas of banks and debt worried them and made them work even harder. Their shops were open long hours and the whole family helped serve customers. This helped their shops become the focus of social life in many communities.

4. Evaluate the usefulness of **Source B** as evidence of the ways immigrants fitted in to Scottish society.   5

    (You may want to comment on who wrote it, when they wrote it, why they wrote it, what they say or what has been missed out.)

[Now go to SECTION 2 starting on *Page eight*]

SECTION 1 — SCOTTISH CONTEXTS — 20 marks

MARKS

Part E — The Era of the Great War, 1910–1928

Attempt the following questions using recalled knowledge and information from the sources where appropriate.

1. Describe the use of new technology on the Western Front.

   5

Source A is from the memoirs of David Lloyd George who was in charge of the Ministry of Munitions in 1915.

Source A

> The courage of the women engaged in these factories has never been sufficiently recognised. They had to work under conditions of real danger to life. What some of them probably dreaded more was horrible disfigurement — for one of the risks of the shell filling factories was toxic jaundice resulting from TNT poisoning. The poor girls were nicknamed "canaries". They were quite proud of this. They had earned it in the path of duty.

2. Evaluate the usefulness of **Source A** as evidence of the impact of the Great War on Scottish women.

   5

   (You may want to comment on who wrote it, when they wrote it, why they wrote it, what they say or what has been missed out.)

Source B is about the treatment of conscientious objectors.

Source B

> Men who refused to enlist in the army had to face military discipline. Some were sentenced to death for refusing orders although the sentence was always reduced if the "conchie" still refused to give in. Many refused non-combatant duty on the grounds that it simply released another man to kill. Special prisons and work camps were opened up in addition to ordinary prisons to which many objectors were sent. Twenty-four objectors died while detained at these work camps.

3. How fully does **Source B** describe how conscientious objectors were treated during the Great War? (Use **Source B** and recall.)

   5

4. Explain the reasons why heavy industry declined in Scotland after the Great War.

   5

[Now go to SECTION 2 starting on *Page eight*]

SECTION 2 — BRITISH CONTEXTS — 20 marks

MARKS

Part A— The Creation of the Medieval Kingdoms, 1066–1406

Attempt the following questions using recalled knowledge and information from the sources where appropriate.

1. To what extent was William I's leadership the main reason why the Normans won the Battle of Hastings?

8

   (You must use recalled knowledge to present a **balanced account** of the influence of different factors and come to a **reasoned conclusion.**)

Source A is from a chronicle written by a royal clerk in 1174.

Source A

> Whilst Henry was dealing with problems elsewhere in his kingdom, the king of Scotland, William the Lion, rebelled and attacked Northumberland. William's army committed terrible crimes wherever they went. Women and children were slaughtered and priests murdered inside their own churches. Next William travelled to Carlisle. His army besieged the castle and, by cutting off their supplies, forced the English to make a treaty with the Scots.

2. Evaluate the usefulness of **Source A** as evidence of the rebellions faced by Henry II during his reign.

6

   (You may want to comment on who wrote it, when they wrote it, why they wrote it, what they say or what has been missed out.)

3. Explain the reasons why there was a Peasants Revolt in 1381.

6

[Now go to SECTION 3 starting on *Page thirteen*]

SECTION 2 — BRITISH CONTEXTS — 20 marks

MARKS

Part B — War of the Three Kingdoms, 1603–1651

Attempt the following questions using recalled knowledge and information from the sources where appropriate.

1. To what extent were arguments between King James VI and I and Parliament the result of religious differences?

   (You must use recalled knowledge to present a **balanced account** of the influence of different factors and come to a **reasoned conclusion**.)

   8

2. Explain the reasons why Charles I was an unpopular monarch by 1640.

   6

Source A is from a letter dated 17 September 1649, written by Oliver Cromwell to the House of Commons.

Source A

> Our army came to Drogheda on 3rd September. On Monday 9th the battering guns began. I sent Sir Arthur Aston a request to surrender the town but received no satisfactory answer. Our guns then beat down the corner tower, and made gaps in the east and south walls. On the following day, after some fierce fighting, we entered the town. Several of the enemy, including Sir Arthur Aston, retreated into Mill Mount, a place very difficult to attack.

3. Evaluate the usefulness of **Source A** as evidence of what happened at Drogheda in Ireland during the Civil War.

   (You may want to comment on who wrote it, when they wrote it, why they wrote it, what they say or what has been missed out.)

   6

[Now go to SECTION 3 starting on *Page thirteen*]

SECTION 2 — BRITISH CONTEXTS — 20 marks   MARKS

Part C — The Atlantic Slave Trade, 1770–1807

Attempt the following questions using recalled knowledge and information from the sources where appropriate.

1. To what extent was the success of the abolitionist campaigns due to the work of campaigners such as Thomas Clarkson?   **8**

   (You must use recalled knowledge to present a **balanced account** of the influence of different factors and come to a **reasoned conclusion**.)

2. Explain the reasons why many people in Britain continued to support the slave trade.   **6**

Source A is from *Black Peoples of the Americas*, a book written by an historian in 1995.

Source A

> The planters in the Caribbean were afraid of a rebellion and they followed a policy of control through fear. Slaves had no rights. They were seen as possessions rather than human beings. Owners could deal with slaves exactly as they pleased and there was no punishment for owners who worked their slaves to death. Until the nineteenth century, no-one questioned owners burning or torturing their slaves.

3. Evaluate the usefulness of **Source A** as evidence of the treatment of slaves on the plantations.   **6**

   (You may want to comment on who wrote it, when they wrote it, why they wrote it, what they say or what has been missed out.)

[Now go to SECTION 3 starting on *Page thirteen*]

SECTION 2 — BRITISH CONTEXTS — 20 marks

MARKS

Part D — Changing Britain, 1760–1900

Attempt the following questions using recalled knowledge and information from the sources where appropriate.

Source A is from a report on housing in Manchester, written by a doctor in 1832.

Source A

> The houses that the mill workers live in are poorly ventilated and do not have toilets. The streets are narrow, unpaved and worn into deep ruts. These ruts become the common resting place of mud, refuse and disgusting rubbish. In Parliament Street there is only one toilet for 380 inhabitants. The flow of muck from this toilet infests close-by houses and must be a source of disease.

1. Evaluate the usefulness of **Source A** as evidence of housing conditions in British cities in the nineteenth century.

   (You may want to comment on who wrote it, when they wrote it, why they wrote it, what they say or what has been missed out.)

   6

2. To what extent was new technology the main reason for improvements in coal mining by 1900?

   (You must use recalled knowledge to present a **balanced account** of the influence of different factors and come to a **reasoned conclusion**.)

   8

3. Explain the reasons why there was a decline in the use of canals after the 1840s.

   6

[Now go to SECTION 3 starting on *Page thirteen*]

SECTION 2 — BRITISH CONTEXTS — 20 marks

Part E — The Making of Modern Britain, 1880–1951

Attempt the following questions using recalled knowledge and information from the sources where appropriate.

1. To what extent was poor health the main cause of poverty by 1900?

    (You must use recalled knowledge to present a **balanced account** of the influence of different factors and come to a **reasoned conclusion**.)

    8

Source A is from the book *From the Cradle to the Grave: Social Welfare in Britain 1890s-1951* by historians and published in 2002.

Source A

> One of the groups of "deserving poor" that the Liberals aimed to help in Britain was the young. The Boer War and the condition of many recruits led politicians to act. The Liberal government knew that poorer children would be the soldiers of the future. Healthy children would grow up to be healthy soldiers and workers, and the British Empire would be stronger as a result.

2. Evaluate the usefulness of **Source A** as evidence of the reasons why the Liberals introduced reforms to help the young.

    (You may want to comment on who wrote it, when they wrote it, why they wrote it, what they say or what has been missed out.)

    6

3. Explain the reasons why the Second World War changed attitudes to welfare reform in Britain.

    6

[Now go to SECTION 3 starting on *Page thirteen*]

SECTION 3 — EUROPEAN AND WORLD CONTEXTS — 20 marks

Part A—The Cross and the Crescent: the Crusades, 1071–1192

Attempt the following questions using recalled knowledge and information from the sources where appropriate.

1. Describe the use of castles in medieval times.

5

2. Explain the reasons why people joined the First Crusade.

5

Source A describes the relationship between Emperor Alexius and the Crusaders.

Source A

> Emperor Alexius was horrified when the Crusader knights arrived at Constantinople. Fearing they would attack his city, Alexius made the Crusaders camp outside and only allowed them to enter in small groups. In a desperate attempt to take charge of the army, Alexius offered treasure and supplies to the Crusaders who agreed to fight for him. Any Crusader who refused was attacked and forced to surrender. Although Alexius had asked the Pope for knights he did not trust them and made plans to remove them from Constantinople.

3. How fully does **Source A** describe the relationship between Emperor Alexius and the Crusaders? (Use **Source A** and recall.)

6

Sources B and **C** are about the character of Richard I.

Source B

> When the king of France left the Crusade, Richard vowed to fulfil his Christian duty and continue to Jerusalem. An excellent military commander, Richard used clever tactics to win key battles and drive the Muslims back. Richard had such a fearsome reputation that the Muslims dreaded facing him on the battlefield. Despite the danger involved Richard always fought alongside his men, courageously attacking the enemy.

Source C

> The Crusaders had been besieging Acre for two years before Richard arrived with his army. Richard immediately took charge of the attack and using his experience and leadership forced the city to surrender. Throughout the fighting Richard showed great bravery by defending his men and killing the enemy. When some Crusaders returned home, Richard refused to leave promising he would keep his oath to God and recapture Jerusalem.

4. Compare the views of **Sources B** and **C** as evidence of the character of Richard I. (Compare the sources overall and/or in detail.)

4

SECTION 3 — EUROPEAN AND WORLD CONTEXTS — 20 marks

MARKS

Part B — "Tea and Freedom": the American Revolution, 1774–1783

Attempt the following questions using recalled knowledge and information from the sources where appropriate.

Source A explains why there was growing tension between Britain and the colonists.

Source A

> The war with France had ended in 1763. Although victory was widely celebrated, there were already voices being raised against British rule in the thirteen colonies. The decision to increase taxes on the colonists was very unpopular. Britain had gone to great expense to protect the colonies and wanted the colonies to pay some of this money back. The decision to maintain a standing army in the colonies also alarmed the colonists. The Stamp Act of 1765 provoked a furious reaction. Colonists responded by organising a boycott of British goods.

1. How fully does **Source A** explain why there was growing tension between Britain and the colonists by 1774? (Use **Source A** and recall.) **6**

2. Describe the events of the Boston Tea Party and the British government's reaction to it. **5**

3. Explain the reasons why Britain lost the war against the colonists. **5**

Sources B and **C** are about the events that led to the British defeat at Saratoga.

Source B

> In June 1777 General Burgoyne set out from Canada with nearly 8,000 men but his progress was then slowed by mountains and dense forest. The British fought off American forces in September. However, unlike the Americans, Burgoyne had no reinforcements. In October, Burgoyne tangled with the Americans once again. He was forced to retreat and his army was trapped against the Hudson River. On 17 October, Burgoyne was forced to surrender almost 6,000 men and 30 cannons.

Source C

> General Burgoyne was eager to win fame for himself. He planned to march south to Albany. Another British army was due to join up with Burgoyne's forces. However, they were stopped by heavy resistance and Burgoyne's army was left on its own. Burgoyne decided to carry on but his progress was slowed by the difficult terrain and lack of supplies. The British were trapped at the little community of Saratoga and had no option but to surrender.

4. Compare the views of **Sources B** and **C** about the British defeat at Saratoga. (Compare the sources overall and/or in detail.) **4**

SECTION 3 — EUROPEAN AND WORLD CONTEXTS — 20 marks

MARKS

Part C — The USA, 1850–1880

Attempt the following questions using recalled knowledge and information from the sources where appropriate.

1. Describe slave life on Southern plantations before the outbreak of the civil war.

    5

2. Explain why there was a growth in tension between the Northern and Southern States by 1860.

    5

Source A describes the reasons why some settlers and prospectors headed west after 1850.

Source A

> After 1850 large numbers of settlers and prospectors were heading west. They were attracted by the promise of a better life. Some were fed up with the cold winters in the east and were attracted by the warmer weather in California. Many farmers went west because they thought the land would be more fertile. Ranch owners, such as Charles Goodnight, quickly realised that the plains could be used to feed their huge herds of cattle. However, it was hard going. One person in ten died before they reached their destination.

3. How fully does **Source A** describe the reasons why large numbers of settlers and prospectors were attracted west after 1850? (Use **Source A** and recall.)

    6

Sources B and C are about the Sand Creek Massacre in 1864.

Source B

> Black Kettle and other chiefs of the Cheyennes were opposed to hostilities with the whites. Yet their village was still attacked by Colonel Chivington, who commanded 900 to 1,000 men. There were 500 people in the village, two-thirds of whom were women and children. I rode over the field after the slaughter was over, and counted from 60 to 70 dead bodies. A large majority of the dead were women and children.

Source C

> In the Cheyenne camp there were about 1,200 people in the village and about 700 were warriors. My reason for making the attack was that I believed they were hostile to the whites. I estimate that there were 500 or 600 people killed. I saw only one woman who had been killed and I saw no dead children. We found the scalps of 19 white people in the camp.

4. Compare the views of **Sources B** and **C** about the events which took place during the Sand Creek Massacre of 1864. (Compare the sources overall and/or in detail.)

    4

SECTION 3 — EUROPEAN AND WORLD CONTEXTS — 20 marks

MARKS

Part D — Hitler and Nazi Germany, 1919–1939

Attempt the following questions using recalled knowledge and information from the sources where appropriate.

1. Describe the rights all Germans had in the Weimar Republic.

5

Sources **A** and **B** are about hyperinflation in Germany.

Source A

> Workers were paid twice a day and when they were given their wages, they threw bundles of banknotes out of factory windows to waiting members of their families who would then rush to the shops to buy food or coal or clothes before the prices went up. Millions of people faced starvation due to hyperinflation. People such as pensioners who were living on fixed incomes found that prices rose much faster than their earnings.

Source B

> Almost overnight the life savings of many Germans became worthless. Some workers were paid twice a day and could spend their wages instantly. People who were paid monthly or depended on savings suffered because these could not keep up with price rises. Pensioners lived on fixed incomes. They always received the same amount of money each week. These incomes were now worth nothing. They faced homelessness and starvation.

2. Compare the views of **Sources A** and **B** on the effects of hyperinflation on the people of Germany. (Compare the sources overall and/or in detail.)

4

3. Explain the reasons why Hitler and the Nazi Party attracted so much support by January 1933.

5

Source C is about Nazi control of people's lives.

Source C

> Hitler and the Nazi Party aimed to control every part of people's lives, and that included their free time. The KDF (Strength through Joy Organisation) controlled most forms of entertainment. Each year around seven million people took part in KDF sports matches. Mass outings to the theatre and the opera were arranged. The KDF had its own symphony orchestra which toured the country. Workers were also provided with affordable holidays including cruises and walking or skiing holidays.

4. How fully does **Source C** describe how the Nazis controlled people's lives? (Use **Source C** and recall.)

6

SECTION 3 — EUROPEAN AND WORLD CONTEXTS — 20 marks

MARKS

Part E — Red Flag: Lenin and the Russian Revolution, 1894–1921

Attempt the following questions using recalled knowledge and information from the sources where appropriate.

1. Describe the methods used by the Tsar to control Russia before 1905.   5

2. Explain the reasons why the Tsar's control of Russia was threatened in 1905.   5

Source A describes some of the effects of the First World War on Russia.

Source A

> The outbreak of the First World War in August 1914 was to have a terrible impact on Russians. Russia went to war to support its friends and allies. Russian armies were in action against Germany and Austria-Hungary within only six days. Heart-breaking losses were suffered by the Tsar's armies during the early years of the war. Thousands of wounded soldiers were left lying untreated on the ground for days. Nurses and doctors lacked enough bandages to treat even a quarter of the wounds.

3. How fully does **Source A** describe the effects of the First World War on Russia? (Use **Source A** and recall.)   6

Sources B and **C** describe the events in Petrograd during February 1917.

Source B

> The disturbances which have begun in Petrograd are becoming more serious. Shortages of bread and flour cause panic. The workers are without jobs, the unemployed take the path to riot and revolt. The capital is in a state of anarchy. The Government is paralysed. The transport system has broken down. The suppliers of fuel and food are completely disorganised. There is wild shooting on the streets and troops are firing at each other.

Source C

> The situation was already very serious. Some of the factories had to close down and there were several thousand workmen unemployed. They wanted bread, but after waiting for hours in the queues outside the bakers' shops, many had been unable to get any. On Thursday, March 8, there had been a stormy sitting in the Duma and it was the bread shortage that was the cause of the unrest.

4. Compare the views of **Sources B** and **C** on the events in Petrograd during February 1917. (Compare the sources overall and/or in detail.)   4

SECTION 3 — EUROPEAN AND WORLD CONTEXTS — 20 marks

MARKS

Part F — Mussolini and Fascist Italy, 1919–1939

Attempt the following questions using recalled knowledge and information from the sources where appropriate.

1. Describe Mussolini's foreign policy up to 1939.　5

2. Explain the reasons why many Italians were unhappy with Mussolini's economic policies.　5

Source A describes the use of propaganda in Fascist Italy.

Source A

> Mussolini had long experience in the newspaper business and so he knew a thing or two about how to make effective propaganda. Mussolini's press office issued official versions of events which all the newspapers were expected to publish without question. The radio and cinema were also used to broadcast Fascist propaganda. News bulletins broadcast a daily diet of Mussolini's speeches and praised him as the saviour of Italy. The media played a very crucial role in the cult of "Il Duce."

3. How fully does **Source A** describe the use of propaganda in Fascist Italy? (Use **Source A** and recall.)　6

Sources B and C are about opposition to Mussolini.

Source B

> The Fascists used terror and violence, but for the most part this was not necessary. Unpopular groups like the Communists and Socialists were treated brutally. Fascist policies benefited the rich to ensure their support. The signing of the Lateran agreement in 1929 was important in winning the support of Catholics. There was some opposition in the army but this was never carried out in a coordinated way.

Source C

> While there was opposition to the Fascists, this never really posed a threat to the government. While some army generals opposed Mussolini, others liked his aggressive attitude. Mussolini changed his policy towards the Roman Catholic Church. This new close relationship with the church reduced the threat of opposition from Catholics. Big businessmen and landowners supported a regime which always seemed to be on their side.

4. Compare the views of **Sources B** and **C** on opposition to Mussolini. (Compare the sources overall and/or in detail.)　4

SECTION 3 — EUROPEAN AND WORLD CONTEXTS — 20 marks

Part G — Free at Last? Civil Rights in the USA, 1918–1968

Attempt the following questions using recalled knowledge and information from the sources where appropriate.

Sources **A** and **B** are about immigrants in American cities in the 1920s.

Source A

> The early twentieth century saw a massive growth in immigration from Southern and Eastern Europe. Immigrants from the same country usually lived in the same areas of the city. These areas contained tenement slums which were damp, dark and filthy with no water supply, toilets or drains. Immigrants had to take any work they could get, usually low paid jobs such as labourers or servants.

Source B

> Finding a well-paid, skilled job was a common problem for poorly educated immigrants. Immigrants tended to live in their own communities: in New York there was a Polish district, a Jewish district and an Italian district. Tenement buildings in these areas were often five or six storeys high with rooms which lacked light or sanitation. Many of the new immigrants found that life in America was not what they expected.

1. Compare the views of **Sources A** and **B** about the living and working conditions of immigrants in American cities.

   4

2. Describe the non-violent protests of the Civil Rights Movement in the 1950s and 1960s.

   5

Source C is about the actions taken by federal authorities to help black Americans.

Source C

> Federal authorities did take action. President Truman issued orders to desegregate the US military in 1948. He also set up a President's Committee on civil rights in 1946 to report to him on how progress towards black civil rights could be made. However no legislation followed. In 1960 Congress passed a Civil Rights Act which established penalties for obstructing black voting. The assassination of President Kennedy in November 1963 came at the time he was preparing a Civil Rights Bill.

3. How fully does **Source C** describe the actions taken by federal authorities to improve civil rights for black Americans between 1945 and 1964? (Use **Source C** and recall.)

   6

4. Explain the reasons why the Black Panthers gained the support of many black Americans.

   5

SECTION 3 — EUROPEAN AND WORLD CONTEXTS — 20 marks   MARKS

Part H — Appeasement and the Road to War, 1918–1939

Attempt the following questions using recalled knowledge and information from the sources where appropriate.

1. Describe the military terms of the Treaty of Versailles.   5

Source A is about the weaknesses of the League of Nations.

Source A

> The USA refused to join as they were not interested in getting involved in the problems of other countries. Initially Russia was not invited to join, so another great country of the world was absent. Therefore, right from the start the League of Nations was actually rather weak. Taking decisions was difficult as the Assembly had to be unanimous and member states often could not agree. A further problem was that the League did not have its own army to back up its decisions.

2. How fully does **Source A** explain the reasons why the League of Nations was weak? (Use **Source A** and recall.)   6

3. Explain the reasons why Britain did not take military action against Germany's reoccupation of the Rhineland.   5

Sources B and **C** are about the Anschluss.

Source B

> Germany and Austria are now one. It was a mistake of the peacemakers at Versailles to forbid the union of Austria and Germany. The population of Austria comprised ethnic Germans, the majority of whom are enthusiastic about the Anschluss. The Austrians will not only feel at home as part of Germany, they will benefit financially too from an increase in trade with their German brothers.

Source C

> That there has been no fighting is proof of the desire of the Austrian people to belong to Germany. Austrians will also benefit from greater markets for their raw materials and manufactured goods. The union of these two countries should never have been forbidden at Versailles. Winston Churchill has argued that Austria is a small country "brutally struck down". I do not see what there is to complain about.

4. Compare the views of **Sources B** and **C** about the Anschluss. (Compare the sources overall and/or in detail.)   4

SECTION 3 — EUROPEAN AND WORLD CONTEXTS — 20 marks

MARKS

Part I — World War II, 1939–1945

Attempt the following questions using recalled knowledge and information from the sources where appropriate.

Sources **A** and **B** are about the German strategy of Blitzkrieg.

Source A

> Blitzkrieg was a tactic based on speed and surprise. It required the effective use of light tank units supported by planes and infantry. The tactic was developed by army officer Hans Guderian. He had written a military pamphlet called "Achtung Panzer" which got into the hands of Hitler. It was used effectively in the first years of the Second World War and resulted in the British and French armies being pushed back in just a few weeks to the beaches of Dunkirk.

Source B

> Hitler had spent four years in World War One fighting a static war with neither side moving far for months on end. He was enthralled by Guderian's plan that was based purely on speed and movement. When Guderian told Hitler that he could reach the French coast in weeks if an attack on France was ordered, fellow officers openly laughed at him. Once a strategic target had been selected, Stuka dive bombers were sent in to "soften" up the enemy, then the tanks approached, supported by infantry.

1. Compare the views of **Sources A** and **B** on the German strategy of Blitzkrieg. (Compare the sources overall and/or in detail.)   **4**

2. Describe what life was like for the ordinary citizens of Nazi occupied Europe.   **5**

Source C is about the activities of the French Resistance.

Source C

> The French Resistance movement developed in 1940. It helped Jews, and Allied airmen who had crash landed in France, to escape. Many resistance workers paid for their courage with their lives. Even school children were recruited to help smuggle people across the borders of northern and southern France. As well as this, the Resistance movement was crucial to undermining Nazi rule by producing publications of news and information. Nazi rule was further challenged by the Resistance who worked together to discover French collaboration.

3. How fully does **Source C** describe the activities of the French Resistance? (Use **Source C** and recall.)   **6**

4. Explain the reasons why the Russian army was able to take over Berlin in 1945.   **5**

SECTION 3 — EUROPEAN AND WORLD CONTEXTS — 20 marks

MARKS

Part J — The Cold War, 1945–1989

Attempt the following questions using recalled knowledge and information from the sources where appropriate.

1. Explain the reasons why a Cold War developed after 1945.

5

Source A is about American intervention in Vietnam.

Source A

> The Americans intervened in Vietnam for several reasons. In a speech in March 1947 President Truman explained that America would resist the spread of Communism. This became known as the Truman Doctrine. In the 1950s the Americans had responded to French requests for assistance in Vietnam by giving money to try to halt the Vietminh. By the early 1960s it was clear that South Vietnam could not resist Communism without the support of American troops. Many in America believed war was necessary to stop the spread of Soviet influence.

2. How fully does **Source A** explain the reasons why Americans intervened in Vietnam? (Use **Source A** and recall.)

6

Sources B and **C** are about the crisis in Berlin in 1961.

> There is peace in Berlin today. The source of world trouble and tension is Moscow, not Berlin. And if war begins, it will have begun in Moscow and not Berlin. For the choice of war or peace is largely theirs, not ours. It is the Soviets who have stirred up this crisis. It is they who are trying to force a change. They have rejected an all-German peace treaty and the rule of international law.

Source C

> We can now look back on the Berlin crisis and say with confidence that this crisis was caused by Moscow. It was the brutal Soviet-backed regime in East Germany which caused so many people to leave. The Soviet domination of East Germany was a clear breach of international law. The Soviets rejected an American proposal for a peace treaty which would have dealt with all of the issues in Germany.

3. Compare the views of **Sources B** and **C** on the crisis in Berlin in 1961. (Compare the sources overall and/or in detail.)

4

4. Describe the impact of the Cuban Missile Crisis on international relations.

5

[END OF QUESTION PAPER]

Page twenty-two

NATIONAL 5

2015

National
Qualifications
2015

X737/75/11

History

FRIDAY, 01 MAY

09:00 AM – 10:45 AM

Total marks — 60

SECTION 1 — SCOTTISH CONTEXTS — 20 marks

Attempt ONE part.

SECTION 2 — BRITISH CONTEXTS — 20 marks

Attempt ONE part.

SECTION 3 — EUROPEAN AND WORLD CONTEXTS — 20 marks

Attempt ONE part.

Write your answers clearly in the answer booklet provided. In the answer booklet you must clearly identify the question number you are attempting.

Use **blue** or **black** ink.

Before leaving the examination room you must give your answer booklet to the Invigilator; if you do not, you may lose all the marks for this paper.

[BLANK PAGE]

DO NOT WRITE ON THIS PAGE

SECTION 1 — SCOTTISH CONTEXTS

PARTS

SECTION 2 — BRITISH CONTEXTS

PARTS

SECTION 3 — EUROPEAN AND WORLD CONTEXTS

PARTS

MARKS

SECTION 1 — SCOTTISH CONTEXTS — 20 marks

Part A—The Wars of Independence, 1286–1328

Answer the following questions using recalled knowledge and information from the sources where appropriate.

Sources **A** and **B** are about Edward I's plans for Scotland after the death of Alexander III.

Source A

> When Alexander III died, Edward I took steps to take control of Scotland. His aim was to unite the kingdoms of Scotland and England by a marriage treaty. Edward plotted to marry his son to Scotland's infant queen, Margaret, Maid of Norway. He secretly asked the Pope's permission for the marriage before any details had been discussed with the Scots. When Margaret's death ended this scheme, he looked for other ways to control Scotland.

Source B

> In 1289 Edward was in France attending to his lands there. Erik, King of Norway, father of Margaret Maid of Norway, sent messengers to him to discuss her safety. He suggested her possible marriage with Edward's son. Edward asked for Scottish representatives to be present before any negotiations began. The Maid would have Edward's protection and this would ensure peace in Scotland. This marriage would mean a union of the kingdoms.

1. Compare the views in **Sources A** and **B** about Edward I's intentions towards Scotland after the death of Alexander III. (Compare the sources overall and/or in detail.)   **4**

2. Describe what happened when Edward I attacked Berwick in 1296.   **5**

MARKS

Source C is about Bruce's campaign to capture the Scottish castles.

Source C

> In 1307, Bruce returned to Scotland. Although many of his leading supporters had been captured by Edward I he still had experienced commanders such as James Douglas. Bruce and his small army marched north and destroyed castles in Inverness and Nairn. He could not spare men to defend castles from attack. Meanwhile, Douglas recaptured his own castle in the south and burned it down. Edward I had taken Stirling castle by using the siege engine, *Warwolf*. Lack of such siege engines forced Bruce to use other methods.

3. How fully does **Source C** describe Bruce's campaign of capturing the Scottish castles? (Use **Source C** and recall.)   6

4. Explain the reasons why English mistakes led to their defeat at the Battle of Bannockburn in 1314.   5

[Now go to SECTION 2 starting on Page fourteen]

MARKS

SECTION 1 — SCOTTISH CONTEXTS — 20 marks

Part B — Mary Queen of Scots and the Scottish Reformation, 1542–1587

Answer the following questions using recalled knowledge and information from the sources where appropriate.

5. Describe the events of the "Rough Wooing". 5

Sources **A** and **B** are about the murder of Riccio.

Source **A**

> Mary was in her chamber enjoying a meal with Riccio and some other friends. Suddenly, Darnley forced his way into the chamber with a large group of followers. One of the intruders held Mary back and a pistol was pointed towards her pregnant belly. Ruthven and another man then attacked Riccio. He was then dragged from the room and stabbed many times. His lifeless body was discovered early next morning.

Source **B**

> Darnley unexpectedly appeared with a group of armed nobles, including Lord Ruthven, and burst into Mary's chamber. Ruthven shouted to Riccio to step forward away from Mary. Riccio was then pulled out of the room and stabbed over 50 times before his body was thrown downstairs. Mary, who was pregnant, could not do anything because she had been seized and had a gun pointed to her stomach.

6. Compare the views of **Sources A** and **B** about what happened to Riccio. (Compare the sources overall and/or in detail.) 4

7. Explain the reasons why Mary was forced to abdicate in 1567. 5

MARKS

Source C describes the events surrounding the trial of Mary, Queen of Scots in 1587.

Source C

> At first Mary thought that she would not attend her trial. However she learned that the trial would be held even in her absence. Mary defended herself but she was not allowed to call her own witnesses. The trial started on the 14th of October and lasted two days. During this time she was not even allowed to consult any documents. Mary told her servants that she knew she would be found guilty because it was too great a risk to let her live.

8. How fully does **Source C** describe the events surrounding the trial of Mary, Queen of Scots in 1587? (Use **Source C** and recall.)

6

[Now go to SECTION 2 starting on Page fourteen]

MARKS

SECTION 1 — SCOTTISH CONTEXTS — 20 marks

Part C — The Treaty of Union, 1689–1715

Answer the following questions using recalled knowledge and information from the sources where appropriate.

9. Explain the reasons why there was tension between Scotland and England by 1705.

5

Source A is about Scottish attitudes towards the Union.

Source A

> Opponents of the Union warned of higher taxes. However supporters of the Union were clear that it would help Scotland to become richer in the future. Many Protestants argued that the main advantage of the Union would be securing the Protestant Succession. They also pointed out that the English had made it clear they would respect the independence of the Church of Scotland. It was also argued that if the Union was rejected England might simply invade and take over anyway.

10. How fully does **Source A** explain the arguments used by supporters of the Union? (Use **Source A** and recall.)

6

MARKS

Sources **B** and **C** are about the Union debate.

Source **B**

> In 1706 the debate over the Union was in full flow. All of the leaflets produced for the public expressed opposition. Many feared that the proposed Union would lead to a rise in taxes. Some feared for the independence of the Church of Scotland. Many leaflets were produced on the subject. They argued that England was the far bigger country and so would control Scotland.

Source **C**

> Many powerful Scots argued for the Union, but their views did not represent the majority. Many Scots felt that the Union would not be a partnership but a takeover. Economic arguments were the most important ones and it was claimed that after Union higher taxes would hit all Scots in the pocket. Religion was very important to many Scots and they did not want the English to interfere in their Church.

11. Compare the views of **Sources B** and **C** on Scottish attitudes to the proposed Union. (Compare the sources overall and/or in detail.)   4

12. Describe the effects of the Treaty of Union on Scotland up to 1715.   5

[**Now go to SECTION 2 starting on Page fourteen**]

MARKS

SECTION 1 — SCOTTISH CONTEXTS — 20 marks

Part D — Migration and Empire, 1830–1939

Answer the following questions using recalled knowledge and information from the sources where appropriate.

Source **A** describes the impact of the Empire on Scotland.

Source A

> Many Scots invested money in the Empire and reinvested their profits in Scotland which added to Scotland's wealth. Scotland's large workforce and the large number of immigrant workers kept wages low. Profits were spent in other ways on luxury houses and impressive public buildings which changed the appearance of Scottish cities. However, profits from trade with the Empire were also used to develop chemical industries and textiles, creating even more jobs. The Empire provided markets for Scottish coal, employing thousands of miners.

13. How fully does **Source A** describe the impact of the Empire on Scotland? (Use **Source A** and recall.)   6

14. Explain the reasons why Lowland Scots emigrated from Scotland between 1830 and 1939.   5

15. Describe how Scots tried to keep their traditional Scottish way of life in their new countries.   5

MARKS

Sources **B** and **C** are about the contribution Scots made to the development of Australia.

Source B

> The links between Scotland and Australia stretch back to the landing of the *Endeavour*. Thomas Mitchell from Stirling was the first European to explore the rich lands of Victoria for new settlement. The Scottish Australia Company was formed in Aberdeen to encourage Scottish investment to businesses in Australia. Education was supported by successful Scots such as Fife-born Sir Peter Russell who gave £100,000 to the University of Sydney to develop the study of engineering.

Source C

> Scots made their mark in shaping modern Australia. Francis Ormond from Aberdeen gave large sums to set up the Working Men's Technical College in Melbourne to support education. Glasgow investors formed the influential New Zealand and Australian Land Company to encourage the wool export trade. The Scottish explorer John McDouall Stuart was the first European to cross Australia. Even "Waltzing Matilda" was written by the son of a Scot.

16. Compare the views in **Sources B** and **C** about the contribution of Scots to the development of Australia. (Compare the sources overall and/or in detail.)   4

[Now go to SECTION 2 starting on Page fourteen]

SECTION 1 — SCOTTISH CONTEXTS — 20 marks

Part E — The Era of the Great War, 1910–1928

Answer the following questions using recalled knowledge and information from the sources where appropriate.

Source A is about the use of tanks on the Western Front.

Source A

> Thirty-six tanks led the way in an attack at Flers. The sudden appearance of the new weapon stunned their German opponents. However, Sir Douglas Haig used them before they were truly battle ready in an attempt to break the trench stalemate. These early tanks were very slow moving. They often broke down. Tanks often became stuck in the heavy mud of no man's land. Conditions for the tank crews were awful. The heat generated inside the tank was tremendous and fumes often nearly choked the men inside.

17. How fully does **Source A** describe the impact tanks had on fighting on the Western Front during the Great War? (Use **Source A** and recall.)   **6**

MARKS

Sources **B** and **C** are about conditions in the trenches.

Source B

> I sincerely hope it will not freeze. It is so hard on the poor men in trenches standing in very deep mud. Water is often up to their waists. A frost will mean so many frozen feet. I spent my New Year's Eve in a dugout lying on a stretcher on the floor with a wounded man over me. Rats were playing about all over. Shells burst all round and shook the place.

Source C

> If anyone had to go to the company on our right he had to walk through thirty yards of waterlogged trench, which was chest-deep in water in some places. The duckboard track was constantly shelled, and in places a hundred yards of it had been blown to smithereens. It was better to keep off the track when walking back and forth. Soldiers had to make their way sometimes through very heavy mud.

18. Compare the views of **Sources B** and **C** about conditions in the trenches. (Compare the sources overall and/or in detail.)   4

19. Explain the reasons why some people were unhappy with government restrictions like DORA.   5

20. Describe the economic difficulties faced by Scotland after the Great War.   5

[Now go to SECTION 2 starting on Page fourteen]

MARKS

SECTION 2 — BRITISH CONTEXTS — 20 marks

Part A — The Creation of the Medieval Kingdoms, 1066–1406

Answer the following questions using recalled knowledge and information from the sources where appropriate.

21. Describe the role of a baron in medieval times. 5

22. Explain the reasons why Henry II and Archbishop Becket quarrelled. 5

Source A describes the duties of a monk.

Source A

> Early in the morning all monks met in the chapter house. When not attending church services, monks were expected to carry out hard physical labour in the field or herb garden. Well-educated monks studied the Bible or spent hours copying and illuminating books. Although monks lived in isolation, they often supported their local community by collecting alms and caring for the poor. Monks also provided the only medical help available at the time, looking after the sick in the monastery's infirmary.

23. How fully does **Source A** describe the duties of a monk in medieval times? (Use **Source A** and recall.) 5

Source B is from a book written by a doctor in 1350.

Source B

> The first sign of death was a swelling called a buboe, under the armpit or in the groin. Usually the swelling grew to the size of an egg or an apple and spread all over the body. Soon after, the victim began to vomit and developed a fever. This was followed by the appearance of black and purple spots on the arms or thighs. No doctor could cure this terrible disease and so thousands died.

24. Evaluate the usefulness of **Source B** as evidence of the symptoms of the Black Death. 5

    (You may want to comment on who wrote it, when they wrote it, why they wrote it, what they say or what has been missed out.)

[Now go to SECTION 3 starting on Page nineteen]

MARKS

SECTION 2 — BRITISH CONTEXTS — 20 marks

Part B — War of the Three Kingdoms, 1603–1651

Answer the following questions using recalled knowledge and information from the sources where appropriate.

25. Describe the changes to the ways Scotland and England were governed after the Union of the Crowns.

5

Source A is from a book written by King James VI and I.

Source A

> The power of the monarchy is the supreme authority on Earth. To question what God may do is to show disrespect to God. Therefore it is treason for a King's subjects to challenge what a King may or may not do. A good King will make decisions according to the law, but he is not obliged to follow that law unless he sees fit to do so.

26. Evaluate the usefulness of **Source A** as evidence of James VI and I's belief in the Divine Right of Kings.

5

(You may want to comment on who wrote it, when they wrote it, why they wrote it, what they say or what has been missed out.)

27. Explain the reasons why Charles I faced opposition to his rule in Scotland.

5

Source B describes the events that led to the outbreak of the Civil War in 1642.

Source B

> In June 1642 the Long Parliament passed a set of demands called the Nineteen Proposals. These demands called for the King's powers to be reduced and more control to be given to Parliament. This event divided Parliament between those who supported the Nineteen Proposals and those who thought Parliament had gone too far. Parliament and Charles then began to raise their own armies. People were then forced to choose sides and on 22nd August 1642 the King raised his standard at Nottingham.

28. How fully does **Source B** describe the events that led to the outbreak of the Civil War in 1642? (Use **Source B** and recall.)

5

[Now go to SECTION 3 starting on Page nineteen]

MARKS

SECTION 2 — BRITISH CONTEXTS — 20 marks

Part C — The Atlantic Slave Trade, 1770–1807

Answer the following questions using recalled knowledge and information from the sources where appropriate.

29. Describe the different stages of the triangular trade.   5

Source A is about the importance of the slave trade to Britain's economy.

Source A

> The slave trade was considered essential to Britain's economy in the eighteenth century. For example, the slave trade had raised Liverpool from a struggling port to one of the richest and most prosperous trading centres in the world. The slave trade provided work in almost every industry in the town. Slave cotton provided work for the mills of Lancashire. However, little thought was given to the suffering of those involved in its production. Merchants made huge profits importing sugar from the Caribbean, a product which was in great demand.

30. How fully does **Source A** explain the importance of the slave trade to Britain's economy? (Use **Source A** and recall.)   5

Source B is from a book written by a modern historian published in 1987.

Source B

> The island of Barbados was transformed by the slave trade. By the eighteenth century, small farms had been replaced by large plantations which grew sugar more profitably. The island had once been a beautiful wilderness. However, accounts tell of how the island was slowly but surely cleared of its native people and its vegetation. These were replaced by plantations. These became the work place, and final resting place, of armies of African slaves.

31. Evaluate the usefulness of **Source B** as evidence of the impact of the slave trade on the Caribbean islands.   5

     (You may want to comment on who wrote it, when they wrote it, why they wrote it, what they say or what has been missed out.)

32. Explain the reasons why resistance was difficult for slaves on plantations.   5

[Now go to SECTION 3 starting on Page nineteen]

Page sixteen

MARKS

SECTION 2 — BRITISH CONTEXTS — 20 marks

Part D — Changing Britain, 1760–1900

Answer the following questions using recalled knowledge and information from the sources where appropriate.

Source A is about the impact of new technology on textile factories.

Source A

> After 1760 there were many inventions that helped to speed up the production of textiles. Spinning was improved by the invention of the Spinning Jenny in 1763, which could spin eight threads at once. In 1769, Arkwright invented the Water Frame which used water power and made much better thread than the Spinning Jenny. A steam engine which was easy to use in factories was developed by Boulton and Watt in the 1780s. This meant that factories did not have to be built near fast-flowing water for a power supply.

33. How fully does **Source A** explain the impact of new technology on textile factories? (Use **Source A** and recall.)   **5**

34. Describe working conditions in coal mines before 1842.   **5**

Source B is from a book by a railway inspector, published in 1870.

Source B

> The comforts, or rather discomforts, of railway travelling about thirty years ago were very different from those of the present day. Third-class carriages were often little different from basic cattle trucks. For a considerable time they were completely open and had no seats. First and second class carriages were covered and had seating. The luggage of the passengers was packed on top of the carriages.

35. Evaluate the usefulness of **Source B** as evidence of railway travel in the nineteenth century.   **5**

    (You may want to comment on who wrote it, when they wrote it, why they wrote it, what they say or what has been missed out.)

36. Explain the reasons why people's health had improved by 1900.   **5**

[Now go to SECTION 3 starting on Page nineteen]

MARKS

SECTION 2 — BRITISH CONTEXTS — 20 marks

Part E — The Making of Modern Britain, 1880–1951

Answer the following questions using recalled knowledge and information from the sources where appropriate.

37. Describe the reforms introduced by the Liberal Government of 1906–1914 to help the sick.

5

Source A is from a book by Flora Thompson about her own life, published in 1939.

Source A

> When pensions began, life was transformed for the old. They were no longer anxious and were suddenly rich. When they went to the Post Office to collect it, tears of gratitude would run down their cheeks and they would say as they picked up their money "God bless that Lord George". They gave flowers from their gardens and apples from their trees to the girl who merely handed them the money.

38. Evaluate the usefulness of **Source A** as evidence of the benefits of the 1908 Old Age Pensions Act.

5

(You may want to comment on who wrote it, when they wrote it, why they wrote it, what they say or what has been missed out.)

Source B is about the Beveridge Report which was published in 1942.

Source B

> The Beveridge Report was published in 1942 and sold over 635,000 copies. The report identified the five "giant evils" facing Britain. Beveridge believed that tackling one of the five giants wouldn't do much good; the government would have to tackle them all. He recommended that there should be a welfare system that would look after people from the "cradle to the grave". He believed that there should be benefits for the unemployed, the sick, the elderly and widows. He also advised the government to adopt a policy of full employment.

39. How fully does **Source B** explain the recommendations of the 1942 Beveridge Report? (Use **Source B** and recall.)

5

40. Explain the reasons why the Labour Government reforms of 1945–1951 did not fully tackle the problem of squalor.

5

MARKS

SECTION 3 — EUROPEAN AND WORLD CONTEXTS — 20 marks

Part A — The Cross and the Crescent: the Crusades, 1071–1192

Answer the following questions using recalled knowledge and information from the sources where appropriate.

41. To what extent did Pope Urban II call for the First Crusade for religious reasons?

    (You must use recalled knowledge to present a **balanced assessment** of the influence of different factors and come to a **reasoned conclusion**.)

    8

42. Explain the reasons why the Crusaders lost control of Jerusalem in 1187.

    6

Source A is from a chronicle written by a Crusader in 1191.

> Despite his promises, Saladin did not pay the ransom agreed for the Muslim hostages and did not return the True Cross to the Crusaders. Instead, Saladin attempted to trick King Richard, sending him gifts and treasures. He hoped that Richard would release the Muslims for free. Eventually King Richard grew tired of Saladin. The next morning the king ordered the Muslims to be led out of the city and beheaded.

43. Evaluate the usefulness of **Source A** as evidence of the massacre at Acre.

    6

    (You may want to comment on who wrote it, when they wrote it, why they wrote it, what they say or what has been missed out.)

MARKS

SECTION 3 — EUROPEAN AND WORLD CONTEXTS — 20 marks

Part B — "Tea and Freedom": the American Revolution, 1774–1783

Answer the following questions using recalled knowledge and information from the sources where appropriate.

44. Explain the reasons why a war broke out between Britain and the American colonists.

6

Source A is from the diary of an American army surgeon during the winter of 1777.

> December 14: The army now begins to grow tired of the continued difficulties they have faced in this winter campaign. Poor food, tough living conditions, cold weather, sickness, fatigue, nasty clothes, nasty cookery, the Devil's in it! I can't endure it! Why are we sent here to starve and freeze? Yet our men still show a great spirit and morale that is unexpected from such young soldiers.

45. Evaluate the usefulness of **Source A** as evidence of the experience of soldiers who fought in the Wars of Independence.

6

(You may want to comment on who wrote it, when they wrote it, why they wrote it, what they say or what has been missed out.)

46. To what extent did the intervention of foreign countries lead to Britain's defeat in the Wars of Independence?

8

(You must use recalled knowledge to present a **balanced assessment** of the influence of different factors and come to a **reasoned conclusion**.)

MARKS

SECTION 3 — EUROPEAN AND WORLD CONTEXTS — 20 marks

Part C — USA, 1850–1880

Answer the following questions using recalled knowledge and information from the sources where appropriate.

47. Explain the reasons why Native Americans opposed westward expansion.

6

48. To what extent did the election of Lincoln as President in 1860 lead to the outbreak of the Civil War?

8

(You must use recalled knowledge to present a **balanced assessment** of the influence of different factors and come to a **reasoned conclusion**.)

Source A is from a report written by an officer of the Freedmen's Bureau in 1866.

> The freed slaves in Texas have been terrorised by attacks from the desperate men of the local area. These freed men are scared to report any murder of a black man. The murderers dislike the fact that they no longer have control over their former slaves. Many of the former slaves are unhappy with their freedom and would prefer to still be slaves as it offered them some protection.

49. Evaluate the usefulness of **Source A** as evidence of the effects of Reconstruction on the Southern States after 1865.

6

(You may want to comment on who wrote it, when they wrote it, why they wrote it, what they say or what has been missed out.)

MARKS

SECTION 3 — EUROPEAN AND WORLD CONTEXTS — 20 marks

Part D — Hitler and Nazi Germany, 1919–1939

Answer the following questions using recalled knowledge and information from the sources where appropriate.

50. Explain the reasons why the Weimar Government was unpopular up to 1925.   **6**

51. To what extent were the social policies of the Nazi Government crucial to their maintenance of power between 1933 and 1939?   **8**

    (You must use recalled knowledge to present a **balanced assessment** of the influence of different factors and come to a **reasoned conclusion**.)

Source A is from a textbook written by a modern historian, published in 2013.

> On buses and park benches, Jews had to sit on seats marked for them. Children at German schools were taught anti-Semitic ideas. Jewish children were ridiculed by teachers. Bullying of Jews in the playground by other pupils went unpunished. If Jewish children then chose not to go to school, the Nazis claimed this proved that Jewish children were lazy and could not be bothered to go to school.

52. Evaluate the usefulness of **Source A** as evidence of the treatment of Jews in Nazi Germany.   **6**

    (You may want to comment on who wrote it, when they wrote it, why they wrote it, what they say or what has been missed out.)

MARKS

SECTION 3 — EUROPEAN AND WORLD CONTEXTS — 20 marks

Part E — Red Flag: Lenin and the Russian Revolution, 1894–1921

Answer the following questions using recalled knowledge and information from the sources where appropriate.

53. Explain the reasons why it was so difficult to oppose the Tsar before 1905.   **6**

54. To what extent did problems caused by the First World War lead to the Tsar's downfall in February 1917?   **8**

(You must use recalled knowledge to present a **balanced assessment** of the influence of different factors and come to a **reasoned conclusion.**)

Source A is from the diary of the British Ambassador to Russia dated 24th October 1917.

> I heard this morning that the Bolsheviks would overthrow the Government in the course of the next few days because they had captured enough weapons. At one o'clock, three Government Ministers arrived. I was not convinced that the Government had enough force behind them to deal with the situation. I told them that I could not understand how the Government could allow Trotsky to go on encouraging the population to murder and steal.

55. Evaluate the usefulness of **Source A** as evidence of the reasons for the Bolshevik seizure of power in October 1917.   **6**

(You may want to comment on who wrote it, when they wrote it, why they wrote it, what they say or what has been missed out.)

MARKS

SECTION 3 — EUROPEAN AND WORLD CONTEXTS — 20 marks

Part F — Mussolini and Fascist Italy, 1919–1939

Answer the following questions using recalled knowledge and information from the sources where appropriate.

56. To what extent was the widespread appeal of Fascism the main reason why Mussolini was able to seize power by 1925?

    (You must use recalled knowledge to present a **balanced assessment** of the influence of different factors and come to a **reasoned conclusion**.)

8

Source A is from a book by a modern historian published in 2006.

> By 1925 Fascist control of Italy was secure. The Battle for Grain began in 1925 and was a major attempt to promote Fascist power and national self-sufficiency. The government tried to boost grain production by giving farmers grants so that they could buy tractors, fertiliser and any other machinery necessary for wheat production. Farmers were also guaranteed a high price for the grain they produced.

57. Evaluate the usefulness of **Source A** as evidence of Mussolini's economic policies.

    (You may want to comment on who wrote it, when they wrote it, why they wrote it, what they say or what has been missed out.)

6

58. Explain the reasons why Mussolini was able to crush opposition in Fascist Italy.

6

MARKS

SECTION 3 — EUROPEAN AND WORLD CONTEXTS — 20 marks

Part G — Free at Last? Civil Rights in the USA, 1918–1968

Answer the following questions using recalled knowledge and information from the sources where appropriate.

59. To what extent was the fear of white violence the main reason for the migration of black Americans to the North?

    (You must use recalled knowledge to present a **balanced assessment** of the influence of different factors and come to a **reasoned conclusion.**)

    8

60. Explain the reasons why the Montgomery Bus Boycott was an important step forward in the campaign for civil rights.

    6

Source A is from a speech made by Malcolm X in December 1962.

> The teaching of the Honourable Elijah Muhammad is making our people, for the first time, proud to be black, and that is most important. I just wanted to point out that whites are a race of devils. It's left up to you and me to decide if we want to integrate with this wicked race or separate to be on our own. If we separate then we have a chance for salvation.

61. Evaluate the usefulness of **Source A** as evidence of the beliefs of Malcolm X.

    6

    (You may want to comment on who wrote it, when they wrote it, why they wrote it, what they say or what has been missed out.)

MARKS

SECTION 3 — EUROPEAN AND WORLD CONTEXTS — 20 marks

Part H — Appeasement and the Road to War, 1918–1939

Answer the following questions using recalled knowledge and information from the sources where appropriate.

62. Explain the reasons why Hitler rearmed Germany after 1933.   6

63. To what extent was public opinion the main reason why Chamberlain followed a policy of appeasement?   8

(You must use recalled knowledge to present a **balanced assessment** of the influence of different factors and come to a **reasoned conclusion**.)

Source A is from a book by a modern historian published in 1989.

> On 15th March 1939, German troops marched in to Prague and within two days Czechoslovakia ceased to exist. After destroying Czechoslovakia, Hitler turned his attention to Poland. On 29th March the British government gave Poland a guarantee to protect it against any threat to its independence. On 22nd May Hitler and Mussolini strengthened the ties between their two countries by signing an agreement which required them to help each other in time of war.

64. Evaluate the usefulness of **Source A** as evidence of the events leading to the outbreak of war in 1939.   6

(You may want to comment on who wrote it, when they wrote it, why they wrote it, what they say or what has been missed out.)

MARKS

SECTION 3 — EUROPEAN AND WORLD CONTEXTS — 20 marks

Part I — World War II, 1939–1945

Answer the following questions using recalled knowledge and information from the sources where appropriate.

Source A is from an interview with a sailor who was on board an evacuation ship at Dunkirk in May 1940.

> The thing that shocked me most was seeing all the soldiers coming back without their equipment. We began to think it was the end of our way of life. We didn't know how long we'd be able to hold Jerry off in England. We knew we had the Navy, and that we could fight. However we didn't know what our soldiers would be able to do if Jerry invaded, because they had nothing.

65. Evaluate the usefulness of **Source A** as evidence of what happened at Dunkirk in May 1940.

    (You may want to comment on who wrote it, when they wrote it, why they wrote it, what they say or what has been missed out.)

    6

66. Explain the reasons why the Japanese attacked the US naval base at Pearl Harbour in December 1941.

    6

67. To what extent was effective planning by the Allies the main reason for the success of the Normandy landings in June 1944?

    8

    (You must use recalled knowledge to present a **balanced assessment** of the influence of different factors and come to a **reasoned conclusion**.)

MARKS

SECTION 3 — EUROPEAN AND WORLD CONTEXTS — 20 marks

Part J — The Cold War, 1945–1989

Answer the following questions using recalled knowledge and information from the sources where appropriate.

68. To what extent was a difference in political beliefs the main reason for the development of the Cold War between 1945 and 1955?

    (You must use recalled knowledge to present a **balanced assessment** of the influence of different factors and come to a **reasoned conclusion**.)

8

Source A is from a newspaper article written by a British journalist, published on 23 October 1956.

> Today I have seen a great event. I have watched the people of Budapest come out into the streets in rebellion against their Soviet masters. As I telephone this report I can hear the roar of crowds marching, shouting complaints against Russia. "Send the Red Army home," they roar. "We want free and secret elections." Leaflets demanding the sacking of the present Government are being thrown from trams into the crowds on the streets.

69. Evaluate the usefulness of **Source A** as evidence of the reasons for the Hungarian revolution of 1956.

    (You may want to comment on who wrote it, when they wrote it, why they wrote it, what they say or what has been missed out.)

6

70. Explain the reasons why America was unable to defeat the Vietcong.

6

[END OF QUESTION PAPER]

NATIONAL 5 | ANSWER SECTION

SQA AND HODDER GIBSON NATIONAL 5 HISTORY 2015

Section 1, Part A

1. *You should try to make 5 separate points from recall.*

You could mention:

- The death of Alexander III
- The death of the Maid of Norway
- The Guardians asked Edward to decide who would be king
- Edward demanded that the (thirteen) Competitors recognise him as overlord
- Edward chose Balliol
- John Balliol did homage to King Edward

You can always get extra marks if you bring in more information to back up a point you are making. E.g. the first event that contributed to Edward becoming overlord was the death of Alexander III (**1 mark**). This severely weakened Scotland as he had no son to succeed him (**1 mark**).

5

2. *Start off by saying that the source partly explains Edward's decision. This allows you to go on to show what is and what is not in the source.*

The source mentions:

- The Scots organised a rebellion against Edward
- The Scots rejected Edward's claim to be Scotland's overlord
- Scotland made an alliance with France against England

However the source does not mention:

- The Scots refused to obey Edward's order to help him fight against the French
- The Scots invaded the north of England
- The Scots attacked Carlisle

5

3. *You should try to make 5 separate points from recall.*

You could mention:

- Wallace organised the army of Scotland
- He defeated the English at Stirling Bridge
- He accepted the position of joint Guardian of Scotland
- He developed the idea of fighting in schiltrons
- He continued to resist Edward until he was executed

You can always get extra marks if you add more information to back up a point you are making. E.g. the leadership of Wallace was important because he managed to organise the army of Scotland (**1 mark**) using guerrilla tactics against the English occupation (**1 mark**).

5

4. *You need to make 5 clear points about the usefulness of the source.*

You would probably start by arguing that the source does provide useful evidence about Bruce's tactics. Comment on who wrote the source, when it was written and why it was written:

- The author is an English monk who was present at the time of the raid
- The source was written at the time of the raid
- The source was written to describe what happened when Bruce's army invaded England

However, you could say that the source is likely to be biased because it was written by an English monk.

You should then comment on the information contained in the source:

- The source tells us that Bruce's army attacked Durham and Richmond
- English people had to resort to paying the Scots not to attack their town

You would gain marks by pointing out that in some ways the source is less useful because of important information that has not been mentioned. E.g. Bruce sent his brother to attack Ireland, and asked the Pope to overturn his excommunication.

5

Section 1, Part B

1. *You should try to make 5 separate points from recall.*

You could mention:

- Henry wanted to break the Auld Alliance between Scotland and France
- The Scots announced that they considered the Treaty of Greenwich was void
- The government of Scotland was becoming more friendly towards France
- The French had bribed Arran to change his mind about the Treaty of Greenwich
- Henry intended to force the Scots into changing their mind

You can always get extra marks if you add more information to back up a point you are making. E.g. the Scots had angered Henry when they claimed that the Treaty of Greenwich was void (**1 mark**). This Treaty had arranged for Mary to marry Henry's son (**1 mark**).

5

2. *You need to make 5 clear points about the usefulness of the source.*

You would probably start by arguing that the source does provide useful evidence about the growth of Protestantism. Comment on who wrote the source, when it was written and why it was written:

- The source was written when Protestantism was growing in Scotland
- It was written by John Knox an important Protestant leader of the time
- It was written to provide an account of the growth of Protestantism

You should then comment on the information contained in the source:

- It tells us that John Knox felt able to return to Scotland and preach openly

However, you could say that the source is likely to be biased because it was written by John Knox who was biased in favour of Protestantism.

You would gain marks by pointing out that in some ways the source is less useful because of important information that has not been mentioned. E.g. Elizabeth I's accession to the throne in England also encouraged the growth of Protestantism in Scotland

5

3. *Start off by saying that the source partly describes how well Mary ruled Scotland. This allows you to go on to show what is and what is not in the source.*

The source mentions:

- She established a successful government
- She defeated nobles who challenged her authority
- Her religious policy was tolerant and ahead of its time

However the source does not mention:

- She was more concerned about furthering her claim to the English throne
- She left the running of Scotland to a small group of nobles
- She failed to deal with religious problems in Scotland

5

4. *You should try to make 5 separate points from recall.*

You could mention:

- Mary was Elizabeth's heir
- Her presence encouraged opposition to Queen Elizabeth in England
- Plots to remove Elizabeth and place Mary on the throne
- There would be dangers in allowing Mary to return to Scotland
- There would be dangers in allowing Mary to go to France

You can always get extra marks if you add more information to back up a point you are making. E.g. there were a number of plots to remove Elizabeth and place Mary on the throne (**1 mark**) for example the Ridolfi Plot (**1 mark**).

5

Section 1, Part C

1. *You should try to make 5 separate points from recall.*

You could mention:

- The English ship, Worcester was seized at Leith
- Captain Green and two of his crew were arrested and put on trial for piracy
- They were found guilty and sentenced to death
- Queen Anne's government in England wanted her to pardon them
- Queen Anne wanted her Scottish Government to pardon them
- Captain Green and the two crewmen were hanged

You can always get extra marks if you bring in more information to back up a point you are making. E.g. Captain Green and two of his crewmen were hanged (**1 mark**). An Edinburgh mob put pressure on the Scottish Government not to pardon them (**1 mark**).

5

2. *You need to make 5 clear points about the usefulness of the source.*

You would probably start by arguing that the source does provide useful evidence about the Treaty of Union. Comment on who wrote the source, when it was written and why it was written:

- Written shortly after the Treaty of Union therefore a primary source
- Written by someone who had traveled in Scotland during the time
- Written to describe reaction to the Treaty in Scotland

You should then comment on the information contained in the source:

- Scots called the people who had negotiated the Union traitors
- Scots wanted to remain Scotsmen

You would gain marks by pointing out that in some ways the source is less useful because of important information that has not been mentioned e.g:

- some Scots supported the Union
- some believed it would make Scotland wealthier

6

3. *Start off by saying that the source partly describes the arguments against the Union. This allows you to go on to show what is and what is not in the source.*

The source mentions:

- Scots feared that they would have little influence over government decisions
- Businesses in Scotland would suffer as a result of English imports
- The Treaty had been signed because of English bribes

However the source does not mention:

- Presbyterians feared a British parliament dominated by Anglican church
- Fears of reduction in status of Scottish nobility in British parliament
- Fear of new taxes
- Fear of taking on English debt

5

4. *You should try to make 5 separate points from recall.*

You could mention:

- Scotland had not become richer
- There was fear that English imports were ruining Scottish businesses
- There were new Customs and Excise taxes
- They disliked the changes in Scotland's weights, measures, money, etc
- Nobles and important politicians had left Edinburgh for London
- The House of Lords had allowed "patronage" in the Church of Scotland (Patronage Act)

You can always get extra marks if you add more information to back up a point you are making. E.g. there were new Customs and Excise taxes (**1 mark**) for example a Malt Tax was introduced (**1 mark**).

5

Section 1, Part D

1. *You should try to make 5 separate points from recall.*

You could mention:

- Scotland was close to Ireland
- Travel was cheap
- There was work to be found in cotton/textile factories
- Many found work as navigators of the canals and railways
- There was work to be found on farms at harvest time
- Many Irish had already settled in Scotland which encouraged more to come

You can always get extra marks if you add more information to back up a point you are making. E.g. there was work to be found in cotton/textile factories (**1 mark**) which often provided jobs for the whole family (**1 mark**).

5

2. *You need to make 5 clear points about the usefulness of the source.*

You would probably start by arguing that the source does provide useful evidence about the impact of the Irish on law and order. Comment on who wrote the source, when it was written and why it was written:

- Comes from a newspaper which reported on events in Scotland
- Published during a time of Irish immigration
- Written to describe the impact of Irish immigrants

You should then comment on the information contained in the source:

- Describes an attack by Irish navvies
- Describes how the police responded to the attack

However, you might point out that the source is taken from a Scottish newspaper and is less likely to give the Irish side of the story.

You would gain marks by pointing out that in some ways the source is less useful because of important information that has not been mentioned. E.g. most Irish immigrants were hardworking and law-abiding.

5

3. *Start off by saying that the source partly explains why Scots emigrated. This allows you to go on to show what is and what is not in the source.*

The source mentions:

- Landlords paid travelling costs
- Rent arrears written off so that emigrants had money
- Landlords often bought their cattle
- Edinburgh and Glasgow made a contribution towards their expenses in emigrating

However the source does not mention:

- Highlands and Islands Emigration Society (HIES) gave assistance
- Charities e.g. Barnardos, helped orphans/young women to emigrate
- Countries such as Australia and Canada sent agents to advise on emigration
- Family members living abroad gave encouragement and sent money for travel

5

4. *You should try to make 5 separate points from recall.*

You could mention:

- Scots brought farming skills to Canada
- Scots developed sheep farming in Australia
- Tradesmen such as stone masons helped the building industry in USA
- Developed businesses, banks and trading companies
- Scots established education system e.g. Canada
- Scots brought a tradition of hard work

You can always get extra marks if you bring in more information to back up a point you are making. E.g. Scots developed businesses in their new countries (**1 mark**) for example Andrew Carnegie's success in the American steel industry (**1 mark**).

5

Section 1, Part E

1. *You need to make 5 clear points about the usefulness of the source.*

You would probably start by arguing that the source does provide useful evidence about the use of new technology during the First World War. Comment on who wrote the source, when it was written and why it was written:

- The source was written by someone who was involved in developing new technology
- It was written in 1918 not long after the invention of the tank
- It was written to explain how the tank was used

You should then comment on the information contained in the source:

- The tank helped to deal with enemy machine guns

You would gain marks by pointing out that in some ways the source is less useful because of important information that has not been mentioned. E.g. early tanks were very unreliable and very slow moving.

5

2. *Start off by saying that the source partly describes the changing role of women during the war. This allows you to go on to show what is and what is not in the source.*

The source mentions:

- Women took over jobs vacated by men
- They carried out vital work in the munitions industry
- They kept transport going
- They had to take on greater responsibility in the home

However the source does not mention:

- Women worked on farms
- They coped with food shortages/ rationing
- They joined the armed services

5

3. *You should try to make 5 separate points from recall.*

You could mention:

- Lack of investment and foreign competition resulted in decline of the coal industry
- The demand for ships declined
- Shipyards were hit by labour disputes
- Other countries increased their steel making

- Jute prices collapsed after the war
- The collapse of foreign markets for herring greatly affected the industry
- Cheap foreign imports of food competed with agriculture when trade was resumed after the war

You can always get extra marks if you bring in more information to back up a point you are making. E.g. the demand for ships declined (**1 mark**) for example Clyde yards produced warships which were no longer needed after the war (**1 mark**).

5

4. *You should try to make 5 separate points from recall.*

You could mention:

- Militancy gained a lot of negative publicity
- Many campaigners felt that militant action undermined their efforts
- Government determined not to give into acts of vandalism/force
- Attacks on MPs alienated support/turned many people against the cause who had previously supported votes for women
- Violent actions e.g. window smashing annoyed the public
- Upset Suffragists/damaged Suffragist campaign
- Once imprisoned Suffragettes could no longer campaign effectively

You can always get extra marks if you add more information to back up a point you are making. E.g. militancy gained a lot of negative publicity (**1 mark**) newspapers such as the Daily Mail condemned the Suffragettes as mad and irresponsible (**1 mark**).

5

Section 2, Part C

1. *You need to make 6 clear points about the usefulness of the source.*

You would probably start by arguing that the source does provide useful evidence about the treatment of slaves on the Middle Passage. Comment on who wrote the source, when it was written and why it was written:

- The source was written by a slave who had experienced the Middle Passage
- Written in 1789 at the time of the slave trade
- Written to describe what the Middle Passage was like

You should then comment on the information contained in the source:

- The source mentions terrible conditions below decks
- It mentions the shrieks of the women

You would gain marks by pointing out that in some ways the source is less useful because of important information that has not been mentioned. E.g. the source does not mention slaves being forced to exercise on deck.

6

2. *You should try to make 5 separate points from recall.*

You could mention:

- Millions of enslaved people taken from Africa
- Mostly strong young males and females
- Some African kings became rich through selling slaves to Europeans
- Europeans sold cloth, alcohol and firearms to Africans
- Some tribes went to war against neighbouring tribes in order to capture people to enslave
- Some tribes carried out raids on other tribes to kidnap people to enslave

You can always get extra marks if you bring in more information to back up a point you are making. E.g. some African Kings grew rich through selling slaves to Europeans (**1 mark**). For example the Kings of Dahomey earned fortunes from enslaving neighbouring tribes (**1 mark**).

5

3. *You should try to make 5 separate points from recall.*

You could mention:

- Slaves were often branded by their owners
- Slaves were punished severely for minor crimes
- Slaves were paired off by their owner for breeding purposes
- Slave families could be split up by their owners
- Female slaves were subjected to sexual abuse by their owners
- Slaves were forced to work very long hours

You can always get extra marks if you add more information to back up a point you are making. E.g. slaves were punished severely for minor crimes (**1 mark**). A runaway might be whipped and forced to wear a collar (**1 mark**).

5

4. *For this type of question you must say whether you think the sources agree or not and then support your decision by making two comparisons using evidence from the sources.*

For this question you would probably decide that the two sources agree. You could then back this up with two of the following comparisons:

- Source A says that plantation owners had political influence and Source B supports this by saying that the plantation owners allied themselves with important groups to promote the case for slavery
- Source A points out that there were British ports which relied on the slave trade and Source B backs this up by mentioning that dozens of British ports relied on the slave trade
- Source A says that people believed that the trade had helped them to make Britain wealthy and prosperous and Source B supports this by pointing out that slavery seemed vital to the continuing prosperity of Britain

4

Section 2, Part D

1. *You should try to make 5 separate points from recall.*

You could mention:

- Revolution in agriculture helped feed the urban population
- Fertility of mothers increased as a result of an improved diet
- Improved medical knowledge e.g. better understanding of the connection between dirt and disease/bacteria
- Vaccinations against killer diseases: 1853 smallpox; 1897 tetanus, etc
- Improvements in sanitation e.g. flushing toilet

You can always get extra marks if you add more information to back up a point you are making. E.g. revolution in agriculture helped feed the urban population (**1 mark**) and scientific farming methods increased the range of food crops (**1 mark**).

5

2. *You need to make 6 clear points about the usefulness of the source.*

You would probably start by arguing that the source does provide useful evidence about working conditions in cotton mills. Comment on who wrote the source, when it was written and why it was written:

- The source was written by a visitor to a cotton mill
- The source was written during a time when working conditions were being improved
- The source was written to describe what a cotton mill was like

You should then comment on the information contained in the source:

- The source mentions that the factory is well ventilated
- The source mentions that there were guards on dangerous machinery

You would gain marks by pointing out that in some ways the source is less useful because of important information that has not been mentioned. E.g. factory acts had been introduced to improve working conditions especially for children, and many mill owners did not obey the new regulations.

6

3. *You should try to make 5 separate points from recall.*

You could mention:

- More use of steam powered machinery for pumping water
- Improvements made to ventilation
- Wider use of mechanical cage lifts
- Davy Lamp which reduced pit explosions
- Metal props made roof falls less likely
- Coal cutting machinery available from the 1880s

You can always get extra marks if you bring in more information to back up a point you are making. E.g. more use of steam powered machinery for pumping water (**1 mark**). This allowed deeper mining to be safer(**1 mark**).

5

4. *For this type of question you must say whether you think the sources agree or not and then support your decision by making two comparisons using evidence from the sources.*

For this question you would probably decide that the two sources agree. You could then back this up with two of the following comparisons:

- Source A mentions working class anger at the Whig government over the 1832 act. Source B describes working class Fury at continuing restriction on voting which remained after the Act
- Source A mentions people's anger at the Poor Law and Source B tells us about the hatred of the poor law
- Source A mentions working class people being confident about forming their own organizations. Source B mentions a working class backlash

4

Section 2, Part E

1. *You need to make 6 clear points about the usefulness of the source.*

You would probably start by arguing that the source does provide useful evidence about the causes of poverty in the early 20th century. Comment on who wrote the source, when it was written and why it was written:

- The source was written by a Liberal MP who would be well informed about problems in Britain
- The source was written in the early 20th century when the causes of poverty were being debated
- The source was written to explain the causes of poverty

You could argue that the source is less useful because the author was a liberal reformer and could be biased.

You should then comment on the information contained in the source:

- The source mentions that some men's earnings are not enough to keep a family
- It mentions that some people find it difficult to find work

You would gain marks by pointing out that in some ways the source is less useful because of important information that has not been mentioned. E.g. the lack of free secondary education made it difficult for young people to escape poverty, and the lack of affordable housing.

6

2. *For this type of question you must say whether you think the sources agree or not and then support your decision by making two comparisons using evidence from the sources.*

For this question you would probably decide that the two sources agree. You could then back this up with two of the following comparisons:

- Source A says that the reforms were in no sense a welfare state and Source B says that reforms were not designed to free people from poverty
- Source A says that the reforms targeted small areas of poverty and Source B mentions that only certain types of worker were supported for sickness and unemployment
- Source A says that the poor law was still necessary and Source B says that only some people were freed from having to seek poor relief

4

3. *You should try to make 5 separate points from recall.*

You could mention:

- Middle class people became more aware of the problems of poverty through the experience of evacuation
- People from different classes also came together to do air-raid duties like firewatching
- People from different classes were brought together in the air-raid shelters
- Both rich and poor faced the same problems such as bomb damage to their homes
- People were more sympathetic towards people living in inadequate housing due to the blitz

You can always get extra marks if you bring in more information to back up a point you are making. E.g. people from different classes were brought together in the air-raid shelters (**1 mark**). Better off people learned about the problems of the poor for themselves (**1 mark**).

5

4. *You should try to make 5 separate points from recall.*

You could mention:

- Beveridge proposed a system which was open to everyone regardless of wealth
- There would be no return to the hated means test
- The National Health Service would be free to everyone meaning that poor people could receive good medical attention
- Proposed a fair insurance scheme where everyone would pay the same contribution to receive the same benefits
- Promised every family an allowance for every child

You can always get extra marks if you add more information to back up a point you are making. E.g. there would be no return to the hated means test (**1 mark**) and benefits would be universal and based on contributions (**1 mark**).

5

Section 3, Part B

1. *You should try to make 6 separate points from recall.*

You could mention:

- Colonists were angered by the passing of the Tea Act in 1773 which allowed the East India Company to undercut the colonial merchants and smugglers
- Bostonians disguised themselves as Mohawk Indians and boarded the three tea ships
- Tea was emptied into the water of Boston harbour
- Some of the tea was stolen
- King George III and Parliament were outraged when they heard of these events
- Lord North rejected the offer of compensation from some of the colonial merchants
- Led to the passing of the "Intolerable Acts"

You can always get extra marks if you bring in more information to back up a point you are making. E.g. led to the passing of the "Intolerable Acts" (**1 mark**) such as the Massachusetts Act (**1 mark**).

6

2. *You need to make 6 clear points about the usefulness of the source.*

You would probably start by arguing that the source does provide useful evidence about what happened at Lexington and Concord in April 1775. Comment on who wrote the source, when it was written and why it was written:

- The source was written only a month after events at Lexington and Concord/written at the start of the year
- The source was written by the leaders of the colonies, who would have detailed/first hand knowledge of what had taken place
- The source was written to condemn the actions of the British army

You might want to point out ways in which the source is less useful, for example the writers of the source were leaders of the colonies so might be biased against the British.

You should then comment on the information contained in the source:

- The attack is described as unprovoked
- The colonists were cruelly slaughtered

You would gain marks by pointing out that in some ways the source is less useful because of important information that has not been mentioned. E.g. militia in Massachusetts had been training for war and spies had warned of the British army's movements and counter-attack was launched at Concord.

6

3. *If the question starts with "To what extent" you must write a balanced answer.*

In this question you should show that you understand that the involvement of foreign countries caused difficulties for Britain in the War of Independence?

You could mention:

- The French attacked British colonies in the Caribbean and elsewhere which undermined Britain's control
- The French harassed British shipping in the Atlantic interfering with trade
- Britain lost control of the seas for the first time that century
- Britain found it more difficult to reinforce and supply its forces in America.
- France provided the colonies with finance
- France provided the colonies with military assistance – soldiers, gunpowder
- Spain distracted Britain by attacking Gibraltar
- A Franco-Spanish force threatened Britain with invasion in 1779

You should then balance your answer by giving other reasons for Britain's defeat such as:

- Leadership qualities of George Washington
- Public opinion with in Britain was split over the war
- Military leadership was poor
- Major defeats at Saratoga and Yorktown
- Supplying an army fighting so far away from Britain posed major problems
- Colonists knew the territory on which battles were fought

Finish with a conclusion giving an overall answer to the question supported with a reason for the judgement you have made. E.g. overall, Spain and France played an important part in the defeat but it was the weaknesses of the British forces as shown in their military disasters at Saratoga and Yorktown, which were the main reasons for the defeat of Britain in the Wars of Independence.

8

Section 3, Part C

1. *You should try to make 6 separate points from recall.*

You could mention:

- White Americans believed in Manifest Destiny
- Native Americans wanted a home where the buffalo roam while the white Americans wanted to farm
- Treaty made with the Native Americans was broken
- White settlers had a 'property attitude' towards land
- Native Americans believed that Great Spirit had created land for their care
- Grants to encourage gold prospecting alarmed Native Americans
- Sacred land had to be protected by the Native Americans
- Many white Americans favoured setting up reservations
- Native Americans objected to reservation life
- Loss of freedoms associated with the move back to reservations

You can always get extra marks if you add more information to back up a point you are making. E.g. white Americans believed in Manifest Destiny (**1 mark**), a belief in being able to occupy land from the Pacific to the Atlantic (**1 mark**).

6

2. *You need to make 6 clear points about the usefulness of the source.*

You would probably start by arguing that the source does provide useful evidence about the impact of Reconstruction on black people in the South. Comment on who wrote the source, when it was written and why it was written:

- The source was written by a visitor to the South
- The source is taken from a diary written at the time of reconstruction
- The source was written to describe the impact of Reconstruction on black people in the South

You should then comment on the information contained in the source:

- The source mentions that black people were living in shabby conditions
- The source mentions violence used against black people

You would gain marks by pointing out that in some ways the source is less useful because of important information that has not been mentioned. E.g. secret organizations were set up in the South to terrorise black people. Black people were too poor to move.

6

3. *If the question starts with "To what extent" you must write a balanced answer.*

In this question you should show that you understand that differing attitudes to the union brought about Civil War.

You could mention:

- North Eastern States were in favour of a strong Union with power exercised from the centre
- Southern States believed States Rights should not be infringed upon by federal government
- Southern States held that it was their right to secede from the union if it was no longer acting in their interests
- Northern states believed that the South had no right to secede

You should then balance your answer by giving other reasons such as:

- North believed in protection of trade through tariffs
- South relied on free trade
- Northerners were opposed to the expansion of slavery
- Southerners believed that the expansion of slavery was necessary

Finish with a conclusion giving an overall answer to the question supported with a reason for the judgement you have made. E.g. overall, attitudes to the union were an important cause of the Civil War but it was the conflicts over the expansion of slavery, which was the main cause of the war.

8

Section 3, Part D

1. *You should try to make 6 separate points from recall.*

You could mention:

- The Spartacists had no organised plan for an armed revolution
- The Government used the Freikorps to crush the revolt
- The well equipped Freikorps quickly crushed the revolt
- The Freikorps used artillery to recapture buildings in Berlin
- The Spartacist leaders Karl Liebknecht and Rosa Luxemburg were arrested
- Both Spartacist leaders were executed/murdered by the Freikorps

You can always get extra marks if you add more information to back up a point you are making. E.g. the Government used the Freikorps to crush the revolt (**1 mark**). The Freikorps received support for their actions from the German army (**1 mark**).

6

2. *You need to make 6 clear points about the usefulness of the source.*

You would probably start by arguing that the source does provide useful evidence about Germany at the end of the First World War. Comment on who wrote the source, when it was written and why it was written:

- The source was written by an eye witness
- The source was written to describe Germany at the end of the war

You might want to argue that in some ways the source is less useful for example:

- The writer of the source is looking back at events which may be less reliable

You should then comment on the information contained in the source:

- The source mentions gunfire on the streets
- The source mentions the authors shock at the announcement of the armistice

You would gain marks by pointing out that in some ways the source is less useful because of important information that has not been mentioned. E.g. Germany had signed the armistice unconditionally. A socialist government took power at the end of the war.

6

3. *If the question starts with "To what extent" you must write a balanced answer.*

In this question you should show that you understand that Hitler's success was due to violence and intimidation.

You could mention:

- Violent activities of the SA
- Destruction of opposition offices and printing presses
- Intimidation of opposition Reichstag deputies

You should then balance your answer by giving other reasons such as:

- Divisions in opposition
- Economic chaos led Germans to support extremism
- Hitler offered simple solutions to Germany's problems

Finish with a conclusion giving an overall answer to the question supported with a reason for the judgement you have made. E.g. overall, violence and intimidation played a major part in Hitler's success but Hitler was also able to convince enough Germans to vote for him to allow him to gain power "legally".

8

Section 3, Part E

1. *You should try to make 5 separate points from recall.*
You could mention:

- Most Russians were religious
- Close link between the Church and the Tsar
- The Church supported the Tsar's rule
- Orthodox Church was the largest in Russia
- Orthodox Church was very wealthy
- Orthodox Church controlled education
- Orthodox Church encouraged the people to regard the Tsar as their "little father"

You can always get extra marks if you add more information to back up a point you are making. E.g. most Russians were religious (**1 mark**) and priests were held in high regard (**1 mark**).

6

2. *If the question starts with "To what extent" you must write a balanced answer.*

In this question you should show that you understand how the Russo-Japanese war caused the 1905 Revolution.

You could mention:

- The Tsar had hoped that a short, successful war would unite the country and boost his popularity
- The war had gone very badly from the start and the Tsar was blamed
- There were stories of soldiers and sailors being killed due to the incompetence of their leaders

You should then balance your answer by giving other reasons such as:

- There was growing poverty among workers and peasants
- There was rising unemployment in the cities
- There were food shortages
- The cruelty of the Tsar's government/secret police

Finish with a conclusion giving an overall answer to the question supported with a reason for the judgement you have made. E.g. overall, the war was the most important cause of the 1905 Revolution because defeat provided the spark which led to the explosion of discontent against the Tsar.

8

3. *You need to make 6 clear points about the usefulness of the source.*

You would probably start by arguing that the source does provide useful evidence about the problems facing the Provisional Government. Comment on who wrote the source, when it was written and why it was written:

- The source was written by the leader of the Provisional Government who would be aware of events in Russia
- The source was written at the time when the Provisional Government was facing problems
- It was written to describe the problems facing the Provisional Government

You should then comment on the information contained in the source:

- The source mentions defeat at the front
- The source also mentions shortages of food and land

You would gain marks by pointing out that in some ways the source is less useful because of important information that has not been mentioned. E.g. opposition groups such as the Bolsheviks were plotting the downfall of the Provisional Government. The Soviets were interfering in the government of Russia.

6

Section 3, Part G

1. *You should try to make 6 separate points from recall.*
You could mention:

- European immigrants often arrived with little wealth or possessions
- They faced discrimination on the grounds of race or religion
- They faced discrimination in most areas of life and work simply because they were immigrants

- They did the poorest jobs with lowest pay
- They lived in poor housing often in unsanitary slums
- They became stereotyped by public and media as a threat
- They were blamed for political extremism e.g. Red Scare

You can always get extra marks if you bring in more information to back up a point you are making. E.g. faced discrimination on the grounds of race or religion (**1 mark**). Many were Catholics or Jews whilst most old immigrants were protestant (**1 mark**).

6

2. *You need to make 6 clear points about the usefulness of the source.*

You would probably start by arguing that the source does provide useful evidence about attitudes towards black Americans in the South at the time of the Civil Rights Movement. Comment on who wrote the source, when it was written and why it was written:

- The source was written by a person from Alabama which is in the deep South
- The source was written at the time of the growth of the Civil Rights Movement
- The source was written to describe the attitude of southerners to black people

You might want to comment on ways in which the source is less useful:

- The source was written by a leader of the KKK who would have extreme views

You should then comment on the information contained in the source:

- Black people should ignore what Northerners say
- Black people should work hard

You would gain marks by pointing out that in some ways the source is less useful because of important information that has not been mentioned. E.g. does not mention support for segregation in the South or that many southerners regarded black people as inferior.

6

3. *If the question starts with "To what extent" you must write a balanced answer.*

In this question you should show that you understand that their experiences in the Second World War encouraged the growth of the Civil Rights Movement.

You could mention:

- Black servicemen overseas had some experience of integration
- Some black people gained employment in war industries where they were treated as equals
- Government propaganda described the war as a fight for freedom which highlighted the lack of freedom for black people

You should then balance your answer by giving other reasons such as:

- Hardship and humiliation caused by the Jim Crow laws
- Segregation of schools, transport, etc
- Inequality faced by black Americans in employment and housing

Finish with a conclusion giving an overall answer to the question supported with a reason for the judgement you have made. E.g. overall, the experience of the Second World War encouraged the growth of the Civil Rights Movement but other reasons such as the injustices of segregation were important in keeping it going.

8

Section 3, Part H

1. *You should try to make 5 separate points from recall.*

You could mention:

- Britain allowed Germany to break the Treaty of Versailles
- British government and public opinion had revised their attitude to the Treaty of Versailles and agreed it was too harsh
- Britain did not protest about the reintroduction of conscription
- Britain took no action over the creation of a German air force
- the Anglo-German Naval Agreement allowed Germany to build a navy
- Britain accepted the reoccupation of the Rhineland

You can always get extra marks if you bring in more information to back up a point you are making. E.g. Britain accepted the reoccupation of the Rhineland (**1 mark**). Members of the government felt Germany was only going into its own backyard (**1 mark**).

6

2. *You need to make 6 clear points about the usefulness of the source.*

You would probably start by arguing that the source does provide useful evidence about Britain's attitude to Czechoslovakia in 1938. Comment on who wrote the source, when it was written and why it was written:

- The source was written by the British ambassador who would reflect British attitudes
- The source was written at the time of the Czech crisis
- The source was written to influence British attitudes towards Czechoslovakia

You might want to comment on ways in which the source is less useful:

- The source was written by a supporter of appeasement

You should then comment on the information contained in the source:

- Says that Czechoslovakia must take some blame
- Says that the Czechs cannot be trusted

You would gain marks by pointing out that in some ways the source is less useful because of important information that has not been mentioned. E.g. Czechs had grievances that were genuine.

6

3. *If the question starts with "To what extent" you must write a balanced answer.*

In this question you should show that you understand that fear of bombing was a reason why British people wanted to avoid war during the 1930s.

You could mention:

- British people felt that the bomber would always get through
- British people overestimated Germany's aerial threat
- British people were frightened by images of air raids from the Spanish Civil War

You should then balance your answer by giving other reasons such as:

- Many British people believed that Germany had genuine grievances which should be settled peacefully
- Many British people supported the League of Nations
- Most British people had memories of the death and destruction caused by the Great War

Finish with a conclusion giving an overall answer to the question supported with a reason for the judgement you have made. E.g. overall, fear of bombing was an important reason why British people wanted to avoid another war but there were also important reasons for them to believe that war was unnecessary.

8

Section 3, Part I

1. *If the question starts with "To what extent" you must write a balanced answer.*

In this question you should show that you understand that sea power played a part in American success in the war with Japan.

You could mention:

- Sea power based on aircraft carriers allowed for air power to support landings and sea battles e.g. Midway
- Sea power victory at the Battle of Midway destroyed major part of Japanese fleets and therefore their ambitions in the Pacific. Four out of five Japanese aircraft carriers sunk, along with cruisers and destroyers
- Sea power allowed for "island hopping" to push Japanese forces back in the Pacific
- Sea power, especially US submarine fleet, contributed to blockade of Japan and led to a lack of resources for Japanese war effort

You should then balance your answer by giving other reasons such as:

- US code breakers successfully intercepted and read most Japanese communication during the war and knew what the enemy plans were
- Codebreakers were vital to victory at Midway
- US used Navaho language in their codes that Japanese could not break
- Codebreakers knew about the journey of Japanese Navy Commander Yamamoto to the South Pacific. He was intercepted, shot down and killed
- US resources and men – better equipped
- US development of A bomb and attack on Hiroshima and Nagasaki

Finish with a conclusion giving an overall answer to the question supported with a reason for the judgement you have made. E.g. overall, sea power was an important reason for American success in the war against Japan but the overall military superiority of the United States and the devastation it was able to inflict on Japan itself was the most important reason for American victory.

8

2. *You need to make 6 clear points about the usefulness of the source.*

You would probably start by arguing that the source does provide useful evidence about attitudes towards the atomic bombing of Japan. Comment on who wrote the source, when it was written and why it was written:

- The source was written by a member of the US government who would be aware of the facts around the use of the bomb
- The source was written shortly after the bomb had been used against Japan
- The source was written to explain why the bomb should not have been dropped

You might want to comment on ways in which the source is less useful:

- The source was written by an opponent of the bomb showing possible bias

You should then comment on the information contained in the source:

- The bomb was unnecessary because Japan was already on the verge of defeat
- The bomb was unnecessary because the blockade was working

You would gain marks by pointing out that in some ways the source is less useful because of important information that has not been mentioned. E.g. the bomb ended the war more quickly than other methods would have done, and probably saved the lives of many US servicemen who would have had to continue with conventional tactics.

6

3. *You should try to make 5 separate points from recall.*

You could mention:

- British and American forces advancing from the west
- Russians were advancing from the east
- Soviets managed to encircle Berlin
- Allied airforces controlled the skies over Germany
- The German defences consisted of several depleted, badly equipped, and disorganised units
- Hitler and a number of his followers committed suicide

You can always get extra marks if you bring in more information to back up a point you are making. E.g. allied airforces controlled the skies over Germany (**1 mark**) and were bombing German cities day and night (**1 mark**).

6

Section 3, Part J

1. *If the question starts with "To what extent" you must write a balanced answer.*

In this question you should show that you understand that the developing arms race was the main cause of the Cold War.

You could mention:

- Stalin was angry with Truman for not informing them about the development of the bomb
- Use of atomic bombs on Hiroshima and Nagasaki started the nuclear arms race
- USSR developed it's own atomic bomb – first test 1949

- Both USA and USSR raced to develop the first hydrogen bomb

You should then balance your answer by giving other reasons such as:

- USA remembered that USSR had made an alliance with Hitler in 1939
- USSR remembered that the USA had supported the white forces during the Civil War
- USA opposed the conquest of Eastern Europe by the USSR at the end of WW2
- USSR felt that USA had deliberately delayed entry into the war against Hitler
- USA was capitalist and USSR was Communist
- USSR wanted control of West Berlin but USA was determined to keep it free
- Berlin blockade and airlift

Finish with a conclusion giving an overall answer to the question supported with a reason for the judgement you have made. E.g. overall, the developing arms race was an important cause of tension but it was the difference in ideologies between communist USSR and capitalist USA that was the main reason for the tension between the two superpowers before 1950. The USA was desperate to stop the spread of communism and the USSR wanted protection against another attack from capitalist countries.

8

2.   *You should try to make 6 separate points from recall.*

You could mention:

- Many of those conscripted avoided enlisting by draft dodging
- Students protested against President Johnson
- Large demonstrations against the war often lead to violent clashes
- Students held protests in many universities across the USA e.g. Kent State
- Prominent figures such as Martin Luther King spoke out against the war
- Many musicians of the time wrote and performed anti-Vietnam songs
- Vietnam veterans spoke out against the war

You can always get extra marks if you bring in more information to back up a point you are making. E.g. many of those conscripted avoided enlisting by draft dodging (**1 mark**) many protestors burned their draft cards to demonstrate their opposition to the war (**1 mark**).

6

3.   *You need to make 6 clear points about the usefulness of the source.*

You would probably start by arguing that the source does provide useful evidence about the Soviet attitude to détente. Comment on who wrote the source, when it was written and why it was written:

- The source was written by the leader of the Soviet Union
- The source was written at the time of détente
- The source was written to explain why the Soviets wanted détente

You should then comment on the information contained in the source:

- The source mentions the need to avoid another war
- The source mentions that progress has already been made with détente

You would gain marks by pointing out that in some ways the source is less useful because of important information that has not been mentioned. E.g. Soviets wanted détente because of the rising cost of defence (**1 mark**). Soviets were fearful that they were falling behind in the arms race (**1 mark**).

6

NATIONAL 5 HISTORY MODEL PAPER 2

Section 1, Part A

1. *You should try to make 5 separate points from recall.*

You could mention:

- Alexander III's sons had all died before him
- Alexander's heir was an infant
- King Edward was the Maid's great uncle
- There were other people who thought they should rule (Balliol, Bruce)
- There was danger of a Civil War in Scotland
- Many Scottish nobles had land in England and looked to Edward for help

You can always get extra marks if you add more information to back up a point you are making. E.g. Alexander's heir was an infant (**1 mark**). Many Scots thought that a girl would not be able to rule (**1 mark**).

2. *You should try to make 5 separate points from recall.*

You could mention:

- John Balliol and the Scots had made an alliance with France against Edward
- John Balliol's men had attacked the north of England
- King Edward had defeated King John's army at Dunbar
- King Edward had pursued King John to the north of Scotland
- King John had surrendered to King Edward
- King Edward had stripped King John of his title and crown

You can always get extra marks if you bring in more information to back up a point you are making. E.g. John Balliol and the Scots had made an alliance with France against Edward (**1 mark**). This was known as the Auld Alliance (**1 mark**).

3. *You need to make 5 clear points about the usefulness of the source.*

You would probably start by arguing that the source does provide useful evidence about what happened at Falkirk. Comment on who wrote the source, when it was written and why it was written:

- The Source was written by an English Chronicler whose job was to record events of the time
- The source was written in 1298 not long after the battle
- The source was written to describe what happened at the Battle of Falkirk

You should then comment on the information contained in the source:

- The source mentions the use of schiltrons
- The source mentions that the Scottish horsemen fled the scene

However, you might mention that the source was written by an English chronicler so may be biased against the Scots.

You would gain marks by pointing out that in some ways the source is less useful because of important information that has not been mentioned. E.g. It does not mention that Edward failed to capture Wallace. It does not mention that the English archers played a decisive part in Edward's victory.

4. *Start off by saying that the source partly explains why it took so long for Bruce to be accepted. This allows you to go on to show what is and what is not in the source.*

The source mentions:

- Bruce had to force many Scots to abandon King John Balliol
- He had to force Scots to reject Edward II as overlord
- Bruce's efforts to spread the war to other parts of Britain were not successful

However the source does not mention:

- It took a long time to drive the English out of their castles in Scotland
- Bruce had been excommunicated so some people could not accept him as King
- Bruce took several years to defeat the Comyns and their allies

Section 1, Part B

1. *You should try to make 5 separate points from recall.*

You could mention:

- Protestantism had been spreading across Scotland
- The Catholic Church had been executing leading Protestants
- Cardinal Beaton had been supporting the French interests in Scotland
- The assassins tricked their way into St Andrews Castle
- Cardinal Beaton barricaded himself in his room
- Protestants broke the door down and stabbed him to death

You can always get extra marks if you bring in more information to back up a point you are making. E.g. the Catholic Church had been executing leading Protestants (**1 mark**) for example George Wishart was burned at the stake (**1 mark**).

2. *You need to make 5 clear points about the usefulness of the source.*

You would probably start by arguing that the source does provide useful evidence about what happened at Falkirk. Comment on who wrote the source, when it was written and why it was written:

- The source was written by a historian who would have studied the details of the murder
- The source was written many years after the event with the advantage of hindsight
- The source was written to describe Mary's actions at the time of Darnley's death

You should then comment on the information contained in the source:

- The source mentions that Mary had the valuable furniture removed from the house
- She had persuaded Darnley to come to Edinburgh

You would gain marks by pointing out that in some ways the source is less useful because of important information that has not been mentioned. E.g. letters were later found which showed Mary's support for the murder of Darnley.

3. *You should try to make 5 separate points from recall.*

You could mention:

- Bothwell was suspected of being involved in the murder of Darnley
- The Scottish nobles persuaded Mary to marry Bothwell
- Bothwell kidnapped Mary
- many believed Mary really wanted to marry Bothwell
- people would not accept being ruled by a murderess
- Mary married Bothwell in a Protestant ceremony

You can always get extra marks if you add more information to back up a point you are making. E.g Bothwell kidnapped Mary (**1 mark**) although some believe that she went with him voluntarily (**1 mark**).

4. *Start off by saying that the source partly describes the plot. This allows you to go on to show what is and what is not in the source.*

The source mentions:

- Mary sent coded letters concealed in a beer keg
- Elizabeth's men knew about the plot from the start because they had a spy in Mary's household
- Mary sent a letter approving the assassination of Elizabeth

However the source does not mention:

- Mary's letter was decoded by a spy
- The letters were presented to Elizabeth

Section 1, Part C

1. *You should try to make 5 separate points from recall.*

You could mention:

- The Worcester was seized in Leith harbour
- The Scots said that Captain Green of the Worcester had sunk one of their ships
- Scots said Green was a pirate
- The Scots thought that Queen Anne was going to order Green to be freed
- Green and two of his crewmen were hanged at Leith

You can always get extra marks if you add more information to back up a point you are making. E.g. the Worcester was seized in Leith Harbour (**1 mark**) this was revenge for English involvement in the seizure of a ship belonging to the Company of Scotland (**1 mark**).

2. *You need to make 5 clear points about the usefulness of the source.*

You would probably start by arguing that the source does provide useful evidence about Scottish attitudes to the Union. Comment on who wrote the source, when it was written and why it was written:

- The source was written by a spy working in Scotland
- The source was written at a time of protests against the Union
- The source was written to describe protests against the Union

You should then comment on the information contained in the source:

- The source describes a large Edinburgh mob protesting against the Union
- The source mentions the Scots calling the English "dogs"

You would gain marks by pointing out that in some ways the source is less useful because of important information that has not been mentioned. E.g. there were protests in many towns across Scotland. Scots feared that the Union would affect trade.

3. *You should try to make 5 separate points from recall.*

You could mention:

- The Jacobites promised to cancel the Act of Union
- Its supporters (Queen Anne and Hanoverians) became unpopular so the Jacobites became popular
- The Scots objected to Excise Duty and other taxes which would go if the Union was ended
- Scottish traders felt threatened by goods coming in from England
- Jacobites were "native"
- Scots felt that their country had been "taken over" by the English

You can always get extra marks if you bring in more information to back up a point you are making. E.g. Jacobites were seen by many Scots as "native" (**1 mark**). The Hanoverians were from Germany (**1 mark**).

4. *Start off by saying that the source partly describes the effects of the Union. This allows you to go on to show what is and what is not in the source.*

The source mentions:

- Money and jobs are going to England
- Scottish manufacturers are ruined
- Scottish troops are in English service

However the source does not mention:

- The Malt Tax and Customs and Excise were unpopular
- The Equivalent was not paid as promised
- Scots were beginning to trade freely with English colonies

Section 1, Part D

1. *You should try to make 5 separate points from recall.*

You could mention:

- Work was available on farms
- There was work in textile factories
- There was building work on the canals and railways
- There was work in the coal mines
- Wages were higher in Scotland
- Housing was available
- Many Irish had already settled in Scotland
- Scotland was close by

You can always get extra marks if you bring in more information to back up a point you are making. E.g. housing was available (**1 mark**) because Scottish towns were growing in size at this time (**1 mark**).

2. *You should try to make 5 separate points from recall.*

You could mention:

- The Irish had a reputation for criminal activity
- Irish navvies were shown as especially violent and lawless
- Scots thought they were taking Scottish jobs
- Scots saw them as competition for housing
- Scots felt the Irish were responsible for lowering wage rates
- Religious tensions

You can always get extra marks if you add more information to back up a point you are making. E.g. there were religious tensions between Scots and Irish (**1 mark**) most Irish were Catholic whereas Scots were Protestant (**1 mark**).

3. *You need to make 5 clear points about the usefulness of the source.*

You would probably start by arguing that the source does provide useful evidence about the reasons for Scottish emigration. Comment on who wrote the source, when it was written and why it was written:

- The source was written by an immigration agent from Canada
- The source was written in 1875 at a time of emigration from Scotland
- The source was written to describe attempts to encourage Scots to emigrate

You should then comment on the information contained in the source:

- The source mentions agents from different countries competing to attract immigrants
- The source mentions posters offering free passages.

You would gain marks by pointing out that in some ways the source is less useful because of important information that has not been mentioned. E.g. push factors such as some landlords were willing to assist their tenants to emigrate and some landlords would buy their tenants cattle from them.

4. *Start off by saying that the source partly describes the impact of Scottish emigrants. This allows you to go on to show what is and what is not in the source.*

The source mentions:

- Scots dominated government in Canada and Australia
- Scots dominated the Canadian fur trade
- A Scot founded the Australian sheep industry

However the source does not mention:

- Scots involvement in banking
- Scots helped to develop the education systems

Section 1, Part E

1. *You should try to make 5 separate points from recall.*

You could mention:

- Government organised a poster campaign
- Appeal to patriotism
- Desire to escape boring or difficult jobs
- Peer pressure
- War was not expected to last long
- Proud tradition of soldiering in Scotland

You can always get extra marks if you add more information to back up a point you are making. E.g. the government poster campaign (**1 mark**) for example the poster showing Kitchener saying "your country needs you" (**1 mark**).

2. *You should try to make 5 separate points from recall.*

You could mention:

- Subjected to ridicule/verbal abuse/white feathers
- Newspaper campaigns against them (e.g. articles or cartoons attacking conscientious objectors)
- Many conscientious objectors were physically assaulted
- Objectors were forced to appear before military tribunals
- Many sent to front as stretcher bearers/faced same risks as regular soldiers
- Some accepted non combat duties (e.g. ambulance drivers)
- Imprisonment of absolutists/pacifists

You can always get extra marks if you bring in more information to back up a point you are making. E.g. pacifists were often imprisoned (**1 mark**) they were singled out for harsh treatment for example were not given clothes (**1 mark**).

3. *Start off by saying that the source partly describes the effect of war on employment in Scotland. This allows you to go on to show what is and what is not in the source.*

The source mentions:

- Unemployment was higher in Scotland than elsewhere in the UK
- Unemployment was often long term
- Skilled workers left without work

However the source does not mention:

- Heavy industries laid off many workers
- New opportunities for women e.g. secretarial work

4. *You need to make 5 clear points about the usefulness of the source.*

You would probably start by arguing that the source does provide useful evidence about the contribution of the Suffragettes. Comment on who wrote the source, when it was written and why it was written:

- The source was written by Millicent Fawcett who was involved in the campaign
- The source was written in 1912 at a time of Suffragette militancy
- The source was written to describe the part played by the Suffragettes in the campaign for female suffrage

You should then comment on the information contained in the source.

- The Suffragettes were successful in drawing attention to their cause
- Many campaigners for the vote viewed the Suffragette's methods with disgust

You would gain marks by pointing out that in some ways the source is less useful because of important information that has not been mentioned. E.g. suffragettes won respect by stopping their campaign to support the war effort in 1914.

Section 2, Part C

1. *You need to make 6 clear points about the usefulness of the source.*

You would probably start by arguing that the source does provide useful evidence about resistance on the plantations. Comment on who wrote the source, when it was written and why it was written:

- The source was written by a historian who would have studied the period
- The source was written many years after slavery making it a secondary source
- It was written to describe resistance on the plantations

You should then comment on the information contained in the source:

- The source mentions the strict laws and codes to which slaves were subjected
- It mentions that slaves who broke laws were hunted down

You would gain marks by pointing out that in some ways the source is less useful because of important information that has not been mentioned. E.g. some slaves were successful in escaping and formed communities of escaped slaves such as the Maroons in Jamaica.

2. *If the question starts with "To what extent" you must write a balanced answer.*

In this question you should show that you understand that the abolitionist movement was important in bringing an end to the slave trade for the following reasons:

- Abolitionists such as Clarkson travelled to Britain educating people about what the trade was like
- Freed slaves such as Equiano published stories about their experiences
- Abolitionists such as Wilberforce put the case for abolition in Parliament
- Abolitionists organized petitions to Parliament against the slave trade

You should then balance your answer by giving other reasons for the end to the slave trade:

- The Quakers had campaigned against slavery before the Abolitionist movement began
- The Evangelical Christian movement spoke out against slavery
- Indian sugar was produced more cheaply without the use of slaves

- The rise of new industries such as coal and iron provided more profitable investments than slave produced products

Finish with a conclusion giving an overall answer to the question supported with a reason for the judgment you have made. E.g. overall, the Abolitionist movement was influential in ending the slave trade but economic reasons such as the development of sugar production in India were probably more important.

3. *You should try to make 6 separate points from recall.*

You could mention:

- New, profitable industries were growing in Britain
- The "sugar island" colonies were becoming less important
- Britain began to trade more with India and East Asia
- Slavery was seen as an inefficient way to produce goods
- More and more people began to recognise Africans as fellow human beings

You can always get extra marks if you add more information to back up a point you are making. E.g. Britain began to trade more with India and East Asia (**1 mark**). Sugar could be produced more cheaply in India without the use of slaves (**1 mark**).

Section 2, Part D

1. *If the question starts with "To what extent" you must write a balanced answer.*

In this question you should show that you understand that better sanitation did lead to improvements in health. You could mention:

- Piped water from clean reservoirs
- Piped sewerage systems
- Introduction of water closets

You should then balance your answer by giving other reasons such as:

- Control of the lethal diseases of childhood
- Victorian hospital building programs in Scottish cities
- Local Government Act 1889 – appointment of Medical Officers

Finish with a conclusion giving an overall answer to the question supported with a reason for the judgment you have made. E.g. overall, improvements in sanitation played an important part in tackling killer diseases such as cholera. However, better medical care also played a part in improving health.

2. *You should try to make 6 separate points from recall.*

You could mention:

- The need for fuel boosted the coal industry
- The need for tracks and locomotives boosted iron industry
- Postal services/communication became quicker and more efficient
- Railways provided cheaper transport of raw materials and manufactured goods
- Boost to employment for railway building
- Decline of canals

You can always get extra marks if you bring in more information to back up a point you are making. E.g. the need for fuel boosted the coal industry (**1 mark**). A reliable supply of fuel was needed for the growing number of steam locomotives (**1 mark**).

3. *You need to make 6 clear points about the usefulness of the source.*

You would probably start by arguing that the source does provide useful evidence about the aims of the Chartists. Comment on who wrote the source, when it was written and why it was written:

- written at the time of the growth of Chartism/a year after the people's charter had been written
- written by someone who witnessed a Chartist meeting
- written to report what the Chartists were saying

You should then comment on the information contained in the source:

- Chartists wanted universal suffrage
- Chartists would fight or die for universal suffrage

You would gain marks by pointing out that in some ways the source is less useful because of important information that has not been mentioned. E.g. Chartists had other aims apart from universal suffrage such as the end of property qualifications for MPs.

Section 2, Part E

1. *You need to make 6 clear points about the usefulness of the source.*

You would probably start by arguing that the source does provide useful evidence about poverty at the end of the 19th century. Comment on who wrote the source, when it was written and why it was written:

- The source was produced at a time of poverty
- Aberdeen organisation representative of an industrial city which would experience more poverty
- Produced to show their willingness to help the "deserving poor"/sober and industrious who may become ill

You should then comment on the information contained in the source:

- Source says drinking and laziness are causes of poverty
- Source says only those willing to work and stay sober are to be helped

You would gain marks by pointing out that in some ways the source is less useful because of important information that has not been mentioned. E.g. some believed poverty was not always the fault of the individual (low wages/size of family/irregularity of work). Other causes of poverty as the fault of the individual such as gambling.

2. *You should try to make 5 separate points from recall.*

You could mention:

- Rationing helped encourage the idea of universal sharing of the nation's food supply rich and poor classes were mixing in society who previously had little in common
- War highlighted problems that could be overcome by government action
- The poor health of some city children evacuated to the country highlighted the problems of poverty

- Suffering of war caused a determination to create a better society once the war was over
- Other reforms had been made by the government during the war such as free health care for war wounded and bomb victims, Emergency Milk and Meals scheme, etc

You can always get extra marks if you bring in more information to back up a point you are making. E.g. war highlighted problems that could be overcome by government action (**1 mark**). This was highlighted by the Beveridge Report (**1 mark**).

3. *If the question starts with "To what extent" you must write a balanced answer.*

In this question you should show that you understand that free health care was important in getting people to welcome the Labour reforms.

You could mention:

- Free prescriptions under the new NHS
- Free dental care
- Free optical care

You should then balance your answer by giving other reasons such as:

- Free secondary education for all
- A National Insurance scheme to cover everybody
- A major new house building programme

Finish with a conclusion giving an overall answer to the question supported with a reason for the judgment you have made. E.g. overall, free health care was one of the most important reasons why people welcomed the Labour Reforms because it was a reform which benefitted everyone.

Section 3, Part B

1. *You should try to make 5 separate points from recall.*

You could mention:

- The British had been patrolling the seas to prevent smuggling/impose customs
- The British vessel Gaspée ran aground off the coast of Rhode Island
- The vessel was attacked by a crowd of local men
- The commander of the Gaspée was wounded by a musket shot
- The British government launched an investigation into the incident

You can always get extra marks if you bring in more information to back up a point you are making. E.g. the British government launched an investigation into the incident (**1 mark**) the people of Rhode Island refused to cooperate with the investigation (**1 mark**).

2. *Start off by saying that the source partly describes what happened at Bunker Hill. This allows you to go on to show what is and what is not in the source.*

The source mentions:

- British navy opened fire on the colonists
- The British charged the hill three times
- Eventually the colonists were driven back

However the source does not mention:

- British soldiers were left exposed to American musket fire as they made their way up the hill
- Bright uniforms of British soldiers made them easy targets
- British suffered 1000 casualties
- Colonists only suffered 400 casualties

3. *For this type of question you must say whether you think the sources agree or not and then support your decision by making two comparisons using evidence from the sources.*

For this question you would probably decide that the two sources agree. You could then back this up with two of the following comparisons:

- Source A says Cornwallis' position at Yorktown was deteriorating fast. Source B supports this by saying that Cornwallis ended up being in a poor position
- Source A points out that American forces prevented Cornwallis' Forces from moving inland. Source B backs this up by mentioning American troops moved in quickly to contain Cornwallis
- Source A says that the French defeated the British fleet in Chesapeake Bay and Source B supports this by pointing out that the French defeated the British fleet in a naval battle near Yorktown

4. *You should try to make 5 separate points from recall.*

You could mention:

- Poor leadership of British forces e.g. Howe, Cornwallis
- Tactical errors made by Britain e.g. Yorktown, Saratoga
- British army was small in number
- British soldiers were not properly trained/equipped to cope with terrain and conditions
- Colonial army was effectively led by George Washington
- Colonists had greater forces/able to call on minutemen when required
- Colonists benefited from assistance from foreign powers

You can always get extra marks if you bring in more information to back up a point you are making. E.g. the British army was small in number (**1 mark**) and had to rely on mercenary forces (**1 mark**).

Section 3, Part C

1. *You should try to make 5 separate points from recall.*

You could mention:

- They were chased from territory to territory as their numbers grew
- Their property was attacked
- They were condemned for their polygamy
- They were persecuted because of their beliefs
- They eventually found a place of safety in Utah

You can always get extra marks if you bring in more information to back up a point you are making. E.g. their property was attacked (**1 mark**). For example Mormon banks were burned to the ground (**1 mark**).

2. *Start off by saying that the source partly explains the outbreak of the war. This allows you to go on to show what is and what is not in the source.*

The source mentions:

- Lincoln sent a naval expedition to supply Fort Sumter
- Confederates opened fire on the fort
- Major Anderson surrendered
- The firing on Fort Sumter set off an outburst of patriotic fever in the North

However the source does not mention:

- Lincoln chose to ignore advice not to supply Fort Sumter
- The flying of the Union flag in Charleston harbour was seen as a provocative act by the South
- Lincoln immediately called for volunteers to avenge Fort Sumter

3. *You should try to make 5 separate points from recall.*

You could mention:

- Gave black Americans very few civil rights
- Prevented many black Americans from voting
- Prevented them from serving on juries
- Prevented from owning guns
- Restricted their right to own property
- Restrictions could not be overturned by northern politicians

You can always get extra marks if you bring in more information to back up a point you are making. E.g. restricted their right to own property (**1 mark**) also restricted the rights of black Americans to rent property (**1 mark**).

4. *For this type of question you must say whether you think the sources agree or not and then support your decision by making two comparisons using evidence from the sources.*

For this question you would probably decide that the two sources agree. You could then back this up with two of the following comparisons:

- Source A says the author was dismayed their life had shown no improvement for black people. Source B supports this by saying that attempts to improve conditions for black people had little effect in the South
- Source A points out that many black Americans remained in the South. Source B backs this up by mentioning because they were too poor, many stayed in the South
- Source A says that some white Americans felt justified in lynching and using violence against black people and Source B supports this by pointing out that secret organisations were set up to terrorise black people

Section 3, Part D

1. *You should try to make 5 separate points from recall.*

You could mention:

- Germany lost land to France, Belgium and Poland
- Germany was blamed for starting the First World War and ordered to pay reparations
- Germany's armed forces were reduced in size

- Germany was forbidden from uniting with Austria
- Germany lost all her overseas colonies
- The Rhineland was demilitarised

You can always get extra marks if you bring in more information to back up a point you are making. E.g. Germany lost land to France, Belgium and Poland (**1 mark**). This contributed to the problem of millions of German speaking people living outside Germany (**1 mark**).

2. *You should try to make 5 separate points from recall.*

You could mention:

- Enabling Act meant Hitler could pass laws without agreement of the Reichstag
- All political parties declared illegal
- Nazis employed spies/Gestapo agents
- Fear of the concentration camps deterred dissent
- Opponents arrested which weakened opposition groups
- Nazis controlled the media which inhibited free speech
- Nazis kept tight control of the young/Nazi-controlled education
- Nazi propaganda indoctrinated the German people
- Widespread support for the Nazis

You can always get extra marks if you bring in more information to back up a point you are making. E.g. fear of the concentration camps deterred dissent (**1 mark**) these were used to imprison anyone suspected of opposition to the Nazis (**1 mark**).

3. *Start off by saying that the source partly explains why Germans supported the Nazis. This allows you to go on to show what is and what is not in the source.*

The source mentions:

- The Nazis were seen as preferable to the Communists
- The Nazis appeared to be well disciplined
- Nazi propaganda pamphlets

However the source does not mention:

- Hitler offered simple solutions to economic problems
- Hitler promised to end the shame of the Versailles settlement
- Hitler offered scapegoats for Germany's problems

4. *For this type of question you must say whether you think the sources agree or not and then support your decision by making two comparisons using evidence from the sources.*

For this question you would probably decide that the two sources agree. You could then back this up with two of the following comparisons:

- Source A says that their weekends were crammed full with sporting activities and Source B says there was an emphasis on activity and sport
- Source A says that these were fun and Source B points out that many young Germans enjoyed activity and sport
- Source A says that this had a bad effect on school work and Source B felt that education was being downgraded

Section 3, Part E

1. *Start off by saying that the source partly explains why national minorities disliked Russification. This allows you to go on to show what is and what is not in the source.*

The source mentions:

- Non-Russians had to use the Russian language
- Russian clothing and customs were to be used
- Russian officials were put in to run regional governments
- Poles were told to change and become Russian citizens

However the source does not mention:

- Russians were the minority – only 44% of population
- Catholic Poles and Asiatic Muslims were pressurised to convert to Russian Orthodoxy
- Jews were persecuted for being "anti-Russian"
- Russian was used in schools and law courts

2. *You should try to make 5 separate points from recall.*

You could mention:

- The Tsar announced his October Manifesto
- A limited vote was extended to the peasants and industrial workers
- Many Liberals accepted these terms and ceased opposing the Tsar
- Right wing supporters of the Tsar began a wave of attacks on Jews and liberal intellectuals who had continued their opposition
- Witte was appointed Chairman of the Council of Ministers and arrested the entire St Petersburg soviet
- The troops stayed loyal to the Tsar and crushed opposition in Moscow
- The general strike came to an end as the middle classes withdrew their support
- The government announced the end of redemption dues to placate the peasants

You can always get extra marks if you bring in more information to back up a point you are making. E.g. the Tsar announced the October Manifesto (**1 mark**) this accepted cabinet government, free speech and a constitution for Russia (**1 mark**).

3. *You should try to make 5 separate points from recall.*

You could mention:

- Germany helped him to return to Russia
- Lenin travelled to Finland in a sealed train
- Lenin arrived at the Finland Station in Petrograd
- He made a speech calling for a second revolution
- He called for non cooperation with the Provisional Government
- He called for an end to the war
- He demanded land for the peasants
- He said that the Soviets should take control of Russia

You can always get extra marks if you bring in more information to back up a point you are making. E.g. Germany helped him to return to Russia (**1 mark**) they arranged for him to travel from Switzerland to Finland (**1 mark**).

4. *For this type of question you must say whether you think the sources agree or not and then support your decision by making two comparisons using evidence from the sources.*

For this question you would probably decide that the two sources mainly disagree.

You could then back this up with two of the following comparisons:

- Source A says that the Bolsheviks did not have the support of the Russian people but Source B says they had massive support
- Source A says that the revolution was caused by the chaos of war but Source B says it was brought about by people who had enough of misery/wanted a better life
- Source A says the Bolsheviks led the revolution but Source B says they simply guided it

Section 3, Part G

1. *You should try to make 5 separate points from recall.*

You could mention:

- Campaigned against immigration in the 1920s especially Jews and Roman Catholics
- Acted anonymously e.g. wore robes and hoods/ activities took place at night
- Used violence against opponents
- Used intimidation of black Americans e.g. fiery crosses/house burnings
- Infiltrated government e.g. 16 senators gained election in 1920s with KKK help
- Infiltrated state officials and police
- Large peaceful demonstrations e.g. 1928 march down Pennsylvania Avenue, Washington DC
- KKK was less active after 1925 as membership fell following allegations of corruption amongst Klan leadership

You can always get extra marks if you bring in more information to back up a point you are making. E.g. KKK used violence against its opponents (**1 mark**). For example there were lynchings where black people accused of crimes against whites were whipped and sometimes killed (**1 mark**).

2. *You should try to make 5 separate points from recall.*

You could mention:

- Hardship and humiliation caused by the Jim Crow laws
- Segregation of schools, transport, etc
- Inequality faced by black Americans in employment and housing
- Impact of 2nd World War e.g. black servicemen overseas had some experience of integration
- Refusal of southern states to desegregate following "Brown v Topeka"
- Success of the Montgomery Bus Boycott
- Effective leadership of the movement e.g. Martin Luther King
- Success of protests e.g. Birmingham, Washington, Selma
- Growing support from whites e.g. student groups like CORE

You can always get extra marks if you bring in more information to back up a point you are making. E.g. the hardship and humiliation caused by Jim Crow encouraged the growth of the Civil Rights Movement (**1 mark**). Some of these laws dated back 90 years (**1 mark**).

3. *For this type of question you must say whether you think the sources agree or not and then support your decision by making two comparisons using evidence from the sources.*

For this question you would probably decide that the two sources agree. You could then back this up with two of the following comparisons:

- Source A says this was to be Martin Luther King's first step towards becoming the leading figure in the Civil Rights Movement. Source B supports this by saying that as a result of the boycott, Martin Luther King became involved in the Civil Rights Movement
- Source A points out that the boycott lasted over a year. Source B backs this up by mentioning that the bus company's services were boycotted by 99% of Montgomery's African Americans for over a year
- Source A says that the courts decided that segregation on Montgomery's buses was illegal. Source B supports this by pointing out that the US Supreme Court announced that Alabama's bus segregation laws were illegal

4. *Start off by saying that the source partly explains why Malcolm X opposed non-violent protest. This allows you to go on to show what is and what is not in the source.*

The source mentions:

- Malcolm's mistreatment in his youth gave him different attitudes towards whites from Martin Luther King
- He became influenced by the ideas of Elijah Mohammed who preached hatred of white people
- He believed that support of non violence was a sign that black people were still living in mental slavery
- He believed violent language and threats would frighten the authorities into action

However the source does not mention:

- Malcolm X claimed that even whites who appeared friendly were "wolves in sheep's clothing"
- He believed that non violence deprived black people of their right to self-defense
- He claimed that peaceful protest gained little for most black people
- He didn't think non violent campaigns tackled the problems for black people in the northern cities

Section 3, Part H

1. *Start off by saying that the source partly explains the situation. This allows you to go on to show what is and what is not in the source.*

The source mentions:

- Germany withdrew from the Disarmament Conference
- Germany withdrew from the League
- France lost Poland as an ally

However the source does not mention:

- Hitler announced conscription
- The German army would rise to 500,000
- Hitler tried to take over Austria in 1934
- Hitler reoccupied the Rhineland

2. *You should try to make 5 separate points from recall.*

You could mention:

- German population was growing
- German territory had been restricted
- Germany needed access to food and raw materials
- Hitler wanted to regain territory lost by Versailles Treaty
- Austria should be annexed to Germany
- Belief that the Germans needed Lebensraum
- German minorities had a right to belong to Germany, e.g. Sudeten Germans

You can always get extra marks if you bring in more information to back up a point you are making. E.g. belief that the Germans needed Lebensraum (**1 mark**). Land in Eastern Europe for settlement and raw materials (**1 mark**).

3. *For this type of question you must say whether you think the sources agree or not and then support your decision by making two comparisons using evidence from the sources.*

For this question you would probably decide that the two sources disagree. You could then back this up with two of the following comparisons:

- Source A says Sudeten Germans should return to Germany. Source B disagrees with this by saying that the Sudetenland had never been part of Germany
- Source A points out that Sudeten Germans resented being part of Czechoslovakia since 1919. Source B disagrees by mentioning that Sudeten German unrest originated in the early 1930s
- Source A says that Sudeten Germans had been persecuted as ethnic minority and Source B opposes this by pointing out that they had been treated with respect

4. *You should try to make 5 separate points from recall.*

You could mention:

- Germany invaded Czechoslovakia in March 1939 breaking the Munich Agreement
- Great Britain sped up her rearmaments programme/led to conscription
- Hitler demanded the return of Danzig from Poland
- Germany demanded permission to build a road and railway line through Poland
- Britain promised to defend Poland if she were attacked
- August 1939 Germany and Russia signed the Nazi-Soviet Non Aggression Pact
- September Germany invaded Poland
- Britain declared war on Germany

You can always get extra marks if you bring in more information to back up a point you are making. E.g. August 1939 Germany and Russia signed the Nazi-Soviet Non Aggression Pact (**1 mark**). This left Hitler free to attack Poland without fear of Russian opposition (**1 mark**).

Section 3, Part I

1. *You should try to make 5 separate points from recall.*

You could mention:

- Hitler had given his full backing to Guderian's tactics
- In 1940, Britain and France still had a World War One mentality and didn't recognise the potential of the new weapons
- What tanks they had were poor compared to the German Panzers
- British and French tactics were outdated
- Britain still had the mentality that as an island we were safe as our navy would protect us
- France hid behind the Maginot Line

You can always get extra marks if you bring in more information to back up a point you are making. E.g. what tanks they had were poor compared to the German Panzers (**1 mark**) which had thicker armour plating and superior weaponry (**1 mark**).

2. *Start off by saying that the source partly explains the effectiveness of resistance groups. This allows you to go on to show what is and what is not in the source.*

The source mentions:

- They gathered intelligence for the Allies
- They organised discovered French collaborators
- They killed many ranking Nazi officials
- They destroyed trains used by the German army

However the source does not mention:

- They ran cafes
- They made radio contact with Britain
- They concealed art works stolen by the Nazis

3. *You should try to make 5 separate points from recall.*

You could mention:

- Need for total secrecy
- Preserve element of surprise by landing in Normandy rather than using shortest crossing point
- Lack of natural harbours on Normandy coast
- Need for suitable weather conditions
- Lack of cover for troops on the beaches
- Providing troops with accurate information about enemy positions

You can always get extra marks if you bring in more information to back up a point you are making. E.g. lack of natural harbours on Normandy coast (**1 mark**) need for artificial "mulberry" harbours to land equipment and supplies (**1 mark**).

4. *For this type of question you must say whether you think the sources agree or not and then support your decision by making two comparisons using evidence from the sources.*

For this question you would probably decide that the two sources disagree. You could then back this up with two of the following comparisons:

- Source A says using the atomic bomb was a mistake. Source B disagrees by saying that using the atomic bomb was justified

- Source A points out that Japanese were already defeated and ready to surrender. Source B disagrees with this by mentioning that the Japanese government had decided to fight on to the last man

- Source A says that Hiroshima and Nagasaki was of no real help in our war against Japan and Source B opposes this by pointing out that Hiroshima and Nagasaki made them surrender sooner

Section 3, Part J

1. *You should try to make 5 separate points from recall.*

You could mention:

- The Soviet take-over of Eastern European countries had increased tension between East and West

- Churchill's Iron Curtain speech

- Offer of Marshall aid to all European countries

- Berlin airlift had increased tension between East and West

- Allies merged their zones to form West Germany

- NATO was formed in 1949

- NATO expanded in 1951 to include Greece and Turkey

- West Germany joined NATO in 1955

You can always get extra marks if you bring in more information to back up a point you are making. E.g. allies merged their zones to form West Germany, (**1 mark**). This formalised the division of Germany, increasing tension (**1 mark**).

2. *For this type of question you must say whether you think the sources agree or not and then support your decision by making two comparisons using evidence from the sources.*

For this question you would probably decide that the two sources disagree. You could then back this up with two of the following comparisons:

- Source A says the Soviet Union had the idea of installing a small number of nuclear missiles on Cuba. Source B disagrees with this by saying that Americans believed that the Soviets planned to place a large number of their missiles in Cuba

- Source A points out that Khrushchev did not want to start a war. Source B opposes this view by mentioning Americans regarded Soviet action as a warlike act

- Source A says that purpose of missiles was just to defend Cuba from American attack but Source B disagrees with this pointing out that missiles had an offensive purpose pointed directly at major American cities

3. *Start off by saying that the source partly explains why America became involved in Vietnam. This allows you to go on to show what is and what is not in the source.*

The source mentions:

- France asked America for assistance in Vietnam

- America feared that Vietnam would become communist

- They believed that they could establish a friendly government in South Vietnam, under the leadership of President Diem

- America feared that a civil war was developing in South Vietnam

However the source does not mention:

- America was increasingly concerned about the influence of China in south-east Asia

- There was a widespread belief in the Domino Theory

- There was a fear that other countries e.g. Thailand, Laos, Burma, Cambodia even New Zealand and Australia could fall to communism

- There was a general concern that America was falling behind in the Cold War at this time and needed to make a stand against communism

- American "advisors" had been in Vietnam to support the government of Diem since the early 1960s

- Gulf of Tonkin incident led America to become involved in a full scale war in Vietnam

4. *You should try to make 5 separate points from recall.*

You could mention:

- There had been a massive increase of refugees fleeing to the West

- Many people living in East Berlin saw that West Berlin was wealthier and had a more democratic society

- Many East Germans were unhappy at being separated from friends and family in the West

- It was felt that Berlin was a centre for western spies

- The East German government took the decision to close the border between East and West Berlin and build a wall.

You can always get extra marks if you bring in more information to back up a point you are making. E.g. there had been a massive increase of refugees fleeing to the West (**1 mark**). In the six months up to June 1961, 103,000 East Germans had fled through Berlin (**1 mark**).

NATIONAL 5 HISTORY MODEL PAPER 3

Section 1, Part A

1. *For this type of question you must say whether you think the sources agree or not and then support your decision by making two comparisons using evidence from the sources.*

For this question you would probably decide that the two sources disagree. You could then back this up with two of the following comparisons:

- Source A says that Balliol claimed to be descended from the eldest line of the family of David, Earl of Huntingdon. Source B disagrees with this – it did not matter that he was descended from the eldest of David's daughters
- Source A points out that it did not matter that Balliol was a generation younger than Bruce. Source B disagrees saying that Bruce was one generation closer to royalty than Balliol
- Source A says that the feudal law of primogeniture always supported the eldest line of the family and Source B denies this by pointing out that the feudal law of primogeniture did not apply to kingdoms

4

2. *You should try to make 5 separate points from recall.*

You could mention:

- The Bruces never supported him
- Balliol had accepted Edward as his overlord
- he was unable to stop Edward interfering
- he was defeated at Dunbar
- he was stripped of his title by Edward

You can always get extra marks if you add more information to back up a point you are making. E.g. he was unable to stop Edward interfering (**1 mark**) Edward heard legal appeals from Scots (**1 mark**).

5

3. *Start off by saying that the source partly explains the situation. This allows you to go on to show what is and what is not in the source.*

The source mentions:

- The Scots allowed as many of the English to cross the bridge as they could hope to defeat
- They slaughtered all who had crossed over
- Cressingham was killed
- De Warenne escaped

However the source does not mention:

- Scots hid on the Abbey Craig
- The English chose to cross the forth using the narrow bridge
- The English knights were forced to fight on marshy ground
- The English were defeated

6

4. *You should try to make 5 separate points from recall.*

You could mention:

- He murdered Comyn
- He ruined the Comyns by destroying their lands
- He destroyed the power of the Comyns' friends
- He captured castles
- He defeated Edward at Bannockburn
- He forced Scottish nobles to accept him as king

You can always get extra marks if you bring in more information to back up a point you are making. E.g. he destroyed the power of the Comyns' friends (**1 mark**) for example he defeated the MacDougalls (**1 mark**).

5

Section 1, Part B

1. *Start off by saying that the source partly explains why Henry interfered in Scotland. This allows you to go on to show what is and what is not in the source.*

The source mentions:

- Henry wanted Mary to marry his son
- Henry wanted to reduce French influence in Scotland
- Scotland and England had been at war
- Henry wanted to spread Protestantism

However the source does not mention:

- Mary had become queen in 1542 but had no husband
- Scots had broken their agreement to the marriage
- Henry aimed to enforce the Treaty of Greenwich
- Scottish protestants wanted Henry's support

6

2. *You should try to make 5 separate points from recall.*

You could mention:

- She was a woman so many Scots felt she would be incapable of ruling Scotland
- She was young and lacked experience
- She was Catholic and Scotland had recently become Protestant
- She had strong ties with France and many Scots feared French influence
- Scottish nobles had become used to running the country themselves

You can always get extra marks if you bring in more information to back up a point you are making. E.g. she had strong ties with France and many Scots feared French influence (**1 mark**) as was seen in Huntley's Rebellion (**1 mark**).

5

3. *For this type of question you must say whether you think the sources agree or not and then support your decision by making two comparisons using evidence from the sources.*

For this question you would probably decide that the two sources agree. You could then back this up with two of the following comparisons:

- Source A says Mary's supporters fought on for several years. Source B supports this by saying that Mary's supporters did not give up until 1573

- Source A points out that Moray and Lennox were killed. Source B backs this up by mentioning the death of the two regents
- Source A says that Edinburgh castle was captured and Source B supports this by pointing out that the castle was forced to surrender in 1573

4

4. *You should try to make 5 separate points from recall.*

You could mention:

- Elizabeth was Protestant and Mary was Catholic
- Elizabeth feared that Mary would return to Scotland and make it a base for opposition to her rule
- Elizabeth was supporting the Protestants who were now ruling Scotland
- Elizabeth was aware of plots against her to make Mary Queen of Britain
- Elizabeth feared the consequences of executing Mary

You can always get extra marks if you add more information to back up a point you are making. E.g. Elizabeth feared the consequences of executing Mary (**1 mark**). She did not want to give the idea that it was alright for queens to be executed (**1 mark**).

5

Section 1, Part C

1. *Start off by saying that the source partly explains why Scots invested in Darien. This allows you to go on to show what is and what is not in the source.*

The source mentions:

- Scottish prosperity depended on farming which suffered from bad weather and poor soil
- Scottish overseas trade was limited
- Scots thought that England's prosperity came from its overseas trade based on colonies
- Paterson promised them a colony where "trade will increase and money will make money"

However the source does not mention:

- The Hanoverian years made Scotland poorer
- Scots had seen huge profits made by the East India Company
- Scotland did not have any colonies
- They were told Darien was in a key location on the Isthmus of Panama between two oceans

6

2. *For this type of question you must say whether you think the sources agree or not and then support your decision by making two comparisons using evidence from the sources.*

For this question you would probably decide that the two sources agree. You could then back this up with two of the following comparisons:

- Source A says some Scots believed trading with England's colonies would make Scotland a richer country. Source B supports this by saying that Scots were angry that they could not make money by trading with England's colonies

- Source A points out that Scotland's trade (with France) was badly affected by England's frequent wars. Source B backs this up by mentioning they wanted to reduce the bad effects of England's war on Scotland's trade (Wine Act)
- Source A says that The Act of Security offered a shared monarch in return for access to England's colonies and Source B supports this by pointing out that they demanded access to England's colonies in return for sharing a monarch

4

3. *You should try to make 5 separate points from recall.*

You could mention:

- It promised "the Equivalent"
- It paid arrears of wages to those who supported the Union
- It insisted that government officials in Scotland support the Union
- It sent Argyll and Queensberry to organize support for the Union
- It paid bribes
- It offered well paid jobs
- It threatened military action

You can always get extra marks if you bring in more information to back up a point you are making. E.g. it threatened military action (**1 mark**). It made it clear that it had military forces in northern England and Ireland, which were ready to take action (**1 mark**).

5

4. *You should try to make 5 separate points from recall.*

You could mention:

- Queen Anne was to be succeeded by Hanoverians
- Hanoverians were seen as "foreign" compared to the "Scottish" Stuarts
- Hanoverian succession alarmed Catholics
- James VIII was ready to lead a rebellion
- Scots regretted the loss of their parliament
- The Equivalent had neither been paid promptly nor in cash

You can always get extra marks if you add more information to back up a point you are making. E.g. Hanoverian succession alarmed Catholics (**1 mark**). The Hanoverians were Protestant whereas Queen Ann was tolerant of Catholicism (**1 mark**).

5

Section 1, Part D

1. *You should try to make 5 separate points from recall.*

You could mention:

- Most of the Irish population lived in poverty
- They subsisted on a diet based on milk and potatoes
- They had very poor housing conditions
- There was little industry in the south of Ireland so unemployment was common
- In 1845 the potato crop was ruined by blight
- Millions of Irish people faced starvation

You can always get extra marks if you bring in more information to back up a point you are making. E.g. they had very poor housing conditions (**1 mark**) and large families often shared small hovels with their livestock (**1 mark**).

5

2. *Start off by saying that the source partly explains the importance of the church. This allows you to go on to show what is and what is not in the source.*

The source mentions:

- Church gave them a place to worship
- They could be baptized, married and buried
- Priests would listen to their problems
- Church offered a centre for social life

However the source does not mention:

- Priests could write letters for them
- Priests helped to find housing and work
- Provided charity in time of need

6

3. *You should try to make 5 separate points from recall.*

You could mention:

- The Highland Clearances
- Potato famine in the 1840s
- Decline of highland industries
- Rising cost of farmland
- Assisted passages
- Letters from relatives
- Higher wages

You can always get extra marks if you add more information to back up a point you are making. E.g. decline of highland industries (**1 mark**), for example the kelp industry (**1 mark**).

5

4. *For this type of question you must say whether you think the sources agree or not and then support your decision by making two comparisons using evidence from the sources.*

For this question you would probably decide that the two sources disagree. You could then back this up with two of the following comparisons:

- Source B says land was of poor quality. Source C denies this by saying that he has prepared good land and is preparing more
- Source B points out that he is lonely. Source C disagrees with this by mentioning that the community is doing well
- Source B says that he wants to return to Scotland and Source C disagrees saying that "this is the best place in the whole world"

4

Section 1, Part E

1. *Start off by saying that the source partly explains why so many Scots volunteered. This allows you to go on to show what is and what is not in the source.*

The source mentions:

- Opportunity for adventure
- Dangers were ignored
- War hysteria
- Anti-German propaganda

However the source does not mention:

- Government organised a poster campaign
- Appeal to patriotism
- Desire to escape boring or difficult jobs
- War was not expected to last long

6

2. *You should try to make 5 separate points from recall.*

You could mention:

- Women took on new jobs previously thought to be "male occupations"
- Women had to cope with food shortages
- Women had to cope with rationing
- Women had to keep the family going without male support
- Women had to cope with bereavement

You can always get extra marks if you bring in more information to back up a point you are making. E.g. women took on new jobs previously thought to be "male occupations" (**1 mark**). They drove buses and trams (**1 mark**).

5

3. *You should try to make 5 separate points from recall.*

You could mention:

- Foreign customers had developed their own industries
- Foreign customers had gone elsewhere for heavy goods
- Lack of investment in modernization during the war
- Less demand for warships in peacetime
- New industries were more profitable for investors

You can always get extra marks if you add more information to back up a point you are making. E.g. foreign customers had developed their own industries (**1 mark**). For example, countries in Asia had developed their own textile industry (**1 mark**).

5

4. *For this type of question you must say whether you think the sources agree or not and then support your decision by making two comparisons using evidence from the sources.*

For this question you would probably decide that the two sources partly agree. You could then back this up with two of the following comparisons:

- Source A says that the government feared a socialist rising and Source B supports this by pointing out that the government was worried about the loyalty of the police and armed forces
- Source A says the workers were ready to carry out a socialist rising. Source B disagrees saying that socialist leaders had little support for their plans

- Source A points out that by Saturday, Clydeside could have been in the workers hands. Source B disagrees saying that the workers went to watch football on Saturday

4

Section 2, Part C

1. *You need to make 6 clear points about the usefulness of the source.*

You would probably start by arguing that the source does provide useful evidence about the treatment of slaves on the Middle Passage. Comment on who wrote the source, when it was written and why it was written:

- The source was written by a historian who would have studied the period
- The source was written many years after slavery ended, giving the benefit of hindsight
- It was written to describe what the Middle Passage was like

You should then comment on the information contained in the source:

- The source mentions that slaves were whipped to make them exercise
- It mentions that the slaves were given poor food

You would gain marks by pointing out that in some ways the source is less useful because of important information that has not been mentioned. E.g. female slaves were often subjected to sexual abuse.

6

2. *You should try to make 6 separate points from recall.*

You could mention:

- The main British ports were London, Bristol and Liverpool
- Glasgow did not share in British Empire trade until 1707 and did not trade in large numbers. However the port did profit from the sugar trade which was closely linked to the slave trade
- Until 1698 London was the only port permitted to trade in African slaves. Shipping and support services all profited from the monopoly. Entrepeneurs were prepared to take risks necessary on the triangular trade
- The City of London profited from financial services provided such as insurance and loans. Banks were established such as Barclays to provide loans to other merchants
- Bristol merchants spent profits on fine buildings in the city centre
- Industries around Bristol such as copper smelting, sugar refining and glass making grew as a result of the slave trade
- Liverpool docks were deep and large and could supply, service and unload large slave ships. Those facilities made Liverpool into richest of slave trading centre
- The Liverpool dockland was filled with sugar warehouses

You can always get extra marks if you add more information to back up a point you are making. E.g. the slave trade was very profitable (**1 mark**). Merchants could make a profit at every point of the triangle (**1 mark**).

6

3. *If the question starts with "To what extent" you must write a balanced answer.*

In this question you should show that you understand that the Zong was important to the growth of the abolitionist campaign:

- The Zong case showed the cruelty of the Middle Passage
- The case was widely reported in newspapers
- Abolitionists such as Sharp publicized the case

You should then balance your answer by giving other reasons for this success:

- Importance of the Quaker campaign against the slave trade
- Importance of other court cases which highlighted the cruelty of slavery e.g. Somerset case
- Importance of the contribution of freed slaves in Britain such as Equiano
- Importance of the campaign in Parliament

Finish with a conclusion giving an overall answer to the question supported with a reason for the judgement you have made. E.g. the case of the Zong was important to the growth of the Abolitionist movement because the shocking details of the case were widely publicized and turned people against the trade. However, other factors such as contribution of freed slaves were also important.

8

Section 2, Part D

1. *You should try to make 6 separate points from recall.*

You could mention:

- The increase in urban population had led to severe overcrowding
- Housing was often built to a poor standard e.g. lacked ventilation/sun light
- The lack of proper sanitation
- People in cities often had poor diet e.g. lack of access to fresh milk, fruit and vegetables
- Poor city dwellers had limited access to proper medical care
- Poor working conditions often led to ill-health

You can always get extra marks if you bring in more information to back up a point you are making. E.g. one reason for poor health was the increase in the urban population, which led to overcrowding (**1 mark**). Whole families would often have to share one or two rooms allowing disease to spread (**1 mark**).

6

2. *You need to make 6 clear points about the usefulness of the source.*

You would probably start by arguing that the source does provide useful evidence about improvements in technology in the textile industry. Comment on who wrote the source, when it was written and why it was written:

- The source was written at a time of improvement in the textile industry
- The source was written by an eyewitness
- The source was written to describe how changes in technology in textile manufacture affected people

You should then comment on the information contained in the source:

- The source mentions improvements in living standards
- The source mentions harmful effects of new technology on workers' health

You would gain marks by pointing out that in some ways the source is less useful because of important information that has not been mentioned. E.g. new technology made some skilled workers redundant and there were accidents caused by the new machinery.

6

3. *If the question starts with "To what extent" you must write a balanced answer.*

In this question you should show that you understand that Britain had become more democratic by 1914.

You could mention:

- voting was no longer restricted to the upper and middle classes/many skilled working class men could vote
- men in the countryside had the same right to vote as those living in the towns and cities
- there was a secret ballot
- candidates in elections were not allowed to bribe the voters
- constituencies all had roughly the same numbers of voters
- property qualifications for MPs had been abolished
- the birth of the Labour Party meant there was a party which spoke up for the working class

You should then balance your answer by pointing out the ways in which Britain was still undemocratic such as:

- property qualifications for voters still existed/only householders could vote
- approximately a third of men aged over 21 could still not vote
- no women could vote in parliamentary elections
- the unelected House of Lords could still stop laws being passed

Finish with a conclusion giving an overall answer to the question supported with a reason for the judgement you have made. E.g. overall, Britain was quite democratic by 1914, but it could not be called a true democracy when half the population was prevented from voting on the grounds of gender.

8

Section 2, Part E

1. *You should try to make 6 separate points from recall.*

You could mention:

- The information produced by surveys of poverty by Booth and Rowntree showed the extent of poverty among children and the elderly
- Investigators had drawn attention to the fact that many poor children got no benefit from their education due to hunger/ill-health
- Socialist groups campaigned for school meals and old age pensions
- Recruits for the army during the Boer war failed the basic army medical
- Poor state of workers made it more difficult for Britain to compete with other countries

- Countries like Germany appeared to have benefited from the introduction of pensions
- Some younger Liberal MPs became convinced that direct action to help children and the elderly was necessary

You can always get extra marks if you add more information to back up a point you are making. E.g. Socialist groups campaigned for school meals and old age pensions (**1 mark**). Liberals were concerned that they might lose votes to the new Labour Party (**1 mark**).

6

2. *You need to make 6 clear points about the usefulness of the source.*

You would probably start by arguing that the source does provide useful evidence about attitudes to the welfare state after the Second World War. Comment on who wrote the source, when it was written and why it was written:

- The author was Prime Minister at the beginning of 1945 and would know about welfare reform
- The source comes from a speech made at a time when welfare reform was being debated
- It was written to explain why Welfare Reform was not necessary

You should also comment on what the source says:

- The source tells us that Labour reformers were unrealistic dreamers
- It says that British people should be free to plan their own lives

You could decide however that in some ways the source is less useful because:

- Churchill was campaigning against Labour's plans for reform so he could be biased
- His party was heavily defeated in the election, which suggests that his views were not widely supported

You could also decide that in some ways the source is less useful because of important information that has not been mentioned:

- Many British people supported the idea of welfare reform
- Beveridge Report was very popular in Britain/sold thousands of copies

6

3. *If the question starts with "To what extent" you must write a balanced answer.*

In this question you should show that you understand how rationing helped to change attitudes towards poverty.

You could mention:

- Rationing was introduced by the government to try to ensure that food was distributed equally to everyone
- The government was stepping in to make sure that poor people were not deprived of food because of rising prices
- Many people thought that this kind of intervention by the government was fair

You should then balance your answer by giving other reasons such as:

- Many people agreed with government support for victims of bombing
- Evacuation made more middle class people aware of the effects of poverty

- The war brought a desire for a fairer society after the war
- Many people supported/were influenced by the Beveridge Report of 1942

Finish with a conclusion giving an overall answer to the question supported with a reason for the judgement you have made. E.g. overall, the experience of rationing was very important in changing attitudes to poverty because everybody had to accept that there was need to ration food.

8

Section 3, Part B

1. *Start off by saying that the source partly explains why many colonists had turned against British rule. This allows you to go on to show what is and what is not in the source*

The source mentions:

- People were persuaded by Paine that the British government were abusing the rights of the American people
- Paine's ideas were very popular
- The King had rejected the Olive Branch Petition
- The British were using mercenary soldiers to help them run the colonies

However the source does not mention:

- Anger at unfair taxation
- Colonists felt that actions of the British government were damaging trade
- Anger among the colonists about the growing number of British soldiers in the colonies
- Acts of violence by the British e.g. Boston Massacre
- Lack of representation in the British parliament

5

2. *You need to make 5 clear points about the usefulness of the source.*

You would probably start by arguing that the source does provide useful evidence about why the Boston Massacre took place. Comment on who wrote the source, when it was written and why it was written:

- The source was written by a British officer who was involved in the massacre
- The source was written shortly after the massacre took place
- The source was written to explain why the massacre took place

You should then comment on the information contained in the source:

- A British soldier fired accidently
- The British were attacked by a great number

You might want to comment on ways in which the source is less useful:

- The source was written by a British soldier which makes it biased

You would gain marks by pointing out that in some ways the source is less useful because of important information that has not been mentioned. E.g. there had been a build up of tension between the colonists and the British people in Boston were furious about the new system of taxation that had been imposed.

5

3. *You should try to make 5 separate points from recall.*

You could mention:

- France provided the colonies with military assistance; soldiers, gunpowder, etc
- The French attacked British colonies in the Caribbean and elsewhere
- The French harassed British shipping in the Atlantic
- Foreign intervention caused Britain to lose its control of the seas
- Foreign intervention made it more difficult for Britain to reinforce and supply its forces in America
- Spain distracted Britain by attacking Gibraltar
- A Franco-Spanish force threatened Britain with invasion in 1779

You can always get extra marks if you bring in more information to back up a point you are making. E.g. France provided the colonies with military assistance soldiers, gunpowder etc. (**1 mark**) and loans to pay for military supplies (**1 mark**).

5

4. *You should try to make 5 separate points from recall.*

You could mention:

- Most colonists were of British descent
- Many colonists were becoming wealthy through trade with Britain
- Some loyalists believed that the conflict was the colonists's fault
- Some colonists had loyalty to the British king
- Some colonists feared the spread of revolutionary ideas

You can always get extra marks if you add more information to back up a point you are making. E.g. some colonists had loyalty to the British king (**1 mark**) and they hoped to win favour with the British government (**1 mark**).

5

Section 3, Part C

1. *Start off by saying that the source partly explains the situation. This allows you to go on to show what is and what is not in the source.*

The source mentions:

- Hunters shot buffalo to provide meat for settlers
- Settlers crossed into sacred land of Native Americans
- Settlers shot buffalo for sport

However the source does not mention:

- Settler's attitude to land ownership offended Natives
- Settlers broke treaties
- Building of railroads

5

2. *You should try to make 5 separate points from recall.*

You could mention:

- Many Northerners felt slavery was morally wrong
- It violated the principles of democracy
- Growth in abolitionist feeling
- Horror of slave life intensified sectional feeling
- Dred Scott decision intensified sectional feeling

- Republican party campaigned against the expansion of slavery

You can always get extra marks if you add more information to back up a point you are making. E.g. horror of slave life intensified sectional feeling (**1 mark**). The novel *Uncle Tom's Cabin* was widely read in the North (**1 mark**).

5

3. *You should try to make 5 separate points from recall.*

You could mention:

- Prevent slavery being extended beyond its current limits
- Free land for farmers
- Grant land to build railroads/subsidise the building of transcontinental railway
- Mining and timber companies would get cheap federal land
- High tariffs to protect northern industries
- Preserve the Union
- Encourage westward expansion

You can always get extra marks if you bring in more information to back up a point you are making. E.g. encourage westward expansion (**1 mark**). Republicans were committed to the idea of Manifest Destiny (**1 mark**).

5

4. *You need to make 5 clear points about the usefulness of the source.*

You would probably start by arguing that the source does provide useful evidence about the effects of the Ku Klux Klan's tactics on black Americans. Comment on who wrote the source, when it was written and why it was written:

- Source written by a historian who would have studied the period
- Source written many years after the event with the benefit of hindsight
- Source written to explain the effects of the KKK on black Americans

You should then comment on the information contained in the source:

- The source mentions the Klan wearing robes to conceal their identity
- The source also mentions KKK lynching its victims

You would gain marks by pointing out that in some ways the source is less useful because of important information that has not been mentioned. E.g. KKK had supporters in positions of importance in the South.

5

Section 3, Part D

1. *You should try to make 5 separate points from recall.*

You could mention:

- Hitler and some Nazis interrupted a meeting at a Munich Beer Hall
- Von Kahr and Bavarian leaders were threatened into offering support to the Nazis
- Von Kahr and other leaders later their withdrew support and ordered the putsch to be crushed
- Next day Hitler marched to the town centre in Munich with 3,000 Nazis

- Nazi supporters were forced back by troops and police
- Hitler was later arrested
- Hitler was tried and imprisoned

You can always get extra marks if you bring in more information to back up a point you are making. E.g. Hitler and some Nazis interrupted the meeting (**1 mark**). Goering and 25 Nazis burst in to the Beer Hall (**1 mark**).

5

2. *Start off by saying that the source partly explains the situation. This allows you to go on to show what is and what is not in the source.*

The source mentions:

- No one party was ever able to win a majority of the seats in the Reichstag
- Germany was ruled by a series of coalitions which many thought provided only weak government
- Many felt that politicians were too busy arguing among themselves to solve the country's problems

However the source does not mention:

- Weimar Republic was associated in people's minds with the capitulation in WWI
- It was also blamed for the signing of the Versailles settlement
- Many blamed the government for Germany's economic problems

5

3. *You should try to make 5 separate points from recall.*

You could mention:

- Little cooperation between opposition groups
- Opposition leaders were arrested put in concentration camps or killed
- Opposition groups were often infiltrated by the Gestapo/spies
- All opposition was declared illegal after 1933 (Enabling Act)
- Trade Unions were declared illegal
- Intimidation by the SS
- Nazis controlled the media
- Nazis kept a tight control over the young

You can always get extra marks if you add more information to back up a point you are making. E.g. Nazis controlled the media (**1 mark**), which issued a stream of constant Nazi propaganda (**1 mark**).

5

4. *You need to make 5 clear points about the usefulness of the source.*

You would probably start by arguing that the source does provide useful evidence about militarism in Nazi Germany. Comment on who wrote the source, when it was written and why it was written:

- Source written by historians who would have studied the period
- Source written some years after the events with the benefit of hindsight
- Source written to describe the Nazi regime

You should then comment on the information contained in the source:

- The source mentions military discipline on work-camps
- The source also mentions that workers were encouraged to see themselves as soldiers of work

You would gain marks by pointing out that in some ways the source is less useful because of important information that has not been mentioned. E.g. military style discipline in the Hitler Youth and similar discipline in schools.

5

Section 3, Part E

1. *You need to make 5 clear points about the usefulness of the source.*

You would probably start by arguing that the source does provide useful evidence about Nicholas II. Comment on who wrote the source, when it was written and why it was written:

- The source was written by someone who lived under the Tsar's rule
- The source was written some time after the Tsar's rule with hindsight
- The source was written to describe the Tsar's rule

You might want to comment on ways in which the source is less useful:

- The source was written by an enemy of the Tsar so likely to be biased

You should then comment on the information contained in the source:

- The source mentions the Tsar was unreliable
- The source also mentions his stupidity

You would gain marks by pointing out that in some ways the source is less useful because of important information that has not been mentioned. E.g. the Tsar had been brought up to be an autocrat. The Tsar was dedicated to his family.

5

2. *You should try to make 5 separate points from recall.*

You could mention:

- Striking factory workers in St Petersburg marched to the Winter Palace
- The march was led by Father Gapon, a police spy
- The workers wanted to petition the Tsar about their working conditions/long hours and low pay
- The crowd was large (200,000) but peaceful and included women and children
- Marchers wore their Sunday clothes, sang hymns and carried icons
- Mounted Cossacks at the front charged the marchers
- Soldiers panicked and opened fire, killing and injuring many

You can always get extra marks if you bring in more information to back up a point you are making. E.g. marchers wore their Sunday clothes, sang hymns and carried icons (**1 mark**). Some carried portraits of the Tsar (**1 mark**).

5

3. *You should try to make 5 separate points from recall.*

You could mention:

- The war was going badly
- Defeats and losses blamed on Tsar and Tsarina
- Influence of Rasputin
- Peasants opposed conscription
- Middle classes wanted democratic reforms
- Workers faced shortages, inflation and unemployment

You can always get extra marks if you add more information to back up a point you are making. E.g. workers faced shortages and inflation (**1 mark**), which had reached 300% by February 1917 (**1 mark**).

5

4. *Start off by saying that the source partly explains why the Bolsheviks were able to stay in power in Russia. This allows you to go on to show what is and what is not in the source.*

The source mentions:

- Landlord's right to property was abolished so land could be redistributed
- Sovnarkom could pass new laws
- Elections held to the Constitutional Assembly
- Cheka set up to wipe out counter-revolutionary activity

However the source does not mention:

- Signed armistice with Germany
- Constitutional Assembly was closed down after one meeting
- Censorship of media

5

Section 3, Part G

1. *You should try to make 5 separate points from recall.*

You could mention:

- The laws enforced separate schools for blacks and whites
- They enforced separate toilets and restrooms
- Some states made marriages between whites and blacks illegal
- Ensured that transport facilities – trains and buses – were segregated
- Supreme Court decision in 1896 Plessy case enshrined the "separate but equal" idea in law and made Jim Crow laws acceptable
- Some laws hindered blacks from voting
- Led to black Americans feeling humiliated/feeling like second citizens/feeling inferior
- Led to anger and demands for change

You can always get extra marks if you bring in more information to back up a point you are making. E.g. the Jim Crow laws enforced separate schools for blacks and whites (**1 mark**). Schools for black children were usually poorly equipped compared to white schools (**1 mark**).

5

2. *You need to make 5 clear points about the usefulness of the source.*

You would probably start by arguing that the source does provide useful evidence about the effects of the Birmingham protest. Comment on who wrote the source, when it was written and why it was written:

- The source was written by the President who had to deal with the events at Birmingham
- The source was written at the time of the events
- The source was written to describe the effects of what was happening in Birmingham

You should then comment on the information contained in the source:

- The source mentions events were damaging the reputation of the US
- The source also mentions that events in Birmingham increased the need for equality

You would gain marks by pointing out that in some ways the source is less useful because of important information that has not been mentioned. E.g. segregation was lifted in Birmingham and there were revenge killings of Civil Rights workers by the KKK.

5

3. *Start off by saying that the source partly explains the situation. This allows you to go on to show what is and what is not in the source.*

The source mentions:

- Thousands of buses and many trains were needed to bring the crowd into Washington
- 20% of the protesters were white
- The huge demonstration was peaceful and orderly

However the source does not mention:

- Martin Luther King's speech
- Coverage of the event was international
- Boosted support for a new Civil Rights Act

5

4. *You should try to make 5 separate points from recall.*

You could mention:

- Speeches against peaceful protest by Malcolm X and Stokely Carmichael
- Feeling that the Civil Rights Movement had done little to help black people in the North
- Long hot summers brought black youths on to the streets
- White police patrolled black areas
- Police harassment of black youths

You can always get extra marks if you add more information to back up a point you are making. E.g. police harassment of black youths (**1 mark**). For example the arrest and beating up of a black youth sparked the Watts Riot in LA (**1 mark**).

5

Section 3, Part H

1. *You need to make 5 clear points about the usefulness of the source.*

You would probably start by arguing that the source does provide useful evidence about Nazi ideas on race. Comment on who wrote the source, when it was written and why it was written:

- Source written by Nazis
- Source written in 1934 at the start of the Nazi regime
- Source written to put forward Nazi racial theory

You should then comment on the information contained in the source:

- The source mentions people of German blood had defended Europe in the past
- The source also mentions Aryan race is superior to others

You would gain marks by pointing out that in some ways the source is less useful because of important information that has not been mentioned. E.g. Jews were a target of Nazi ideas on race and Nazis believed in the notion of racial purity.

4

2. *Start off by saying that the source partly explains why Hitler wanted to rearm Germany. This allows you to go on to show what is and what is not in the source.*

The source mentions:

- Germany had been disarmed in 1919
- Hitler wanted to take every opportunity to attack the Treaty of Versailles
- Germany was surrounded by "hostile" enemies
- A strong Germany would safeguard European civilisation

However the source does not mention:

- Rearmament was a long term goal of Hitler's foreign policy
- Hitler interpreted the lack of disarmament by the allied powers as a breech of Versailles
- Hitler claimed that Europe was under threat from Communist USSR

5

3. *You should try to make 5 separate points from recall.*

You could mention:

- British public opinion favoured peace
- Memories of the horrors of the Great War
- Britain was weakened by economic depression
- British armed forces were over-stretched by the need to defend the empire
- Defence chiefs warned politicians against the war
- Britain lacked reliable allies

You can always get extra marks if you add more information to back up a point you are making. E.g. Britain lacked reliable allies (**1 mark**) as the USA was isolationist and France favoured defence (**1 mark**).

5

4. *You should try to make 5 separate points from recall.*

You could mention:

- Nazi agitation in Sudetenland organised by Henlein
- Runciman mission failed to persuade Czechs to hand over Sudetenland
- First meeting between Hitler and Chamberlain – agreement to transfer Sudetenland
- Second meeting – Hitler makes new demands
- Munich Conference – arranges for transfer of Sudetenland
- March 1939 – Hitler invades Czech territory

You can always get extra marks if you bring in more information to back up a point you are making. E.g. at the second meeting between Hitler and Chamberalain, Hitler made new demands (**1 mark**). He required the immediate hand over of the Sudetenland (**1 mark**).

5

Section 3, Part I

1. *You need to make 5 clear points about the usefulness of the source.*

You would probably start by arguing that the source does provide useful evidence about Blitzkrieg tactics. Comment on who wrote the source, when it was written and why it was written:

- The source was written by a German tank commander
- The source was written at the time of Blitzkrieg attacks
- The source was written to describe the effectiveness of Blitzkrieg

You might want to comment on ways in which the source is less useful:

- The source was written by a German soldier who may be biased

You should then comment on the information contained in the source:

- The source mentions terror caused to French soldiers and civilians
- The source also mentions the speed of the attack

You would gain marks by pointing out that in some ways the source is less useful because of important information that has not been mentioned. E.g. importance of air power and the use of Blitzkrieg in other campaigns during 1940 e.g. Denmark and the Netherlands.

5

2. *You should try to make 5 separate points from recall.*

You could mention:

- Shortages of food and fuel
- Presence of enemy soldiers
- Severe punishment for "crimes" committed against the occupying force
- Censorship of newspapers and radio
- Restrictions on travel

You can always get extra marks if you bring in more information to back up a point you are making. E.g. Shortages of food and fuel (**1 mark**). Fore example, the "hongerwinter" 1944 in the Netherlands (**1 mark**).

5

3. *Start off by saying that the source partly explains the situation. This allows you to go on to show what is and what is not in the source.*

The source mentions:

- Rescue and sheltering of Jews
- Manufacture of false papers
- Distribution of secret documents
- Involvement of over 50,000 individuals in the resistance

However the source does not mention:

- Rescuing and concealing allied airmen
- Sabotage of enemy installations
- Assassination of enemy officers

5

4. *You should try to make 5 separate points from recall.*

You could mention:

- Japan faced severe shortage of war materials
- Army and airforce had taken huge losses
- Destruction of the Japanese fleet
- Devastating air raids on Japanese cities
- US economy in full war production
- Atomic bombs dropped on Hiroshima and Nagasaki

You can always get extra marks if you add more information to back up a point you are making. E.g. Japan faced a severe shortage of war materials (**1 mark**) and was still involved in a costly war in China (**1 mark**).

5

Section 3, Part J

1. *Start off by saying that the source partly explains the situation. This allows you to go on to show what is and what is not in the source.*

The source mentions:

- A new labour law preventing strikes had caused unrest in the factories
- There were shortages of food and higher prices
- There had been a massive increase of refugees fleeing to the West
- In the six months up to June 1961, 103,000 East Germans had fled through Berlin

However the source does not mention:

- Many people living in East Berlin saw that West Berlin was wealthier and had a more democratic society
- Many East Germans were unhappy at being separated from friends and family in the West
- It was felt that Berlin was a centre for western spies
- The East German government took the decision to close the border between East and West Berlin and build a wall

5

2. *You should try to make 5 separate points from recall.*

You could mention:

- The Soviet Union had developed an alliance with Cuba following Castro's seizure of power
- With Castro's agreement, the Soviet Union constructed missile launch sites on Cuba

- Soviet cargo ships with missiles on board headed for Cuba, despite American protests
- U2 spy plane shot down by Soviet missile over Cuba
- Khrushchev thought he could take advantage of youth and inexperience of American President, Kennedy
- Khrushchev eventually backed down
- Soviet missiles were removed from Cuba in exchange for the removal of American ones in Europe

You can always get extra marks if you bring in more information to back up a point you are making. E.g. Khrushchev eventually backed down (**1 mark**) when Kennedy held firm to his blockade around Cuba (**1 mark**).

5

3. *You should try to make 5 separate points from recall.*

You could mention:

- US forces seemed to be making little progress in the war
- Thousands of American casualties
- War was widely reported on TV
- Disgust at the use of chemical weapons such as Napalm
- Student protests against the war
- Prominent figures such as Martin Luther King spoke out against the war

You can always get extra marks if you add more information to back up a point you are making. E.g. disgust at the use of chemical weapons such as Napalm (**1 mark**) and Agent Orange, which was shown to cause birth defects in Vietnamese children (**1 mark**).

5

4. *You need to make 5 clear points about the usefulness of the source.*

You would probably start by arguing that the source does provide useful evidence about why the process of détente had come to a halt by the early 1980s. Comment on who wrote the source, when it was written and why it was written:

- Source written by the President of the United States who dealt directly with the Soviet leadership
- Source written in 1983 when détente was collapsing
- Source written to explain why détente could no longer continue

You should then comment on the information contained in the source:

- The source mentions the build up of Soviet military might
- The source also mentions that the freeze on nuclear weapons made peace less secure

You would gain marks by pointing out that in some ways the source is less useful because of important information that has not been mentioned. E.g. the Soviet invasion of Afghanistan had increased tension and the USA boycott of Moscow Olympics increased tension.

5

NATIONAL 5 HISTORY 2014

Section 1, Context A, The Wars of Independence, 1286–1328

1. *Candidates can be credited in a number of ways up to a maximum of 5 marks.*

Candidates must show a causal relationship between events.

Up to a **maximum of 5 marks in total**, **1 mark** should be given for each accurate, relevant reason, and a **second mark** should be given for reasons that are developed. Candidates may achieve full marks by providing five straightforward reasons, three developed reasons, or a combination of these.

Possible reasons may include:
1. Alexander III had died without a surviving male heir/ Scots had agreed the infant Margaret was his heir, Edward approached for help
2. Edward had been Alexander's brother-in-law and a friend
3. Edward was a strong king who could use his authority to subdue Scottish troublemakers/there was a threat of civil war
4. Edward was Margaret's great uncle so could claim an interest as a relative
5. The Scots agreed to the Treaty of Birgham and the marriage of Margaret to Edward's infant son
6. Margaret died before she reached Scotland so there was now no direct heir – a further opportunity for Edward's involvement
7. Bishop Fraser invited Edward to help choose from the claimants to the throne
8. Edward insisted the claimants/competitors accepted him as their overlord before he would begin to judge the claims
9. Edward insisted the Scottish castles be handed over to him, to hold for the eventual king
10. All the competitors accepted that Edward was overlord
11. Edward judged that John Balliol had the best claim
12. Balliol paid homage to Edward for Scotland after his coronation, making Edward's superiority clear

2. *Candidates can be credited in a number of ways up to a maximum of 5 marks.*

They may take different perspectives on the events and may describe a variety of different aspects of the events.

1 mark should be given for each accurate relevant key point of knowledge. **A second mark** should be given for each point that is developed, up to a maximum of **5 marks**. Candidates may achieve full marks by making five straightforward points, by making three developed points, or a combination of these.

Possible points of knowledge may include:
1. Wallace and Murray joined forces on the north side of the River Forth
2. The Scots were on the high ground of Abbey Craig/the English assembled on the south side of the river
3. The English delayed the start of the battle/Surrey slept in
4. The English could not decide whether to use the narrow bridge or travel further upstream and cross at the broader ford

5. Cressingham did not want any further expenses and wanted to get the battle over as quickly as possible in case the Scots escaped so opted for the bridge
6. The English partly crossed, turned back and then began again, making their plans clear to the Scots
7. The English crossed the bridge slowly/only three abreast
8. The Scots attacked before all the English were over
9. The Scots attacked the end of the bridge trapping the English who had crossed and preventing the rest from crossing to help them
10. English soldiers who attempted to escape across the river were drowned/weighed down by waterlogged tunics
11. Bridge collapsed and English fled
12. The English were defeated/Cressingham was killed

3. *Candidates can be credited in a number of ways **up to a maximum of 5 marks**.*

Candidates must make a judgement about the usefulness of the source and support this by making evaluative comments on identified aspects of the source.

1 mark should be given for each relevant comment made, up to a **maximum of 5 marks in total**.

- A maximum of **4 marks** can be given for evaluative comments relating to the author, type of source, purpose and timing.
- A maximum of **2 marks** may be given for comments relating to the content of the source.
- A maximum of **2 marks** may be given for comments relating to points of significant omission.

Examples of aspects of the source and relevant comments:

Aspect of the source	Possible comment
Author: Walter of Guisborough	Churchman in Guisborough Priory in Yorkshire, so not an eyewitness, so perhaps less useful
Type of Source: Chronicle	Contains details of events, generally thought to be reliable so more useful
Purpose: To record	Keep a record of events as a history, so may be more useful, but an English version so may be biased against Bruce
Timing: Early 14th century	Written during the Wars of Independence at the time of Bruce taking the throne, so more useful.

Content	Possible comment
He lured him to a meeting in Greyfriars Church	Suggests Bruce planned a deception so shows bias so less useful
Bruce accused Comyn of telling lies about him	May not be accurate so less useful
He struck him with his sword	Puts blame on Bruce so may be biased and less useful

Possible points of significant omission may include:
1. Comyn was his main rival so more useful
2. Comyn was killed by Bruce/Bruce's men
3. Comyn's body was left at the altar
4. Bruce was excommunicated for sacrilege
5. Bruce had himself crowned king

4. *Candidates can be credited in a number of ways **up to a maximum of 5 marks**.*

Candidates must make an overall judgement about how fully the source explains the events. **1 mark** may be given for each valid point interpreted from the source or each valid point of significant omission provided. The candidate can achieve **up to 3 marks** for their interpretation of the parts of the source they consider are relevant in terms of the proposed question where there is also at least one point of significant omission identified to imply a judgement has been made about the limitations of the source. For full marks to be given each point needs to be discretely mentioned in terms of the question.

A maximum of 2 marks may be given for answers which refer only to the source or in which no judgement has been made.

Possible points which may be identified in the source include:
1. Bruce's parliament agreed that Scots nobles who had not made peace with him would lose their lands in Scotland
2. Bruce gave this forfeited land to his own supporters
3. Scots nobles would no longer be allowed to have English estates so their loyalties would not be divided
4. Continued to raid the north of England to put pressure on Edward

Possible points of significant omission may include:
1. Defeated English army at Bannockburn
2. Secured release of his wife and daughter/Wishart, in exchange for ransomed English prisoners
3. Recaptured Berwick from English occupation
4. Added to Scottish exchequer by accepting protection money from northern English towns
5. Encouraged production of Declaration of Arbroath
6. Renewed Alliance with France
7. Agreed Treaty of Edinburgh with England in 1328
8. Made a marriage treaty for his son/heir

Section 1, Context B, Mary Queen of Scots and the Scottish Reformation, 1542-1587

1. *Candidates can be credited in a number of ways **up to a maximum of 5 marks**.*

They may take different perspectives on the events and may describe a variety of different aspects of the events.

1 mark should be given for each accurate relevant key point of knowledge. **A second mark** should be given for each point that is developed, up to a maximum of **5 marks**. Candidates may achieve full marks by providing five straightforward points, by making three developed points, or a combination of these.

Possible points of knowledge may include:
1. English wanted Mary to marry Edward, son of Henry VIII, Treaty of Greenwich
2. Scots cancelled their agreement for Mary to marry Edward, this angered Henry
3. Henry VIII sent armies to destroy Scottish cities/punish the Scots – known as the 'Rough Wooing'
4. English armies tried to capture Mary
5. English armies burned Edinburgh/Borders Abbeys, St Andrews etc
6. English defeated the Scots at the Battle of Pinkie, 1547
7. Scots needed French help/French agreed if Mary married the French Dauphin (Treaty of Haddington)
8. Mary left for France from Dumbarton in August 1548

2. *Candidates can be credited in a number of ways up to a maximum of 5 marks.*

Candidates must make an overall judgement about how fully the source explains the events. **1 mark** may be given for each valid point interpreted from the source or each valid point of significant omission provided. The candidate can achieve **up to 3 marks** for their interpretation of the parts of the source they consider are relevant in terms of the proposed question where there is also at least one point of significant omission identified to imply a judgement has been made about the limitations of the source. For full marks to be given each point needs to be discretely mentioned in terms of the question.

A maximum of 2 marks may be given for answers which refer only to the source or in which no judgement has been made.

Possible points which may be identified in the source include:
1. The Protestant form of worship meant that people could participate much more in services.
2. The Bible was available in English, not Latin; therefore people who could not read Latin could still understand it
3. Some people began to criticise the Catholic Church because of its great wealth
4. Local priests were resented for charging people for christening their children.

Possible points of significant omission may include:
1. Some Scots began to resent the wealth of the Catholic Church eg excessive spending on decoration
2. Some priests & nuns attacked for setting bad example eg spent wealth on themselves not the poor/broke vow of chastity
3. Resentment at the way Protestant preachers had been treated led to more sympathy for Protestants eg Wishart burned as a heretic
4. Resentment at Catholic foreign influence at court (French)
5. Creation of the Lords of the Congregation/many favoured Protestantism
6. Scottish Parliament that met in 1560 was controlled by men who had sympathised with the Reformation
7. Scottish Parliament banned the celebration of mass in 1560/agreed to end the power of the Pope over the Church in Scotland
8. Lack of priests or poor quality of priests caused resentment

3. *Candidates can be credited in a number of ways up to a maximum of 5 marks.*

Candidates must make a judgement about the usefulness of the source and support this by making evaluative comments on identified aspects of the source.

1 mark should be given for each relevant comment made, up to a **maximum of 5 marks in total**.
- A maximum of 4 marks can be given for evaluative comments relating to the author, type of source, purpose and timing.
- A maximum of 2 marks may be given for comments relating to the content of the source.
- A maximum of 2 marks may be given for comments relating to points of significant omission.

Examples of aspects of the source and relevant comments:

Aspect of the source	Possible comment
Author: John Knox	Useful as he was an influential Protestant reformer/hated Mary as a Catholic ruler
Type of Source: Sermon	Useful as heard by Protestant followers/ public expression of Knox's views
Purpose: To persuade	Less useful as it is biased/ enthusiastically condemns Mary and her Catholic religion/to persuade people to turn against Mary
Timing: 1560s	Useful as it was delivered when the Protestant faith was growing in Scotland

Content	Possible comment
In the north of the country, where Mary had travelled before harvest time, the famine was hardest with great suffering. Many people died	Less useful as Knox blames Mary for causing famine – extreme and much exaggerated view/but perhaps useful as many Protestants also held these views
Thus did God punish the many sins of our wicked Queen and her followers	Less useful as he claims God is punishing Scotland for having a Catholic Queen – extreme and much exaggerated view/but perhaps useful as many Protestants also held these views
The excessive celebrations and huge feasts in the palace and in the country provoked God into this action	Less useful as he claims God punished Scotland because of Mary's behaviour – extreme and much exaggerated view/but perhaps useful as many Protestants also held these views

Possible points of significant omission may include:
1. John Knox denounced Mary for her whole way of life, she was an 'ungodly ruler', eg dancing criticised
2. Knox would often lecture Mary on religion, condemning Catholicism (Mary reduced to tears by him on one occasion)
3. Some Protestants were happy with Mary eg she tolerated their religion/ ensured the Protestant Church had an income

4. *Candidates can be credited in a number of ways up to a maximum of 5 marks.*

Candidates must show a causal relationship between events.

Up to a **maximum of 5 marks in total**, **1 mark** should be given for each accurate, relevant reason, and a **second mark** should be given for reasons that are developed. Candidates may achieve full marks by providing five straightforward reasons, three developed reasons, or a combination of these.

Possible reasons may include:
1. Nobles persuaded Darnley that Riccio was too friendly with Mary/implied they were having an affair
2. Riccio was humiliating the Scottish nobles by making them ask him to see Mary
3. Riccio was boasting about his influence over Mary
4. Riccio was dressing and behaving like a nobleman which angered the nobles as he w as below them in status

5. Darnley thought Riccio had persuaded Mary not to give him the crown matrimonial, which angered Darnley
6. Some nobles thought Riccio was a spy sent by the Pope so were suspicious of Riccio

Section 1, Context C, The Treaty of Union, 1689–1715

1. *Candidates can be credited in a number of ways up to a maximum of 5 marks.*

They may take different perspectives on the events and may describe a variety of different aspects of the events.

1 mark should be given for each accurate relevant key point of knowledge. **A second mark** should be given for each point that is developed, up to a maximum of **5 marks**. Candidates may achieve full marks by providing five straightforward points, by making three developed points, or a combination of these.

Possible points of knowledge may include:
1. King William wanted to remain on good terms with the Spanish and so deliberately sabotaged the Darien colony
2. English officials prevented investment in the Darien scheme
3. There was a feeling that the English had not done enough to help Scotland during the Ill Years of the 1690s
4. William took little positive interest in Scotland eg Glencoe massacre
5. Anne had declared herself to be "entirely English"
6. The strength of Jacobitism in Scotland caused tension
7. Scots loyalties were suspect after the rebellion of 1689
8. The Scots were angry that the English Parliament passed the succession to Sophia of Hanover without consulting them
9. The English were angry when the Scots Parliament passed the Act of Security
10. Scottish trade badly affected by England's French wars (no Scottish gains in the peace treaties)
11. Worcester incident

2. *Candidates can be credited in a number of ways up to a maximum of 5 marks.*

Candidates must make a judgement about the usefulness of the source and support this by making evaluative comments on identified aspects of the source.

1 mark should be given for each relevant comment made, up to a **maximum of 5 marks in total.**
- A maximum of **4 marks** can be given for evaluative comments relating to the author, type of source, purpose and timing.
- A maximum of **2 marks** may be given for comments relating to the content of the source.
- A maximum of **2 marks** may be given for comments relating to points of significant omission.

Examples of aspects of the source and relevant comments:

Aspect of the source	Possible comment
Author: Andrew Fletcher	Useful as he was one of the leading opponents of the Union.
Type of Source: Leaflet	Useful as this was a common method of trying to communicate political ideas at this time.
Purpose: To persuade	Less useful as the writer is biased against the Union/designed to persuade the reader that the Union will be bad for Scotland

Timing: One year before Union was agreed	Useful as it is written when the Union was being debated in Scotland.
Content	**Possible comment**
Scotland needs to keep its own separate law and church	Useful as it was a commonly held view at the time.
If the Scots agree to these interests being controlled by a single Parliament they will surrender control to the English	Useful as it reflects the fears of many Scots.
The English will have a vast majority.	Useful as it is an accurate statement about the parliamentary arithmetic after Union.

Possible points of significant omission may include:
1. Scotland had always been an independent nation and its identity would be subsumed if there was a new united Parliament.
2. Public opinion in Scotland was against a union.
3. Some Scots would have preferred a Federal Union eg Andrew Fletcher.
4. Episcopalians in Scotland opposed union as it would secure the Hanoverian succession and only a return to the Stuart dynasty could restore episcopacy to the Scottish church.
5. Some Presbyterians feared over the position of the Church of Scotland. The English Parliament was dominated by the Episcopalian church with Bishops' seats in the House of Lords.

3. *Candidates can be credited in a number of ways **up to a maximum of 5 marks**.*

Candidates must make an overall judgement about how fully the source explains the events. **1 mark** may be given for each valid point interpreted from the source or each valid point of significant omission provided. The candidate can achieve **up to 3 marks** for their interpretation of the parts of the source they consider are relevant in terms of the proposed question where there is also at least one point of significant omission identified to imply a judgement has been made about the limitations of the source. For full marks to be given each point needs to be discretely mentioned in terms of the question.

A maximum of 2 marks may be given for answers which refer only to the source or in which no judgement has been made.

Possible points which may be identified in the source include:
1. By this union we will all have access to all the advantages of trade that the English enjoy at the moment
2. We will be able to improve our wealth
3. We will have our liberty, our property and our religion secured
4. Scotland will be under the protection of one sovereign and one Parliament of Great Britain.

Possible points of significant omission may include:
- If Scotland failed to accept Union voluntarily they might be forced to accept it on unfavourable terms after an English invasion.
- The Scots knew that Ireland had been conquered by England and wanted to avoid this fate.

- Presbyterians wanted to solve the problem of the succession and ensure that the exiled Stuarts did not return
- The Union guaranteed the position of the Presbyterian Church
- Fear of the reintroduction of the Alien Act if Union was not approved by the Scots
- Many Scots believed the Scottish economy would benefit from Union
- Scots attracted by guarantee of free trade with the UK and the colonies
- Some felt that failure of Darien proved that Scotland could no longer go it alone/some influential Scots saw it as only way to recover from the financial disaster of the Darian Scheme
- The position of Scots Law had been guaranteed

4. *Candidates can be credited in a number of ways up to a maximum of 5 marks.*

Candidates must show a causal relationship between events.

Up to a **maximum of 5 marks in total**, **1 mark** should be given for each accurate, relevant reason, and a **second mark** should be given for reasons that are developed. Candidates may achieve full marks by providing five straightforward reasons, three developed reasons, or a combination of these.

Possible reasons may include:
1. The 1707 Union was deeply unpopular. It had failed to bring economic prosperity to Scotland
2. Many participated as they were anti-Union. James VIII promised to end the Union
3. Dislike of the Campbells (especially in the Highlands)
4. Episcopalians offered support as the return of James seemed to provide the best prospect of an Episcopalian church settlement
5. Loyalty to the House of Stuart. Jacobites did not accept William, Anne or George. They believed James was the rightful King
6. Highland clansmen felt loyalty to the exiled King
7. Some participants were "forced out"
8. The Earl of Mar fought for selfish political reasons as he had lost his government position under George I
9. Dislike of new currency, weights etc
10. Disappointment at failure of payment of the Equivalent motivated some to participate

Section 1, Context D, Migration and Empire, 1830-1939

1. *Candidates can be credited in a number of ways **up to a maximum of 5 marks.***

Candidates must show a causal relationship between events.

Up to a **maximum of 5 marks in total**, **1 mark** should be given for each accurate, relevant reason, and a **second mark** should be given for reasons that are developed. Candidates may achieve full marks by providing five straightforward reasons, three developed reasons, or a combination of these.

Possible reasons may include:
1. Scots accused them of taking Scots' jobs, so resented immigrants
2. Scots accused them of working for less money/lowering wages, so suspicious of immigrants
3. Immigrants were exploited as strike breakers/did not join in with strikes so were unpopular
4. Some had a reputation for drunkenness, so many Scots were wary of immigrants
5. Some had a reputation for violence/fighting, so some Scots were afraid of immigrants
6. Accused them of causing overcrowding/pressure on limited housing stock/ putting up rents, which caused resentment
7. Immigrants were said to spread disease/unhygienic way of life/'brought down' the Scots, so viewed with suspicion
8. Accused some of claiming poor relief intended for Scots, so were resented
9. Some immigrants practised a different religion, which made Scots suspicious of them
10. Some immigrants failed to fit in/kept to themselves/ kept their own customs, so were viewed with suspicion

2. *Candidates can be credited in a number of ways up to a maximum of 5 marks.*

They may take different perspectives on the events and may describe a variety of different aspects of the events.

1 mark should be given for each accurate relevant key point of knowledge. **A second mark** should be given for each point that is developed, up to a maximum of **5 marks**. Candidates may achieve full marks by providing five straightforward points, by making three developed points, or a combination of these.

Possible points of knowledge may include:
1. Fares were paid by landlords in the Highlands
2. HIES – sent poor crofter families to Australia
3. Glasgow Emigration Society – gave assistance to settle in Canada
4. British Government/Colonial Land and Emigration Commissioners – 'Bounty' settlers to Australia
5. Emigrants' Information Office – gave advice and assistance on aspects of emigration
6. Empire Settlement Act 1922 – gave loans and grants to help with passages and training
7. Barnardos/Quarriers – sent orphan boys and girls to Australia and Canada
8. YMCA – helped young men to emigrate as farm workers/Big Brother scheme supported boys who emigrated/'Dreadnought' boys supported as farm workers
9. Personal loans from family paid for fares etc
10. Cheap rail/steamer fares offered by transport companies eg Anchor-Donaldson Line
11. Subsidised passages paid for by Australian and Canadian governments
12. Free passage for domestic servants to New Zealand, Lewis girls as servants to Canada etc

3. *Candidates can be credited in a number of ways **up to a maximum of 5 marks.***

Candidates must make an overall judgement about how fully the source explains the events. **1 mark** may be given for each valid point interpreted from the source or each valid point of significant omission provided. The candidate can achieve **up to 3 marks** for their interpretation of the parts of the source they consider are relevant in terms of the proposed question where there is also at least one point of significant omission identified to imply a judgement has been made about the limitations of the source. For full marks to be given each point needs to be discretely mentioned in terms of the question.

A maximum of 2 marks may be given for answers which refer only to the source or in which no judgement has been made.

Possible points which may be identified in the source include:

1. Alexander Spark was a leading member of the business community/ prominent in banking
2. By 1840 owned £40,000 of land
3. Became the local agent for a variety of companies
4. Scottish Agents in Australia handled the interests of many Scots who invested money in Australian businesses without ever leaving Scotland.

Possible points of significant omission may include:

1. Scots introduced merino sheep to Australia/developed sheep farming in New Zealand
2. Scots developed shipping companies/developed refrigerated sea transport for meat
3. Scots pioneered the sugar industry in Australia/ introduced sugar mills/ refineries
4. Scots were involved in developing the wine industry/ brewing in Australia
5. Scots set up universities in Canada/New Zealand/ education systems variously
6. Scots developed engineering companies in Canada, Australia/developed shipbuilding in New Zealand
7. Scots developed Canadian Pacific railroad as engineers and financiers
8. Scots cleared and developed virgin land in Canada, Australia, New Zealand
9. Scots masons built prestigious public buildings in new cities
10. Scots developed the jute industry in India
11. Scots' were active in politics/reached high positions eg JA MacDonald, Prime Minister of Canada

4. *Candidates can be credited in a number of ways **up to a maximum of 5 marks.***

Candidates must make a judgement about the usefulness of the source and support this by making evaluative comments on identified aspects of the source.

1 mark should be given for each relevant comment made, up to a **maximum of 5 marks in total.**

- A maximum of **4 marks** can be given for evaluative comments relating to the author, type of source, purpose and timing.
- A maximum of **2 marks** may be given for comments relating to the content of the source.
- A maximum of **2 marks** may be given for comments relating to points of significant omission.

Examples of aspects of the source and relevant comments:

Aspect of the source	Possible comment
Author: Mary Contini	Personal recollection of her own family history so useful
Type of Source: Memoirs about her grandparents' experience	Not describing a first-hand experience so may be less accurate, so less useful
Purpose: Informs why they worked hard	Simple explanation, not exaggerated, so useful
Timing: Reflection on early 20th century	Grandparents arrived around time of peak Italian immigration to Scotland so fairly typical and more useful/looking back with the benefit of hindsight

Content	Possible comment
Many of them made their living selling fish and chips	Useful as true of many Italian immigrants
Debt worried them and made them work even harder	Useful as explains concerns of immigrants to succeed
Shops were open long hours/the whole family helped serve customers/shops became the focus of social life	Useful as explains why families had so much contact with new communities/useful as accurate

Possible points of significant omission may include:

1. Italian cafes became very stylish and fashionable eg Nardini's in Largs
2. Names changed to Scottish versions/nicknames were used to seem less foreign
3. Second generation immigrants spoke Scots English
4. Some intermarriage, especially Scots and Irish
5. Worked with Scots in Trade Union movement/ Temperance movement
6. Worked with Scots in politics/Women's suffrage movement
7. Scots and immigrants served together in the Great War

Section 1, Context E, The Era of the Great War, 1910-1928

1. *Candidates can be credited in a number of ways up to a maximum of 5 marks.*

They may take different perspectives on the events and may describe a variety of different aspects of the events.

1 mark should be given for each accurate relevant key point of knowledge. **A second mark** should be given for each point that is developed, up to a maximum of **5 marks**. Candidates may achieve full marks by providing five straightforward points, by making three developed points, or a combination of these.

Possible points of knowledge may include:

1. **Use of Tanks:**
   - Able to cross trenches/crush barbed wire
   - Use fascines to cross trenches
   - Scattered German infantry
   - Achieved some success/at Cambrai
   - Protected the infantry going forward
   - Were armoured/bullet proof/equipped with machine guns/six pound guns
   - However were easily bogged down/inefficient/ unreliable/dangerous or uncomfortable for the crew
2. **Use of Machine guns:**
   - Vickers was highly efficient/successful/accurate weapon
   - Could fire up to 600 bullets a minute
   - Killed thousands of men
   - Development of portable machine guns
3. **Use of Aircraft**
   - Used for reconnaissance, ascertain enemy actions
   - Used to photograph enemy lines
   - Used to protect troops in the trenches
   - Fighter planes built to shoot down enemy planes
   - Used to bomb enemy trenches
   - Used to strafe enemy trenches

4. **Use of Gas**
   - Germans were first to use gas at Ypres in 1915 British use of gas eg ...
   - operation of gas canisters/shells; delivery; unreliability
   - different types of gas used (chlorine, mustard, phosgene, tear)
   - surprise/fear/panic factor of gas
   - importance of weather/wind direction
   - effects of gas (suffocating/choking, blinding, blisters/burns)
   - use of gas masks; soldiers urinated on hankies
   - gas rarely used after 1917 as the Germans ran out of chemicals
   - (initially) killed thousands
   - (overall) more injuries than deaths
5. Development of range finding techniques for heavy artillery
6. Flamethrowers used to clear out enemy trenches

2. *Candidates can be credited in a number of ways **up to a maximum of 5 marks**.*

Candidates must make a judgement about the usefulness of the source and support this by making evaluative comments on identified aspects of the source.

1 mark should be given for each relevant comment made, up to a **maximum of 5 marks in total**.
- A maximum of 4 marks can be given for evaluative comments relating to the author, type of source, purpose and timing.
- A maximum of 2 marks may be given for comments relating to the content of the source.
- A maximum of 2 marks may be given for comments relating to points of significant omission.

Examples of aspects of the source and relevant comments:

Aspect of the source	Possible comment
Author: David Lloyd George	Useful as he is an eyewitness/a government minister soon to be Prime Minister so an expert on women's war effort
Type of Source: Memoir extract	Useful as based on Lloyd George's feelings/as a memoir could be less useful as could be coloured by subsequent events
Purpose: To record	Useful as it is an accurate account of the dangers faced by the women/ to record DLG's admiration of the women who worked in the munitions factories
Timing: Memoir from his time as Minister of Munitions (from 1915)	Useful as it is an account of his wartime experiences

Content	Possible comment
They had to work under conditions of real danger to life	Useful as it tells of the dangers of explosions which were common
One of the risks of shell filling factories was toxic jaundice resulting from the TNT poisoning/ The poor girls were nicknamed 'canaries'	Useful as it explains the dangers of the TNT poisoning
They were quite proud of this/They had earned it in the path of duty	Useful as it shows the women were proud of the jobs they were doing, despite the danger

Possible points of significant omission may include:
1. Details of other jobs done by women eg the Land Army, Nursing etc
2. Mourning for lost loved ones
3. Women became head of the family/struggled to juggle children, jobs, bills etc
4. Women got the vote as a result of contribution

3. *Candidates can be credited in a number of ways **up to a maximum of 5 marks**.*

Candidates must make an overall judgement about how fully the source explains the events. **1 mark** may be given for each valid point interpreted from the source or each valid point of significant omission provided. The candidate can achieve **up to 3 marks** for their interpretation of the parts of the source they consider are relevant in terms of the proposed question where there is also at least one point of significant omission identified to imply a judgement has been made about the limitations of the source. For full marks to be given each point needs to be discretely mentioned in terms of the question.

A maximum of 2 marks may be given for answers which refer only to the source or in which no judgement has been made.

Possible points which may be identified in the source include:
1. Men who refused to enlist in the army had to face military discipline
2. Some were sentenced to death for refusing orders although the sentence was always reduced if the 'conchie' still refused to give in
3. Special prisons and work camps were opened up in addition to the ordinary prisons to which many objectors were sent
4. Twenty four objectors died while detained at work camps

Possible points of significant omission may include:
1. In their communities conscientious objectors were often subject to a torrent of verbal and sometimes physical abuse
2. They were often ignored or refused service in shops
3. Women would give these men white feathers to signify cowardice

4. *Candidates can be credited in a number of ways up to a maximum of 5 marks.*

Candidates must show a causal relationship between events.

Up to a **maximum of 5 marks in total**, **1 mark** should be given for each accurate, relevant reason, and a **second mark** should be given for reasons that are developed. Candidates may achieve full marks by providing five straightforward reasons, three developed reasons, or a combination of these.

Possible reasons may include:

1. Post-war lack of demand/orders for shipbuilding eg 1921–23 tonnage of ships built on the Clyde declined/from 510,000 to 170,000
2. Poor industrial relations (eg demarcation disputes) created difficulties
3. Failure to invest in new technology/lack of investment
4. Lack of demand led to iron and steel production declining/plants closing
5. Lack of orders led to decline in railway production eg by two-thirds at the North British Locomotive company
6. New fuels, so coal production also declined/pits closed
7. Foreign competition challenged Scottish industry
8. International markets lost during the war were not recovered
9. The jute factories in Dundee were in need of fresh investment and repair/lack of demand for sandbags reduced demand for jute
10. At the same time jute prices fell around the world
11. The management of Scottish industry suffered from disproportionate effect of losses of middle-class officers

Section 2, Context A, The Creation of the Medieval Kingdoms, 1066–1406

1. *Candidates can be credited in a number of ways up to a maximum of 8 marks.*

Candidates must use knowledge to present a balanced assessment of the influence of different possible factors and come to a reasoned conclusion.

Up to 5 marks are allocated for relevant points of knowledge used to address the question. **1 mark** should be given for each relevant, factual key point of knowledge used to support a factor. **If only one factor is presented, a maximum of 3 marks should be given for relevant points of knowledge.**

Possible factors may include:	Relevant, factual, key points of knowledge to support this factor may include:
William's leadership skills	1. William was experienced in battle and had previously defeated the French king 2. William feigned retreat during the battle tricking the Anglo-Saxons
William's superior army	3. William's army was well trained and wore chain mail armour 4. William's cavalry rode specially bred horses. The horses also had a saddle on them keeping the knights in position and allowing them to fight 5. William had brought supplies with him from Normandy and so his army was well fed and rested
Harold's inferior army	6. Harold's army was a mixture of professional soldiers/bodyguards and ordinary men 7. The army was not as well trained as the Normans 8. Death of Harold and his brothers meant there was no clear leadership during the battle
Harold's army were tired	9. Harold's army had only just fought the Battle of Stamford Bridge 10. Harold's army had been forced to march quickly to the south to meet the Normans
Any other valid factor	

Up to 3 marks should be given for presenting the answer in a structured way, leading to a conclusion which addresses the question, as follows:

1 mark for the answer being presented in a structured way, with knowledge being organised in support of different factors.
1 mark given for a valid judgement or overall conclusion.
1 mark given for a reason being provided in support of the conclusion.

2. *Candidates can be credited in a number of ways up to a maximum of 6 marks.*

Candidates must make a judgement about the usefulness of the source and support this by making evaluative comments on identified aspects of the source.

1 mark should be given for each relevant comment made, up to a **maximum of 6 marks in total.**

- A maximum of 4 marks can be given for evaluative comments relating to the author, type of source, purpose and timing.
- A maximum of 2 marks may be given for comments relating to the content of the source.
- A maximum of 2 marks may be given for comments relating to points of significant omission.

Examples of aspects of the source and relevant comments:

Aspect of the source	Possible comment
Author: Royal clerk	Useful because he was well placed to gather information
Type of Source: Chronicle	Useful because it was an official record of events
Purpose: To describe	Less useful as clearly biased description of rebellions/author may have exaggerated when describing the actions of the Scots
Timing: 1174	At the time that Henry II was facing rebellion
Content	**Possible comment**
William rebelled and attacked Northumberland	Useful because it gives details of William's rebellion
Women and children were slaughtered/priests murdered inside their own churches	Less useful because it could be exaggerating what happened.

His army besieged the castle/by cutting off their supplies/forced the English to make a treaty with the Scots.	Useful because it provides details on what William did next.

Possible points of significant omission may include:
1. Henry II's sons rebelled against him/the Great Rebellion 1173
2. Further rebellions by Henry's sons in 1183 and 1187

3. *Candidates can be credited in a number of ways up to a maximum of 6 marks.*

Candidates must show a causal relationship between events.

Up to a **maximum of 6 marks in total**, **1 mark** should be given for each accurate, relevant reason, and a **second mark** should be given for reasons that are developed. Candidates may achieve full marks by providing five straightforward reasons, three developed reasons, or a combination of these.

Possible reasons may include:
1. Effects of the Black Death eg some peasants were free some were not
2. Peasants prevented from earning higher wages than they had before the Black Death eg 1351 Statute of Labour (ie wages were cut), so unhappy
3. Peasants' discontent with war with France
4. Peasants had been taxed in 1377, 1379 and 1381, so unhappy
5. 1381 tax targeted new groups eg over 15s/craftsmen/ women taxed whether they worked or not, which was resented
6. Peasants unhappy as wanted an end to forced labour/ greater access to forests
7. Lack of faith in King Richard II who was a boy
8. Hatred of the King's advisor/allegations of corruption
9. Inspired by speakers who criticised the Church and monarchy eg John Ball/ Waldergrave

Section 2, Context B, War of the Three Kingdoms, 1603–1651

1. *Candidates can be credited in a number of ways up to a maximum of 8 marks.*

Candidates must use knowledge to present a balanced assessment of the influence of different possible factors and come to a reasoned conclusion.

Up to **5 marks** are allocated for relevant points of knowledge used to address the question. **1 mark** should be given for each relevant, factual key point of knowledge used to support a factor. **If only one factor is presented, a maximum of 3 marks should be given for relevant points of knowledge.**

Possible factors may include:	Relevant, factual, key points of knowledge to support this factor may include:
Religious differences	1. Some in Parliament were offended by James' belief in the Divine Right of Kings 2. Millenary Petition 1603 demanded changes to church practices – rejected by James VI and I
Religious differences *(continued)*	3. Archbishops Canons – clergy had to subscribe to 39 articles and Prayer Book, James licensed the Canons, which provoked the clergy 4. 1622 – Direction of Preachers issued, gave Bishops more control, which worried Puritans 5. Demands of Presbyterians for the removal of Bishops 6. Demands from Catholics for more lenient treatment 7. Gunpowder plot
Financial grievances	8. Extravagant spending and debts built up by James eg clothing banquets 9. Gave money and power to his favourites at court 10. Bates Case 1606 – judges agreed that impositions (new source of revenue of additional tax on imports and exports) were legal 11. Failure of Great Contract 1610 – reciprocal distrust 12. Monopolies caused anger and resentment
Political factors	13. James dismissed Parliament in 1610 14. Failure of 'Addled Parliament' in 1614 15. James' insistence on creating a legal and administrative Union with Scotland caused suspicions in England
Any other relevant factor	

Up to 3 marks should be given for presenting the answer in a structured way, leading to a conclusion which addresses the question, as follows:
1 mark for the answer being presented in a structured way, with knowledge being organised in support of different factors.
1 mark given for a valid judgement or overall conclusion.
1 mark given for a reason being provided in support of the conclusion.

2. *Candidates can be credited in a number of ways up to a maximum of 6 marks.*

Candidates must show a causal relationship between events.

Up to a **maximum of 6 marks in total**, **1 mark** should be given for each accurate, relevant reason, and a **second mark** should be given for reasons that are developed. Candidates may achieve full marks by providing six straightforward reasons, three developed reasons, or a combination of these.

Possible reasons may include:
1. Believed in the Divine Right of Kings, which was resented
2. Married to Henrietta Maria – a Catholic, unpopular with Protestants
3. Spending habits eg paintings and expensive clothes were resented

4. 1629-1640 – ruled without Parliament (Personal Rule), so was unpopular
5. Forced Ship Money, those who refused went to prison, created resentment
6. Appointed Laud as Archbishop of Canterbury, who was unpopular
7. Laud changed Church of England services (statues, music and candles introduced) – offended some Protestants
8. Introduced New Prayer Book – in Scotland this caused riots
9. Scots attacked English because of religious changes (Bishops' Wars)
10. Charles called Parliament to get money to fight the Scots, which was resented
11. Earl of Strafford ruled Ireland for Charles – Strafford unpopular with the Irish and the Long Parliament

3. *Candidates can be credited in a number of ways* **up to a maximum of 6 marks.**

Candidates must make a judgement about the usefulness of the source and support this by making evaluative comments on identified aspects of the source.

1 mark should be given for each relevant comment made, up to a **maximum of 6 marks in total.**
- A maximum of 4 marks can be given for evaluative comments relating to the author, type of source, purpose and timing.
- A maximum of 2 marks may be given for comments relating to the content of the source.
- A maximum of 2 marks may be given for comments relating to points of significant omission.

Examples of aspects of the source and relevant comments:

Aspect of the source	Possible comment
Author: Oliver Cromwell	Useful as he was the leader of the Parliamentary forces (who was an extreme Puritan and who hated the Irish Catholics)
Type of Source: Letter (to the House of Commons)	Useful as an official account of the events of the battle, so should be accurate/less useful as may be biased based on Cromwell's actions
Purpose: To inform	Useful as provides reasons for victory at Drogheda/ Cromwell justifying his actions
Timing: September 1649	Useful as written soon after the battle took place
Content	Possible comment
On Monday 9th the battering guns began/Our guns then beat down the corner tower, and made gaps in the east and south walls	Useful as it provides accurate details of when the battle began/weapons used
I sent Sir Arthur Aston a request to surrender the town but received no satisfactory answer	Useful as Sir Arthur Aston ignored Cromwell's order to surrender
On the following day, after some fierce fighting, we entered the town/several of the enemy, including Sir Arthur Aston, retreated into Mill Mount	Useful as it describes the successful storming of the city by Cromwell's forces

Possible points of significant omission may include:
1. Cromwell ordered his men to kill everyone remaining in the town who had weapons
2. Cromwell's men killed approximately 2000 men after the surrender
3. The Church of St. Peters was set on fire, burning alive a group of defenders who had barricaded themselves in
4. Parliamentarian losses are regarded to be around 150
5. Sir Arthur Aston reported to have been beaten to death with his own wooden leg

Section 2, Context C, The Atlantic Slave Trade, 1770-1807

1. *Candidates can be credited in a number of ways up to a maximum of 8 marks.*

Candidates must use knowledge to present a balanced assessment of the influence of different possible factors and come to a reasoned conclusion.
Up to 5 marks are allocated for relevant points of knowledge used to address the question. **1 mark** should be given for each relevant, factual key point of knowledge used to support a factor. **If only one factor is presented, a maximum of 3 marks should be given for relevant points of knowledge.**

Possible factors may include:	Relevant, factual, key points of knowledge to support this factor may include:
Role of Thomas Clarkson	1. Visited ports such as Liverpool to collect evidence about the cruelties of the slave trade 2. Interviewed sailors who were involved in the slave trade 3. Risked his life to campaign for the abolition of slavery 4. Clarkson published his evidence about the slave trade 5. Clarkson's influence on Wilberforce and others
Role of other campaigners	6. William Wilberforce led the campaign against the slave trade in parliament. 7. Wilberforce presented bills to abolish the slave trade 8. Wilberforce used his friendship with the prime minister and the monarchy to win support for abolition 9. Wilberforce became leader of the Society for the Abolition of the Slave Trade 10. Former slave ship captain, John Newton, preached against the evils of the trade/wrote the hymn, Amazing Grace 11. Freed slaves such as Olaudah Equiano published personal accounts about the terrible nature of the slave trade 12. Granville Sharp campaigned against slavery in British courts 13. Many people across Britain signed petitions against the slave trade.

Role of other campaigners (continued)	14. Pamphlets, posters, newspaper adverts were used to campaign against the slave trade 15. Slogans such as 'Am I not a man and a brother' were used/appeared on Wedgwood crockery 16. Boycotts of slave produced goods such as sugar
Changing attitudes	17. Christian teaching led people to change their attitudes to the slave trade 18. People began to think of Africans as fellow human beings 19. Plantation agriculture became less important to the British economy 20. People began to regard slave labour as an inefficient way to produce goods
Any other relevant factor	

Up to 3 marks should be given for presenting the answer in a structured way, leading to a conclusion which addresses the question, as follows:

1 mark for the answer being presented in a structured way, with knowledge being organised in support of different factors.
1 mark given for a valid judgement or overall conclusion.
1 mark given for a reason being provided in support of the conclusion.

2. *Candidates can be credited in a number of ways up to a maximum of 6 marks.*

Candidates must show a causal relationship between events.

Up to a **maximum of 6 marks in total**, **1 mark** should be given for each accurate, relevant reason, and a **second mark** should be given for reasons that are developed. Candidates may achieve full marks by providing six straightforward reasons, three developed reasons, or a combination of these.

Possible reasons may include:
1. The slave trade brought wealth to Britain, so was popular with those who became wealthy
2. The slave trade brought employment to Britain in areas such as shipyards, ports, mills, manufacturing, so was supported by many involved in these industries
3. Cities profited from the slave trade (eg Bristol, Liverpool and Glasgow), so many in these cities wished to see slavery continue
4. The products of the slave trade were in great demand (eg cotton, tobacco and sugar) and many believed that slavery was needed in order to meet demand for these products
5. Involvement in the slave trade helped Britain to remain a world power, so many continued to support slavery
6. The slave trade was seen as a valuable training ground for the Royal Navy, so it was supported
7. Many MPs had financial interests in the slave trade, so wished to see it continue
8. Many MPs were being bribed to ensure that they continued to give their support for the continuation of the trade

9. The slave trade still enjoyed the support of the King
10. Profits from the trade were essential to fund the war with France

3. *Candidates can be credited in a number of ways up to a maximum of 6 marks.*

Candidates must make a judgement about the usefulness of the source and support this by making evaluative comments on identified aspects of the source.

1 mark should be given for each relevant comment made, up to a **maximum of 6 marks in total**.
- A maximum of **4 marks** can be given for evaluative comments relating to the author, type of source, purpose and timing.
- A maximum of **2 marks** may be given for comments relating to the content of the source.
- A maximum of **2 marks** may be given for comments relating to points of significant omission.

Examples of aspects of the source and relevant comments:

Aspect of the source	Possible comment
Author: Historian	Useful as modern historians are likely to be experts on the issue and have carried out research
Type of Source: Textbook	Factual account of the treatment of slaves on the plantations
Purpose: To inform	Useful as evidence of harsh treatment of slaves on the plantations
Timing: 1995	A secondary source written with the benefit of hindsight
Content	**Possible comment**
They followed a policy of control through fear	Useful as this shows how harsh the treatment of slaves was
Slaves had no rights. They were seen as possessions rather than human beings	Useful as this shows slaves were not treated equally
There was no punishment for owners who worked their slaves to death/ no one questioned owners burning or torturing their slaves	Useful as this shows how cruel plantation owners were/not answerable for their actions towards their slaves

Possible points of significant omission may include:
1. Slaves were forced to work long hours
2. Slaves were often whipped for not working hard enough
3. Slave families were often broken up when slaves were bought and sold from plantations

Section 2, Context D, Changing Britain, 1760-1900

1. *Candidates can be credited in a number of ways up to a maximum of 6 marks.*

Candidates must make a judgement about the usefulness of the source and support this by making evaluative comments on identified aspects of the source.

1 mark should be given for each relevant comment made, up to a **maximum of 6 marks** in total.

- A maximum of 4 marks can be given for evaluative comments relating to the author, type of source, purpose and timing.
- A maximum of **2 marks** may be given for comments relating to the content of the source.
- A maximum of **2 marks** may be given for comments relating to points of significant omission.

Examples of aspects of the source and relevant comments:

Aspect of the source	Possible comment
Author: Doctor	Useful as it was written by an eyewitness to poor housing conditions in Manchester
Type of Source: Report	Useful as it was part of an official document by someone with medical expertise/reports tend to be factual
Purpose: To record	May be less useful, as report only focuses on one area of Manchester/ but useful because factual record of poor housing conditions in Manchester
Timing: 1832	Useful as it was written at the time of urbanisation/growth of cities/ industrial revolution/time when there was a lot of poor housing in British cities
Content	**Possible comment**
The houses that the mill workers live in are poorly ventilated and do not have toilets	Useful as fairly typical of urban housing in poorer areas at this time
The streets are narrow, unpaved and worn into deep ruts, which become the resting place of mud, refuse and rubbish	Useful as typical of cities at this time with poor sanitation
In Parliament Street there is only one toilet for 380 inhabitants. The flow of muck from this toilet infests close-by houses and must be a source of disease	May be less useful as may have been exaggerated for effect but could also say useful as fairly typical of concerns about dirt and disease at this time

Possible points of significant omission may include:
1. Lack of clean water
2. Overcrowding
3. Poorly constructed homes
4. Impact of these living conditions on health – eg rickets/ cholera/TB, vermin spread other diseases

2. *Candidates can be credited in a number of ways up to a maximum of 8 marks.*

Candidates must use knowledge to present a balanced assessment of the influence of different possible factors and come to a reasoned conclusion.

Up to 5 marks are allocated for relevant points of knowledge used to address the question. **1 mark** should be given for each relevant, factual key point of knowledge used to support a factor. **If only one factor is presented, a maximum of 3 marks should be given for relevant points of knowledge.**

Possible factors may include:	Relevant, factual, key points of knowledge to support this factor may include:
Technology	1. Iron rails underground made it easier to transport coal 2. Steam power to raise cages 3. Wire rope to raise cages 4. Steam-powered drainage pumps 5. Davy safety lamp 6. Metal pit props 7. Gunpowder used to loosen rock 8. Technology enabled deeper shafts to be dug, reaching into seams of coal below water-bearing ground 9. Chain coal-cutting machines from the 1880s 10. Better ventilation systems 11. Electric lighting from the 1890s 12. Electric hauling from the 1890s
Legislation	13. 1842 – banned women and children under 10 from working underground/fatalities reduced as fewer children employed 14. 1850 – Mine Inspectors appointed, which improved safety 15. 1860 – boys under 12 forbidden to go underground 16. 1862 – mines must have at least two exits 17. 1872 – mine managers required a certificate, which improved safety 18. from 1894 – minimum wage for miners
Animals	19. Canaries used to detect pockets of suffocating gas (Choke Damp) 20. Ponies used (instead of putters) to move wagons of coal
Pressure groups	21. Trade unions campaigned for shorter working hours/better conditions
Any other valid factor	

Up to 3 marks should be given for presenting the answer in a structured way, leading to a conclusion which addresses the question, as follows:

1 mark for the answer being presented in a structured way, with knowledge being organised in support of different factors.

1 mark given for a valid judgement or overall conclusion.
1 mark given for a reason being provided in support of the conclusion.

3. *Candidates can be credited in a number of ways* **up to a maximum of 6 marks.**

Candidates must show a causal relationship between events.

Up to a **maximum of 6 marks in total, 1 mark** should be given for each accurate, relevant reason, and a **second mark** should be given for reasons that are developed. Candidates may achieve full marks by providing six straightforward reasons, three developed reasons, or a combination of these.

Possible reasons may include:
1. Canals very slow means of transport – railways much faster
2. Canals could not go everywhere, especially in hilly country
3. A more extensive network of railways developed
4. Canals often different widths and depths, so goods had to be transferred from one size of boat to another
5. Even short journeys involved several canal companies/ inconvenient paperwork/expensive
6. Locks slowed up movement considerably
7. Canal transport more expensive than railways/railways carried more goods so more cost effective
8. Factories could have their own railway sidings – more convenient than canals
9. Canal companies failed to invest their profits back into widening and deepening canals/Investment needed to widen canals was diverted to railways

Section 2, Context E, The Making of Modern Britain, 1880-1951

1. *Candidates can be credited in a number of ways* **up to a maximum of 8 marks.**

Candidates must use knowledge to present a balanced assessment of the influence of different possible factors and come to a reasoned conclusion.

Up to **5 marks** are allocated for relevant points of knowledge used to address the question. **1 mark** should be given for each relevant, factual key point of knowledge used to support a factor. **If only one factor is presented, a maximum of 3 marks should be given for relevant points of knowledge.**

Possible factors may include:	Relevant, factual, key points of knowledge to support this factor may include:
Poor health	1. Absence from work due to sickness could lead to loss of job/earnings 2. Poor could not afford doctors/ medicine 3. Many occupations dangerous/ few safety precautions eg miners/shipyards so greater chance of accidents/injury
Old age	4. Those on low wages unable to save, so when too old to work, fell into poverty 5. Limited poor relief 6. Caring for elderly relatives was an added burden on poor households
Death of wage-earner	7. Death of the main wage-earner would cause families to fall into poverty 8. Only limited compensation available for illness or accidents caused through work
Family size	9. Large families often lived below poverty-line, especially when children were very young 10. No easily available child-care, so mother often prevented from working
Irregular/ low earnings/ unemployment	11. Work was often cyclical/ irregular or seasonal – causing temporary poverty 12. Wages were often below subsistence-level 13. Considerable time often had to be spent looking for work/ queuing outside factory gates 14. Women were particularly low paid half or even less of male wages 15. Unemployment meant a lack of income
Other causes	16. Secondary poverty caused when earnings spent/wasted on other things – eg drinking or gambling 17. High rents used up a lot of family income 18. Discrimination could add to unemployment eg Irish in Scotland

Up to **3 marks** should be given for presenting the answer in a structured way, leading to a conclusion which addresses the question, as follows:

1 mark for the answer being presented in a structured way, with knowledge being organised in support of different factors.
1 mark given for a valid judgement or overall conclusion.
1 mark given for a reason being provided in support of the conclusion.

2. *Candidates can be credited in a number of ways* **up to a maximum of 6 marks.**

Candidates must make a judgement about the usefulness of the source and support this by making evaluative comments on identified aspects of the source.

1 mark should be given for each relevant comment made, up to a **maximum of 6 marks in total.**
- A maximum of **4 marks** can be given for evaluative comments relating to the author, type of source, purpose and timing.
- A maximum of **2 marks** may be given for comments relating to the content of the source.
- A maximum of **2 marks** may be given for comments relating to points of significant omission.

Examples of aspects of the source and relevant comments:

Aspect of the source	Possible comment
Author: Historians	Useful because they would have researched the subject thoroughly
Type of Source: Modern history book	Useful as published sources tend to be factual
Purpose: To inform	Useful as will be a balanced/ comprehensive account of reasons for Liberals passing reforms to help the young
Timing: Published in 2002	Useful as written with the benefit of hindsight

Content	Possible comment
The Boer War and the condition of many recruits led politicians to act	Useful as the Boer War did raise concern about the fitness of recruits/national stock/efficiency
The children would be the soldiers of the future	Useful as this was a typical/ important concern at the time of international tensions
Healthy children would grow up to be healthy soldiers and workers and the British Empire would be stronger as a result	Useful as there was great concern about Britain's status in the world

Possible points of significant omission may include:
1. Rowntree's report in particular revealed that families with young children often fell below the poverty line.
2. Children regarded as 'deserving' poor.
3. Report of the 1904 Inter-departmental Committee on Physical Deterioration recommended reforms to improve the health of children/ free school meals and medical inspections.
4. School leaving age 13/desire to improve access to free secondary education for some.
5. High levels of juvenile crime/often caused by poverty.
6. Desire to alter justice system which treated juvenile criminals in the same way as adult criminals.
7. Work of Margaret McMillan in pushing for school meals and medical inspections.

3. *Candidates can be credited in a number of ways **up to a maximum of 6 marks.***

Candidates must show a causal relationship between events.

Up to a maximum of **6 marks in total**, **1 mark** should be given for each accurate, relevant reason, and a **second mark** should be given for reasons that are developed. Candidates may achieve full marks by providing six straightforward reasons, three developed reasons, or a combination of these.

Possible reasons may include:
1. Sense of determination/will to 'build a better Britain' after the war.
2. Evacuation highlighted the poor health/physical condition of children and the problem of poverty, so opened eyes/changed attitudes
3. Rich and poor subject to bombing/created need for reform
4. Rationing ensured a fair supply of food for all – rich and poor alike, levelled classes/created expectation of further government intervention

5. Social classes mixed more than ever before during the war – raised awareness of social problems and need for welfare reform
6. Government had been forced to intervene more during the war – eg Ministry of Food, rationing, and free health care for war-wounded/War forced government to change laissez-faire attitudes
7. Greater acceptance of government control during wartime was accepted to tackle post-war problems
8. War highlighted social problems that only the state could tackle – eg poverty, housing, people accepted this
9. Beveridge Report of 1942 highlighted social problems/ Beveridge Report popular and created an expectation of government action

Section 3, Context A, The Cross and the Crescent; the Crusades, 1071–1192

1. *Candidates can be credited in a number of ways **up to a maximum of 5 marks.***
They may take different perspectives on the events and may describe a variety of different aspects of the events.

1 mark should be given for each accurate relevant key point of knowledge.

A second mark should be given for each point that is developed, up to a maximum of **5 marks**. Candidates may achieve full marks by providing five straightforward points, by making three developed points, or a combination of these.

Possible points of knowledge may include:
1. Castles used as a home
2. Castles used for protection/defence against an enemy eg control of river crossings
3. Castles were used as barracks for knights
4. Castles were a symbol of power/wealth
5. Castles were administrative centres
6. Castles were used to hold courts
7. Castles were used to store food
8. Castles held feasts

2. *Candidates can be credited in a number of ways **up to a maximum of 5 marks.***

Candidates must show a causal relationship between events.

Up to a **maximum of 5 marks in total**, **1 mark** should be given for each accurate, relevant reason, and a **second mark** should be given for reasons that are developed. Candidates may achieve full marks by providing five straightforward reasons, three developed reasons, or a combination of these.

Possible reasons may include:
1. Inspired by the Pope's speech/preachers such as Peter the Hermit
2. To recapture Jerusalem/free eastern Christians from Muslim rule
3. Religious motives/desire to fulfil Christian duty to God eg Raymond of Toulouse
4. To have sins forgiven/to be able to enter heaven in the afterlife
5. To gain land eg younger sons or those disinherited eg Bohemond of Taranto/Baldwin of Boulogne
6. Peer pressure/to represent a family eg Hugh of Vermandois/Stephen of Blois
7. Military skills/to fight in battle with the Church's blessing eg Tancred wanted to escape the limitations of the Peace of God movement

8. Social mobility eg peasants wanted better life/"land of milk and honey"

3. *Candidates can be credited in a number of ways up to a maximum of 6 marks.*

Candidates must make an overall judgement about how fully the source explains the events. **1 mark** may be given for each valid point interpreted from the source or each valid point of significant omission provided. The candidate can achieve **up to 3 marks** for their interpretation of the parts of the source they consider are relevant in terms of the proposed question where there is also at least one point of significant omission identified to imply a judgement has been made about the limitations of the source. For full marks to be given each point needs to be discretely mentioned in terms of the question.

A maximum of 2 marks may be given for answers which refer only to the source or in which no judgement has been made.

Possible points which may be identified in the source include:
1. Alexius feared they would attack his city/made them camp outside the city and only allowed them to enter in small groups
2. Offered treasure and supplies to Crusaders who agreed to fight for him
3. Any Crusader who refused was attacked and forced to surrender
4. Alexius did not trust the Crusaders/made plans to remove them from Constantinople

Possible points of significant omission may include:
1. Crusaders blamed Alexius for the failure of the People's Crusade
2. Made Crusaders take an oath of loyalty/made Crusaders take an oath they would capture land for him
3. Provided the Crusaders with a guide/troops/supplies
4. Provided the Crusaders with boats to blockade Nicaea
5. Negotiated with the Muslims inside Nicaea/took the city behind the Crusaders' back
6. Baldwin broke his oath and captured Edessa
7. Alexius did not arrive at Antioch to help the Crusaders
8. Bohemond broke his oath and claimed Antioch

4. *Candidates can be credited in a number of ways up to a maximum of 4 marks.*

Candidates must make direct comparisons of the two sources, either overall or in detail. A simple comparison will indicate what points of detail or overall viewpoint they agree or disagree about and should be given **1 mark**.

A developed comparison of the points of detail or overall viewpoint should be given **2 marks**. Candidates may achieve full marks by making four simple comparisons, two developed comparisons or by a combination of these.

Possible points of comparison may include:

Overall: The sources agree about the character of Richard I	
Source B	**Source C**
Vowed to fulfil his Christian duty	Promised he would keep his oath to God
Excellent military commander who used clever tactics to win key battles	Used his experience and leadership to force the city to surrender
Always fought alongside his men, courageously attacking the enemy	Richard showed great bravery by defending his men and killing the enemy

Section 3, Context B, "Tea and Freedom,": the American Revolution, 1774-83

1. *Candidates can be credited in a number of ways up to a maximum of 6 marks.*

Candidates must make an overall judgement about how fully the source explains the events. **1 mark** may be given for each valid point interpreted from the source or each valid point of significant omission provided. The candidate can achieve **up to 3 marks** for their interpretation of the parts of the source they consider are relevant in terms of the proposed question where there is also at least one point of significant omission identified to imply a judgement has been made about the limitations of the source. For full marks to be given each point needs to be discretely mentioned in terms of the question.

A maximum of 2 marks may be given for answers which refer only to the source or in which no judgement has been made.

Possible points which may be identified in the source include:
1. The decision to increase taxes was very unpopular
2. The decision to maintain a standing army alarmed colonists
3. The Stamp Act provoked a furious reaction
4. Colonists organised a boycott of British goods

Possible points of significant omission may include:
1. Colonists felt that actions of the British government were damaging trade
2. The colonists were unhappy that the British were stopping them from moving West
3. There was anger among the colonists about the Quartering Act which allowed British soldiers to invade private property
4. There was anger among the colonists about a lack of representation in the British parliament
5. Events such as the Boston Massacre increased tension

2. *Candidates can be credited in a number of ways up to a maximum of 5 marks.*

They may take different perspectives on the events and may describe a variety of different aspects of the events.

1 mark should be given for each accurate relevant key point of knowledge. **A second mark** should be given for each point that is developed, up to a maximum of **5 marks**. Candidates may achieve full marks by providing five straightforward points, by making three developed points, or a combination of these.

Possible points of knowledge may include:
1. Colonists were angered by the passing of the Tea Act in 1773 which allowed the East India Company to undercut colonial merchants and smugglers
2. Bostonians disguised themselves as Mohawk Indians and boarded the three tea ships
3. Tea was emptied into the water of Boston harbour
4. Some of the tea was stolen
5. King George III and Parliament were outraged when they heard of these events
6. Lord North rejected the offer of compensation from some of the colonial merchants
7. Led to the passing of the 'Intolerable Acts' eg Massachusetts Act/ Administration of Justice Act/ Quartering Act/Quebec Act
8. Port of Boston closed

3. *Candidates can be credited in a number of ways **up to a maximum of 5 marks.***

Candidates must show a causal relationship between events.

Up to a **maximum of 5 marks in total**, **1 mark** should be given for each accurate, relevant reason, and a **second mark** should be given for reasons that are developed. Candidates may achieve full marks by providing five straightforward reasons, three developed reasons, or a combination of these.

Possible reasons may include:
1. The British forces were poorly led so poorer tactics/communication
2. There were tactical errors by Britain eg at Yorktown, so battles were lost
3. British army had to rely on mercenary forces, so less loyalty
4. British soldiers were not properly trained, so less effective
5. Colonial army was effectively led by George Washington, strong leader
6. British generals underestimated the bravery of the Americans
7. Rebel tactics also made life very difficult/rebels often used guerrilla tactics against British which were successful
8. Colonists had greater forces/able to call on minutemen when required, so more effective
9. Fighting a war so far from home made it difficult to supply British forces
10. Attacks by French and Spanish weakened/distracted British forces
11. Assistance from French and Spanish navies gave colonists control of the seas

4. *Candidates can be credited in a number of ways **up to a maximum of 4 marks.***

Candidates must make direct comparisons of the two sources, either overall or in detail. A simple comparison will indicate what points of detail or overall viewpoint they agree or disagree about and should be given **1 mark**.

A developed comparison of the points of detail or overall viewpoint should be given **2 marks**. Candidates may achieve full marks by making four simple comparisons, two developed comparisons or by a combination of these.

Possible points of comparison may include:

Overall: The sources agree that there were a number of reasons for the British defeat at Saratoga	
Source B	**Source C**
Progress was then slowed by mountains and dense forest	Progress was slowed by the difficult terrain
Burgoyne had no reinforcements	Burgoyne's army was left on its own
Army was trapped against the Hudson River	British found themselves trapped at the little community of Saratoga

Section 3, Context C, USA 1850–1880

1. *Candidates can be credited in a number of ways **up to a maximum of 5 marks.***

They may take different perspectives on the events and may describe a variety of different aspects of the events.

1 mark should be given for each accurate relevant key point of knowledge.

A second mark should be given for each point that is developed, up to a maximum of **5 marks**. Candidates may achieve full marks by providing five straightforward points, by making three developed points, or a combination of these.

Possible points of knowledge may include:
1. Many subject to strict rules and regulations/had no freedom
2. Slaves could be bought and sold/seen as property
3. Worked long hours at hard work with only short breaks
4. Subject to harsh/inhuman discipline eg whipping common
5. Runaway slaves were beaten/maimed: use of dogs to hunt runaways
6. Slaves needed permission to get married
7. Slave marriages had no legal status
8. Slave owners often named slave children
9. Slave families often broken up/separated
10. Slaves unable to visit family/relatives on other plantations
11. Female slaves sometimes sexually abused by owners/overseers
12. Children born to a slave, fathered by white owner, were still slaves
13. Pregnant slaves were expected to work until the child was born.

2. *Candidates can be credited in a number of ways **up to a maximum of 5 marks.***

Candidates must show a causal relationship between events.

Up to a **maximum of 5 marks in total**, **1 mark** should be given for each accurate, relevant reason, and a **second mark** should be given for reasons that are developed. Candidates may achieve full marks by providing five straightforward reasons, three developed reasons, or a combination of these.

Possible reasons may include:
1. Kansas – Nebraska Act allowed States to decide if slave state or free state, which caused tension.
2. Violence in Kansas (Bleeding Kansas) had led to a number of deaths, which increased tension
3. Dred Scott Case caused unhappiness among abolitionists and Northern States
4. Attack on Harpers Ferry by John Brown heightened tension
5. Growth of Republican Party which favoured Northern Interests upset South
6. Election of Lincoln upset South
7. South felt North was infringing on states' rights, caused resentment
8. Growth of militant abolitionism in North increased tension
9. Southern planters resented Northern trade tariffs which affected their trade
10. Expansion of Northern cities and immigration worried the South

3. *Candidates can be credited in a number of ways up to a maximum of 6 marks.*

Candidates must make an overall judgement about how fully the source explains the events. **1 mark** may be given for each valid point interpreted from the source or each valid point of significant omission provided. The candidate can achieve **up to 3 marks** for their interpretation of the parts of the source they consider are relevant in terms of the proposed question where there is also at least one point of significant omission identified to imply a judgement has been made about the limitations of the source. For full marks to be given each point needs to be discretely mentioned in terms of the question.

A maximum of 2 marks may be given for answers which refer only to the source or in which no judgement has been made.

Possible points which may be identified in the source include:
1. Attracted by the promise of a better life
2. Attracted by the warmer weather in California
3. Went west because they thought the land would be more fertile
4. Ranch owners realised that the plains could be used to feed their huge herds of cattle

Possible points of significant omission may include:
1. Gold in California attracted many. Later gold discoveries in Black Hills also attracted prospectors
2. Cheap land available in the west for farmers
3. Belief in Manifest Destiny eg many Americans saw it as a duty to spread their way of life
4. Mormons wished to find new lands to settle away from other people
5. Railways encouraged many settlers west
6. Government Acts offered land to settlers
7. The Homestead Act of 1862/Timber and Culture Act of 1875 each offered cheap/free land to settlers
8. Railroad companies sold land cheaply to settlers
9. Freed slaves headed west after 1865 to escape persecution
10. Shopkeepers and hotel owners travelled west to exploit the demand of the settlers
11. Overcrowding of cities in East
12. Sense of adventure

4. *Candidates can be credited in a number of ways up to a maximum of 4 marks.*

Candidates must make direct comparisons of the two sources, either overall or in detail. A simple comparison will indicate what points of detail or overall viewpoint they agree or disagree about and should be given **1 mark**.

A developed comparison of the points of detail or overall viewpoint should be given **2 marks**. Candidates may achieve full marks by making four simple comparisons, two developed comparisons or by a combination of these.

Possible points of comparison may include:

Overall: The sources disagree about the events which took place during the Sand Creek massacre of 1864.	
Source B	**Source C**
In the village there were 500 people	In the Cheyenne camp there were about 1200 people
Two-thirds of whom were women and children.	700 were warriors
Counted from 60 to 70 dead bodies, a large majority of whom were women and children.	I estimate there were 500 or 600 people killed/I saw only one woman who had been killed and I saw no dead children

Section 3, Context D, Hitler and Nazi Germany, 1919-1939

1. *Candidates can be credited in a number of ways up to a maximum of 5 marks.*

They may take different perspectives on the events and may describe a variety of different aspects of the events.
1 mark should be given for each accurate relevant key point of knowledge.

A second mark should be given for each point that is developed, up to a maximum of **5 marks**. Candidates may achieve full marks by providing five straightforward points, by making three developed points, or a combination of these.

Possible points of knowledge may include:
1. All men and women over 20 had the vote/over 35 in Presidential elections
2. All Germans were equal before the law
3. People had the right to vote by secret ballot
4. Everyone had the right of freedom of speech/to express opinions freely and openly
5. Freedom of association/people had the right to hold peaceful meetings
6. Freedom of press
7. Everyone had the right of freedom of religion
8. Letters and correspondence could not be opened and read
9. No one could be arrested without good reason/unless they broke the law
10. People had the right to join trade unions and societies
11. No one could be imprisoned without trial
12. Rights of privacy/people had the right of privacy in their own homes
13. People had the right to form political parties.

2. *Candidates can be credited in a number of ways up to a maximum of 4 marks.*

Candidates must make direct comparisons of the two sources, either overall or in detail. A simple comparison will indicate what points of detail or overall viewpoint they agree or disagree about and should be given **1 mark**.

A developed comparison of the points of detail or overall viewpoint should be given **2 marks**. Candidates may achieve full marks by making four simple comparisons, two developed comparisons or by a combination of these.

Possible points of comparison may include:

Overall: The sources agree that hyperinflation caused people difficulties	
Source B	**Source C**
Workers were paid twice a day/ rushed to shops before prices went up	Some workers were paid twice a day/could spend their wages instantly.
Millions of people faced starvation due to hyperinflation	They faced homelessness and starvation.
Pensioners who were living on fixed incomes found that prices rose much faster than their earnings	Pensioners lived on fixed incomes and received the same amount each week; these incomes were now worth nothing

3. *Candidates can be credited in a number of ways **up to a maximum of 5 marks**.*

Candidates must show a causal relationship between events.

Up to a **maximum of 5 marks in total**, **1 mark** should be given for each accurate, relevant reason, and a **second mark** should be given for reasons that are developed. Candidates may achieve full marks by providing five straightforward reasons, three developed reasons, or a combination of these.

Possible reasons may include:
1. Hitler appeared to offer Germany strong leadership, which was appealing
2. Offered solutions to Germany's economic problems, so popular
3. Promised to provide jobs for the unemployed , which was popular
4. Promised to overthrow the Treaty of Versailles, which was welcomed
5. Nazi rallies, eg Nuremberg, impressed people
6. Hitler was a superb speaker
7. Effective use of propaganda to get over his message
8. Hitler had a clear, simple message which appealed to many people
9. Promised support for the farmers, shopkeepers, etc, which was popular
10. Businessmen were attracted by Hitler's promise to destroy trade unions
11. Young people were attracted to the Hitler Youth
12. Promised to restore Germany as a world power, which was welcomed
13. Germany's best defence against Communism/support from middle classes
14. Discipline/uniforms of the SA impressed people
15. Widespread support from nationalists for his racial theories/anti-Semitism
16. Tired of the chaos of the Weimar Government and wanted a change/belief that democracy weak

4. *Candidates can be credited in a number of ways **up to a maximum of 6 marks**.*

Candidates must make an overall judgement about how fully the source explains the events. **1 mark** may be given for each valid point interpreted from the source or each valid point of significant omission provided. The candidate can achieve **up to 3 marks** for their interpretation of the parts of the source they consider are relevant in terms of the proposed question where there is also at least one point of significant omission identified to imply a judgement

has been made about the limitations of the source. For full marks to be given each point needs to be discretely mentioned in terms of the question.

A maximum of 2 marks may be given for answers which refer only to the source or in which no judgement has been made.

Possible points which may be identified in the source include:
1. The KDF (Strength through Joy Organisation) controlled most forms of entertainment
2. Each year around seven million people took part in KDF sports matches
3. Mass outings to the theatre and the opera were arranged
4. Workers were also provided with affordable holidays including cruises and walking or skiing holidays

Possible points of significant omission may include:
1. Other Strength through Joy programmes such as: Evening classes for adults The Peoples Car (Volkswagen) hire purchase scheme which turned out to be a swindle
2. Nuremberg Laws
3. Hitler Youth later made compulsory
4. Role of Gestapo
5. Propaganda (examples of)
6. Censorship of newspapers/films/books/films
7. Books considered unacceptable were burned
8. Complaining about the Nazis against the law
9. Penalty for anti-Hitler jokes was death
10. National Labour Service
11. Compulsory Military Service

Section 3, Context E, Red Flag: Lenin and the Russian Revolution, 1894-1921

1. *Candidates can be credited in a number of ways **up to a maximum of 5 marks**.*

They may take different perspectives on the events and may describe a variety of different aspects of the events.

1 mark should be given for each accurate relevant key point of knowledge.

A second mark should be given for each point that is developed, up to a maximum of **5 marks**. Candidates may achieve full marks by providing five straightforward points, by making three developed points, or a combination of these.

Possible points of knowledge may include:
1. The Pillars of Autocracy controlled the Russian people
2. The Civil Service controlled everyday life eg censorship of newspapers
3. Use of secret police the Okhrana to spy on opponents
4. Support from church who taught peasants that Tsar should be obeyed
5. Use of army/Cossacks to crush uprisings or opponents
6. Use of exile to get rid of opponents

2. *Candidates can be credited in a number of ways **up to a maximum of 5 marks**.*

Candidates must show a causal relationship between events.

Up to a **maximum of 5 marks in total**, **1 mark** should be given for each accurate, relevant reason, and a **second mark** should be given for reasons that are developed. Candidates may achieve full marks by providing five straightforward reasons, three developed reasons, or a combination of these.

Possible reasons may include:
1. Peasants unhappy due to redemption payments and high taxes (bad harvests made situation worse)
2. Peasant 'land hunger' caused discontent
3. Workers unhappy with poor wages and working conditions
4. Violent strikes due to long hours and low wages (government reaction made situation worse eg by arresting leaders)
5. Radical politics among university students caused further discontent
6. Defeat in the Russo – Japanese War led to unrest
7. Policy of Russification caused discontent amongst nationalities eg Poles
8. Some sections of military become discontented – Potemkin Mutiny.
9. Events of Bloody Sunday in January 1905 led to discontent and strikes
10. Set up of St Petersburg & Moscow Soviets
11. October Manifesto split middle classes from workers and socialists

3. *Candidates can be credited in a number of ways up to a maximum of 6 marks.*

Candidates must make an overall judgement about how fully the source explains the events. **1 mark** may be given for each valid point interpreted from the source or each valid point of significant omission provided. The candidate can achieve **up to 3 marks** for their interpretation of the parts of the source they consider are relevant in terms of the proposed question where there is also at least one point of significant omission identified to imply a judgement has been made about the limitations of the source. For full marks to be given each point needs to be discretely mentioned in terms of the question.

A maximum of 2 marks may be given for answers which refer only to the source or in which no judgement has been made.

Possible points which may be identified in the source include:
1. First World War was to have a terrible impact on Russia
2. Heart-breaking losses were suffered by the Tsars armies
3. Thousands of wounded soldiers were left lying untreated on the ground for days
4. Not even quarter enough bandages

Possible points of significant omission may include:
1. Military defeat at Tannenburg and Masurian lakes
2. Collapse of the economy
3. Inflation affected prices
4. Population suffered shortages of food and fuel
5. Tsar took control of the armies and was then blamed for defeats
6. Tsarina took charge and was unpopular as she was German-born/thought to be under the influence of Rasputin
7. Political instability – regular changes to both Prime Ministers and Ministers/ministerial 'leapfrog'
8. Allegations of government corruption eg Rasputin weakened Tsar's authority
9. Conscripting millions of peasants led to shortage of grain
10. Inability of the government to organise procurement/movement of supplies to civilians or war production for the military

4. *Candidates can be credited in a number of ways up to a maximum of 4 marks.*

Candidates must make direct comparisons of the two sources, either overall or in detail. A simple comparison will indicate what points of detail or overall viewpoint they agree or disagree about and should be given **1 mark**.

A developed comparison of the points of detail or overall viewpoint should be given **2 marks**. Candidates may achieve full marks by making four simple comparisons, two developed comparisons or by a combination of these.

Possible points of comparison may include:

Overall: The sources agree the situation was serious with shortages and unrest	
Source B	**Source C**
Disturbances...are becoming more serious	The situation was already very serious
Shortages of bread	They wanted bread but... many had been unable to get any
Workers are without jobs	Several thousand workmen unemployed

Section 3, Context F, Mussolini and Fascist Italy, 1919-1939

1. *Candidates can be credited in a number of ways up to a maximum of 5 marks.*

They may take different perspectives on the events and may describe a variety of different aspects of the events.

1 mark should be given for each accurate relevant key point of knowledge.

A second mark should be given for each point that is developed, up to a maximum of **5 marks**. Candidates may achieve full marks by providing five straightforward points, by making three developed points, or a combination of these.

Possible points of knowledge may include:
1. Mussolini aimed to make Italy a great power/wanted control of Mediterranean
2. Mussolini wanted to expand Italy's colonial empire in Africa/increase Italian influence in the Balkans
3. In 1924 Mussolini took control of the Yugoslavian port of Fiume
4. Wished to appear as a statesman in early years eg Locarno 1925
5. Mussolini supported King Zog in Albania (by signing a Treaty of Friendship in 1926 Mussolini made Albania into an Italian satellite state)
6. Mussolini funded Croat nationalists in order to create trouble for Yugoslavia
7. Mussolini settled the border dispute with Britain over Libya and Egypt
8. Mussolini aided Dolfuss in order to provide a bulwark against Nazi aggression
9. In 1935 concluded Stresa Front with France and Britain (wished to be recognised as a great power)
10. Launched attack on Ethiopia
11. Intervened in Spanish Civil War
12. Agreed Anti-Comintern Pact with Japan and Germany in 1937
13. Posed as mediator at Munich Conference Sept 1938
14. Invaded Albania in 1939
15. Pact of Steel with Germany concluded May 1939

2. *Candidates can be credited in a number of ways **up to a maximum of 5 marks**.*

Candidates must show a causal relationship between events.

Up to a **maximum of 5 marks in total**, **1 mark** should be given for each accurate, relevant reason, and a **second mark** should be given for reasons that are developed. Candidates may achieve full marks by providing five straightforward reasons, three developed reasons, or a combination of these.

Possible reasons may include:
1. Many were unhappy when trade unions were outlawed
2. Revaluation of the lira in 1927 led to decline in exports, causing discontent
3. Increase in unemployment 1926-28. By 1933 unemployment had reached 2 million, causing unpopularity
4. High tariffs restricted imports, so people unhappy
5. Real wages fell, so people unhappy
6. Sick pay and paid holidays were not introduced until 1938, so people were unhappy
7. The failure to make Italy self-sufficient – embarrassment/unpopularity
8. As part of the Battle For Grain land in central and southern regions was turned over to wheat production despite being unsuitable (traditional agricultural exports declined), unpopular in these areas
9. Increasing government control of industry was resented

3. *Candidates can be credited in a number of ways **up to a maximum of 6 marks**.*

Candidates must make an overall judgement about how fully the source explains the events. **1 mark** may be given for each valid point interpreted from the source or each valid point of significant omission provided. The candidate can achieve **up to 3 marks** for their interpretation of the parts of the source they consider are relevant in terms of the proposed question where there is also at least one point of significant omission identified to imply a judgement has been made about the limitations of the source. For full marks to be given each point needs to be discretely mentioned in terms of the question.

A maximum of 2 marks may be given for answers which refer only to the source or in which no judgement has been made.

Possible points which may be identified in the source include:
1. Mussolini's press office issued official versions of events which all the newspapers were expected to publish without question
2. The radio and the cinema were also used to broadcast Fascist propaganda
3. News bulletins broadcast a daily diet of Mussolini's speeches and praised him as the saviour of Italy
4. The media played a crucial role in the cult of "Il Duce"

Possible points of significant omission may include:
1. Mussolini started a new calendar with Year 1 beginning in 1922
2. The regime made propagandist feature films
3. The Duce was shown as a great athlete and musician (cult of personality)
4. Brainwashing/indoctrination of young at school/ textbooks or youth groups
5. The newspapers suggested that Mussolini was infallible
6. An image of youthfulness was portrayed by not referring to Mussolini's age or the fact he wore glasses/usually seen in uniform
7. It was said that Mussolini worked 16 hour days – his light was left on after he had gone to bed to maintain this fiction

8. Use of RC church to support Fascists policies eg against communism at home or in Spain

4. *Candidates can be credited in a number of ways **up to a maximum of 4 marks**.*

Candidates must make direct comparisons of the two sources, either overall or in detail. A simple comparison will indicate what points of detail or overall viewpoint they agree or disagree about and should be given **1 mark**.

A developed comparison of the points of detail or overall viewpoint should be given **2 marks**. Candidates may achieve full marks by making four simple comparisons, two developed comparisons or by a combination of these.

Possible points of comparison may include:

Overall: The sources agree that there was a limited opposition to the regime	
Source A	**Source B**
Fascist policies benefited the rich to ensure their support.	Big businessmen and landowners supported a regime which always seemed to be on their side.
The signing of the Lateran agreement in 1929 was important in winning the support of Catholics.	This new close relationship with the church reduced the threat of opposition from Catholics.
There was some opposition in the army, but this was never carried out in a coordinated way	While some army generals opposed Mussolini others liked his aggressive attitude.

Section 3, Context G, Free at Last? Civil Rights in the USA, 1918-1968

1. *Candidates can be credited in a number of ways **up to a maximum of 4 marks**.*

Candidates must make direct comparisons of the two sources, either overall or in detail. A simple comparison will indicate what points of detail or overall viewpoint they agree or disagree about and should be given **1 mark**.

A developed comparison of the points of detail or overall viewpoint should be given **2 marks**. Candidates may achieve full marks by making four simple comparisons, two developed comparisons or by a combination of these.

Possible points of comparison may include:

Overall: The sources agree about the poor living and working conditions of immigrants	
Source A	**Source B**
Immigrants from the same country usually lived in the same areas of the city	Immigrants tended to live in their own communities: in New York there was a Polish district, a Jewish district and an Italian district
These areas contained tenement slums which were damp, dark and filthy with no water supply, toilets or drains	Tenements buildings in these areas were often five or six storeys high with rooms which lacked light or sanitation
Immigrants had to take any work they could get, usually low paid jobs such as labourers or servants	Finding a well-paid, skilled job was a common problem for poorly educated immigrants

2. *Candidates can be credited in a number of ways **up to a maximum of 5 marks**.*

They may take different perspectives on the events and may describe a variety of different aspects of the events.

1 mark should be given for each accurate relevant key point of knowledge.

A second mark should be given for each point that is developed, up to a maximum of **5 marks**. Candidates may achieve full marks by providing five straightforward points, by making three developed points, or a combination of these.

Possible points of knowledge may include:
1. Legal action leading to the decision of the Supreme Court in 1954 to declare segregation in schools unconstitutional
2. Bus boycott in Montgomery
3. Little Rock, Arkansas – attempt by black students to enter Central High School
4. Sit-downs/Sit-ins eg deliberately holding up traffic/ the occupation of lunch counters and other segregated places
5. Freedom rides – travel on buses through southern states using segregated facilities at bus stations
6. Project C – sit-ins and marches in Birmingham, Alabama led by Martin Luther King
7. March on Washington

3. *Candidates can be credited in a number of ways **up to a maximum of 6 marks**.*

Candidates must make an overall judgement about how fully the source explains the events. **1 mark** may be given for each valid point interpreted from the source or each valid point of significant omission provided. The candidate can achieve **up to 3 marks** for their interpretation of the parts of the source they consider are relevant in terms of the proposed question where there is also at least one point of significant omission identified to imply a judgement has been made about the limitations of the source. For full marks to be given each point needs to be discretely mentioned in terms of the question.

A maximum of 2 marks may be given for answers which refer only to the source or in which no judgement has been made.

Possible points which may be identified in the source include:
1. President Truman issued orders to desegregate the US military
2. He also set up a President's Committee on civil rights in 1946 to report to him on how progress towards black civil rights could be made
3. In 1960 Congress passed a Civil Rights Act which established penalties for obstructing black voting.
4. The assassination of President Kennedy in November 1963 came at the time he was preparing a Civil Rights Bill

Possible points of significant omission may include:
1. Supreme Court decision declared that schools could no longer be segregated
2. In 1957 President Eisenhower sent in federal troops to Little Rock in Arkansas to ensure that nine black children could safely enter a recently desegregated high school
3. Federal Marshalls were sent to escort James Meredith through the gates of Mississippi University
4. Civil Rights Act passed in 1964

4. *Candidates can be credited in a number of ways **up to a maximum of 5 marks**.*

Candidates must show a causal relationship between events.

Up to a maximum of **5 marks** in total, **1 mark** should be given for each accurate, relevant reason, and a **second mark** should be given for reasons that are developed. Candidates may achieve full marks by providing five straightforward reasons, three developed reasons, or a combination of these.

Possible reasons may include:
1. Black Panthers gained support for their demand for the release of black prisoners
2. Black Panthers gained support due to their efforts to give practical help to poor blacks eg breakfast clubs in schools
3. Black Panthers had charismatic leaders who gained attention and popularity
4. The Black Panthers encouraged blacks to be proud of the colour of their skin and their African American culture. This appealed to many
5. Black Panthers condoned violence and this appealed to many blacks who were frustrated by the non-violent methods of the Civil Rights Movement
6. Black Panthers attracted further support after gaining the much publicised support of athletes at the Olympic Games in 1968

Section 3, Context H, Appeasement and the Road to War, 1918–1939

1. *Candidates can be credited in a number of ways **up to a maximum of 5 marks**.*

They may take different perspectives on the events and may describe a variety of different aspects of the events.

1 mark should be given for each accurate relevant key point of knowledge.

A second mark should be given for each point that is developed, up to a maximum of 5 marks. Candidates may achieve full marks by providing five straightforward points, by making three developed points, or a combination of these.

Possible points of knowledge may include:
1. The German army was limited to 100,000 men
2. The German army was forbidden from having tanks
3. The German army was forbidden from being situated in the Rhineland
4. The German navy was forbidden from having submarines
5. The German navy was limited to six battleships
6. Germany was forbidden from having an air force

2. *Candidates can be credited in a number of ways **up to a maximum of 6 marks**.*

Candidates must make an overall judgement about how fully the source explains the events. **1 mark** may be given for each valid point interpreted from the source or each valid point of significant omission provided. The candidate can achieve **up to 3 marks** for their interpretation of the parts of the source they consider are relevant in terms of the proposed question where there is also at least one point of significant omission identified to imply a judgement has been made about the limitations of the source. For full marks to be given each point needs to be discretely mentioned in terms of the question.

A maximum of 2 marks may be given for answers which refer only to the source or in which no judgement has been made.

Possible points which may be identified in the source include:

1. The USA refused to join as they were not interested in getting involved in the problems of other countries
2. Initially Russia was not invited to join, so another great country of the world was absent
3. Taking decisions was difficult as the Assembly had to be unanimous and member states often could not agree
4. A further problem was that the League did not have its own army to back up its decisions

Possible points of significant omission may include:

1. Germany was not allowed to join until 1926, so another major power was absent
2. Member countries were reluctant to agree to economic sanctions for fear of damaging their own economies
3. Member countries were reluctant to take action against a powerful member state
4. The two most powerful member countries Britain and France were reluctant to commit troops to fight for the League
5. Countries lost faith in the League with each failure

3. *Candidates can be credited in a number of ways **up to a maximum of 5 marks.***

Candidates must show a causal relationship between events.

Up to a **maximum of 5 marks in total**, **1 mark** should be given for each accurate, relevant reason, and a **second mark** should be given for reasons that are developed. Candidates may achieve full marks by providing five straightforward reasons, three developed reasons, or a combination of these.

Possible reasons may include:

1. There was a belief that although Germany had broken the Treaty, they had been too severely punished at Versailles
2. It was argued that Germany had done little more than liberate her own territory
3. Many believed that the Franco-Soviet Pact had unduly provoked Hitler
4. Many within Britain saw a stronger Germany as a useful barrier against the spread of communism
5. It was hoped that a conciliatory approach might persuade Germany to re-enter the League and resume disarmament talks
6. It was felt that the relative weakness of the British armed forces restricted the opportunity for direct action
7. There was little sign that public opinion would have supported military action against Hitler

4. *Candidates can be credited in a number of ways **up to a maximum of 4 marks.***

Candidates must make direct comparisons of the two sources, either overall or in detail. A simple comparison will indicate what points of detail or overall viewpoint they agree or disagree about and should be given **1 mark**.

A developed comparison of the points of detail or overall viewpoint should be given **2 marks**. Candidates may achieve full marks by making four simple comparisons, two developed comparisons or by a combination of these.

Possible points of comparison may include:

Overall: The sources agree that Anschluss was a positive event which should be welcomed	
Source B	**Source C**
The population of Austria comprised ethnic Germans, a majority of whom are enthusiastic about the Anschluss/The Austrians will not only feel at home as part of Germany/Their German brothers	That there has been no fighting is proof of the desire of the Austrian people to belong to Germany
It was a mistake of the peacemakers at Versailles to forbid the union of Austria and Germany	The union of these two countries should never have been forbidden at Versailles
They will benefit financially too from an increase in trade	Austrians will also benefit from greater markets for their raw materials and manufactured goods

Section 3, Context I, World War II, 1939–1945

1. *Candidates can be credited in a number of ways **up to a maximum of 4 marks.***

Candidates must make direct comparisons of the two sources, either overall or in detail. A simple comparison will indicate what points of detail or overall viewpoint they agree or disagree about and should be given **1 mark**.

A developed comparison of the points of detail or overall viewpoint should be given **2 marks**. Candidates may achieve full marks by making four simple comparisons, two developed comparisons or by a combination of these.

Possible points of comparison may include:

Overall: The sources agree that the tactic of Blitzkrieg was effective at the beginning of the war.	
Source A	**Source B**
Blitzkrieg was a tactic based on speed and surprise	Hitler was very excited by a plan of attack that was based purely on speed and movement
It required the effective use of Stuka dive bombers	Stuka dive bombers were sent in to 'soften' up the enemy
These were supported by light tank units and infantry	Then the tanks attacked, supported by infantry

2. *Candidates can be credited in a number of ways **up to a maximum of 5 marks.***

They may take different perspectives on the events and may describe a variety of different aspects of the events.

1 mark should be given for each accurate relevant key point of knowledge.

A second mark should be given for each point that is developed, up to a maximum of **5 marks**. Candidates may achieve full marks by providing five straightforward points, by making three developed points, or a combination of these.

Possible points of knowledge may include:
1. Citizens in the west placed under German military rule
2. Eastern European civilians more brutally governed under German civil administrations
3. Vichy regime set up in southern France where citizens lived under German controlled French Government
4. Economies controlled: industry and agriculture supervised and the people often left to go hungry
5. Workers issued with work cards and free deployment of labour was prohibited
6. In western Europe workers pressured to 'volunteer' for work in Germany/ pressure on young men to join 'crusade' against communism in East
7. Almost all food was rationed
8. Curfews in place
9. All citizens had to carry an identity card
10. Gestapo operated under Night and Fog Decree of 1941, giving them powers to seize anyone endangering German security
11. Media censorship
12. SS brutality and the Police State ruled over occupied citizens
13. Jews and other 'undesirables' deported to concentration camps mostly in the east/willing collaboration in deportation Jews eg Vichy
14. Jewish Poles dispossessed, property and belongings confiscated
15. Jews in Poland forced to live in ghettos then deported to camps in the east/examples of life in the ghettos
16. Special forces in Eastern Europe killed Jews and other undesirables in mass killings eg gypsies

3. *Candidates can be credited in a number of ways **up to a maximum of 6 marks**.*

Candidates must make an overall judgement about how fully the source explains the events. **1 mark** may be given for each valid point interpreted from the source or each valid point of significant omission provided. The candidate can achieve **up to 3 marks** for their interpretation of the parts of the source they consider are relevant in terms of the proposed question where there is also at least one point of significant omission identified to imply a judgement has been made about the limitations of the source. For full marks to be given each point needs to be discretely mentioned in terms of the question.

A maximum of 2 marks may be given for answers which refer only to the source.

Possible points which may be identified in the source include:
1. It helped Jews or Allied airmen who had crash landed in France, to escape
2. School children were recruited to help smuggle people across the borders of northern and southern France
3. The Resistance movement produced anti-German propaganda which was crucial in undermining Nazi rule
4. Nazi control was further challenged by the Resistance who worked to punish any French collaboration

Possible points of significant omission may include:
1. Key intelligence link for Allied spy networks
2. Sabotaged German military operations eg blowing up trains, convoys, ships etc
3. Targeted and killed many high ranking Nazi officials
4. Carried out acts of sabotage prior to and during the D-Day landings to help Allied establish a foothold in Normandy/pinned down vital German forces
5. Radio operators (pianists) to send messages of German activities and other communications back to Britain

6. Telephone workers sabotaged telephone lines and intercepted German military messages
7. Postal workers intercepted important military communications
8. Rail workers diverted freight shipments/caused derailments/destroyed tracks/blew up bridges
9. Created labs to manufacture explosives/stole explosives and other resources from German army

4. *Candidates can be credited in a number of ways **up to a maximum of 5 marks**.*

Candidates must show a causal relationship between events.

Up to a **maximum of 5 marks in total**, **1 mark** should be given for each accurate, relevant reason, and a **second mark** should be given for reasons that are developed. Candidates may achieve full marks by providing five straightforward reasons, three developed reasons, or a combination of these.

Possible reasons may include:
1. Russian army encircled the city by mid-April due to their success in previous battles
2. Stalin had prioritised capturing Berlin before the Allies
3. Russians advanced easily against poor German defences at the Oder River/German units chose to concentrate fighting to the west of the city so they could surrender to Allied forces rather than Russian
4. Defence of the city of Berlin relied upon disorganised/poorly armed units from the German army and Hitler Youth members/elderly men or boys
5. City of Berlin defences in panic and disarray, so easier
6. Allied aerial bombing of the city assisted the Russian army
7. Artillery barrage into the city began on April 16th and pushed back the German defences further
8. Hitler sacked commanders, created confusion
9. Loss of morale after Hitler committed suicide

Section 3, Context J, The Cold War, 1945–1989

1. *Candidates can be credited in a number of ways **up to a maximum of 5 marks**.*

Candidates must show a causal relationship between events.

Up to a **maximum of 5 marks in total**, **1 mark** should be given for each accurate, relevant reason, and a **second mark** should be given for reasons that are developed. Candidates may achieve full marks by providing five straightforward reasons, three developed reasons, or a combination of these.

Possible reasons may include:
1. The only thing that kept them together was over – the Second World War
2. Disagreements at Potsdam eg over Poland
3. The Americans had developed the atomic bomb and this angered/ worried the Soviet Union
4. Soviet troops were occupying most of Eastern Europe and this caused tension
5. Truman, the new American President was more anti-communist than Roosevelt
6. An arms race developed causing further tension
7. Different ideas – capitalism versus communism
8. The Soviets saw Marshall Aid as an American attempt to dominate Europe/Soviet satellites prevented from accepting Marshall Aid
9. Berlin Blockade, 1948-1949, deepened the divisions between East and West

10. The establishment of NATO by America and its allies in 1949 caused further division
11. Establishment of Warsaw Pact 1955 heightened tensions
12. The Soviets and the Americans involved on different sides in proxy wars eg Korea

2. *Candidates can be credited in a number of ways **up to a maximum of 6 marks.***

Candidates must make an overall judgement about how fully the source explains the events. **1 mark** may be given for each valid point interpreted from the source or each valid point of significant omission provided. The candidate can achieve **up to 3 marks** for their interpretation of the parts of the source they consider are relevant in terms of the proposed question where there is also at least one point of significant omission identified to imply a judgement has been made about the limitations of the source. For full marks to be given each point needs to be discretely mentioned in terms of the question.

A maximum of 2 marks may be given for answers which refer only to the source or in which no judgement has been made.

Possible points which may be identified in the source include:
1. President Truman explained that America would resist the spread of Communism
2. The Americans had responded to French requests for assistance in Vietnam
3. It was clear that South Vietnam could not resist Communism without the support of American troops
4. Many in America believed war was necessary to stop the spread of Soviet influence

Possible points of significant omission may include:
1. America feared that a civil war was developing in South Vietnam.
2. America was increasingly concerned about the influence of China in south-east Asia
3. There was a widespread belief in the Domino Theory eg Thailand, Laos, Burma, Cambodia even New Zealand and Australia could fall to communism
4. There was a general concern that America was falling behind in the Cold War at this time
5. Gulf of Tonkin incident led America to become involved in a full scale war in Vietnam.

3. *Candidates can be credited in a number of ways **up to a maximum of 4 marks.***

Candidates must make direct comparisons of the two sources, either overall or in detail. A simple comparison will indicate what points of detail or overall viewpoint they agree or disagree about and should be given **1 mark**.

A developed comparison of the points of detail or overall viewpoint should be given **2 marks**. Candidates may achieve full marks by making four simple comparisons, two developed comparisons or by a combination of these.

Possible points of comparison may include:

Overall: The sources agree that the Soviets were at fault	
Source A	Source B
The source of world trouble and tension is Moscow	We now say with confidence that this crisis was caused by Moscow.
They have rejected an all-German peace treaty	The Soviets rejected an American proposal for a peace treaty
It is they who have rejected … the rule of international law.	The Soviet domination of East Germany was a clear breach of international law

4. *Candidates can be credited in a number of ways **up to a maximum of 5 marks.***

They may take different perspectives on the events and may describe a variety of different aspects of the events.

1 mark should be given for each accurate relevant key point of knowledge.

A second mark should be given for each point that is developed, up to a maximum of **5 marks**. Candidates may achieve full marks by providing five straightforward points, by making three developed points, or a combination of these.

Possible points of knowledge may include:
1. Cuba stayed Communist/Castro's position strengthened as Kennedy promised not to invade
2. American missiles withdrawn from Turkey/Italy
3. Kennedy greatly improved his reputation in America and the West
4. Khrushchev was able to claim he prevented America from taking over Cuba, a useful ally so close to America
5. Krushchev seemed weak as American missiles removed in secret/led directly to Krushchev's fall 2 years later
6. Led to a thaw in the Cold War
7. 'Hot line' set up between the White House and the Kremlin
8. Nuclear Test Ban Treaty signed in 1963

NATIONAL 5 HISTORY 2015

Section 1, Part A, The Wars of Independence, 1286-1328

1. *Candidates can be credited in a number of ways up to a maximum of 4 marks.*

Candidates must make direct comparisons of the two sources, either overall or in detail. A simple comparison will indicate what points of detail or overall viewpoint they agree or disagree about and should be given **1 mark**.

A developed comparison of the points of detail or overall viewpoint should be given **2 marks**. Candidates may achieve full marks by making four simple comparisons, two developed comparisons or by a combination of these.

Possible points of comparison may include:

Source A	Source B
Overall: The sources agree that Edward wanted to unite the kingdoms through marriage/the sources disagree over his methods	
His aim was to unite the kingdoms with a marriage treaty	This marriage would mean a union of the kingdoms
Edward had secretly asked the Pope's permission for the marriage before any terms had been discussed with the Scots	Edward asked for Scottish representatives to be present before any negotiations began
He plotted to arrange the marriage of his son to Scotland's infant queen, Margaret, Maid of Norway	Erik, King of Norway, father of Margaret the Maid, sent messengers to him to suggest her possible marriage with Edward's son

2. *Candidates can be credited in a number of ways up to a maximum of 5 marks.*

They may take different perspectives on the events and may describe a variety of different aspects of the events.

1 mark should be given for each accurate relevant key point of knowledge.

A second mark should be given for each point that is developed, up to a maximum of **5 marks**. Candidates may achieve full marks by providing five straightforward points, by making three developed points, or a combination of these.

Possible points of knowledge may include:
1. Edward had mustered a very large army for the invasion
2. Edward had ships waiting to enter the harbour and attack
3. Edward gave the inhabitants three days to surrender
4. the castle garrison surrendered without reprisal
5. the townspeople refused to surrender/mocked Edward's offer of surrender
6. three of Edward's ships ran aground and were burned by the townspeople
7. Edward's troops were sent in to take the town
8. there was little resistance to the attack
9. the townspeople were slaughtered/the slaughter lasted for three days
10. thirty Flemish merchants fired arrows at the English/ were burned to death in the Red Hall
11. the town was burned to the ground

3. *Candidates can be credited in a number of ways up to a maximum of 6 marks.*

Candidates must make an overall judgement about how fully the source explains the events. **1 mark** may be given for each valid point interpreted from the source or each valid point of significant omission provided. The candidate can achieve **up to 3 marks** for their interpretation of the parts of the source they consider are relevant in terms of the proposed question where there is also at least one point of significant omission identified to imply a judgement has been made about the limitations of the source. For full marks to be given each point needs to be discretely mentioned in terms of the question.

A maximum of 2 marks may be given for answers which refer only to the source.

Possible points which may be identified in the source include:
1. Bruce destroyed castles in Inverness and Nairn
2. Bruce could not spare men to defend castles from attack.
3. Douglas recaptured his own castle in the south (and burned it down)
4. lack of siege engines forced Bruce to use other methods.

Possible points of significant omission may include:
1. castles that were destroyed could not later be used against him by his enemies
2. Douglas burned all the stores with the English garrisons' bodies in his castle – the 'Douglas Larder'
3. Perth castle was captured by Bruce's men wading across the river at night/scaled riverside wall at night with ladders
4. Roxburgh castle was captured by Bruce's men hiding among cattle at dusk to get close to walls/used rope ladders at night to scale walls and open gates
5. Linlithgow castle was captured by jamming the gate and portcullis with a haycart/men were hidden in the cart to fight till reinforcements arrived
6. Edinburgh castle was captured with a daring climb up the rock face/ diversionary attack on other side
7. Stirling, Bothwell and Berwick castles were recaptured later

4. *Candidates can be credited in a number of ways up to a maximum of 5 marks.*

Candidates must show a causal relationship between events.

Up to a maximum of 5 marks in total, 1 mark should be given for each accurate, relevant reason, and a second mark should be given for reasons that are developed. Candidates may achieve full marks by providing five straightforward reasons, three developed reasons, or a combination of these.

Possible reasons may include:
1. there was no battle plan as Edward did not think the Scots would fight
2. the English were overconfident due to their superior numbers
3. Edward did not take charge himself but appointed favourites to key commands, causing resentment
4. Edward ignored warnings not to attack across Bannockburn
5. marshy ground not suitable for heavy cavalry or infantry

6. there was confusion among the commanders about attacking the Scots on the first day/whether the battle was to take place that day
7. de Bohun charged Bruce without being ordered to and his defeat contributed to lowered morale among the English
8. English commanders argued among themselves and were forced to retreat on the first day of the battle by Scottish pikemen
9. Edward moved his army to the Carse during the night, so they were tired
10. the commanders did not learn from the forced retreat against the Scots pikemen on the first day of the battle so repeated the same mistake/cavalry made no headway against schiltrons
11. the English army was badly positioned
12. the English footsoldiers/archers/cavalry had no room to manoeuvre
13. huge numbers became a handicap when they attempted to retreat **across the Bannockburn**

Section 1, Part B, Mary Queen of Scots and the Scottish reformation, 1542–1587

5. *Candidates can be credited in a number of ways **up to a maximum of 5 marks**.*

They may take different perspectives on the events and may describe a variety of different aspects of the events.

1 mark should be given for each accurate relevant key point of knowledge. **A second mark** should be given for each point that is developed, up to a maximum of **5 marks**. Candidates may achieve full marks by providing five straightforward points, by making three developed points, or a combination of these.

Possible points of knowledge may include:
1. the Scots broke the Treaty of Greenwich which stated that Mary would marry Edward, Henry VIII's son
2. Henry VIII ordered the Earl of Hertford to invade Scotland and burn Edinburgh
3. the English attacked Scotland and destroyed abbeys/towns in the south of Scotland
4. Henry VIII encouraged the assassination of Cardinal Beaton
5. Battle of Pinkie Cleugh 1547 – large Scottish army defeated
6. the Palace of Holyrood in Edinburgh was looted/large parts of Edinburgh were burned
7. the pier at Leith in Edinburgh was destroyed
8. Berwick upon Tweed was attacked and burned
9. Scots received help from the French who sent a force to Edinburgh in 1548
10. Treaty of Haddington was signed by the Scots and French which agreed Mary would marry the heir to the French throne
11. Mary was sent to France for protection

6. *Candidates can be credited in a number of ways **up to a maximum of 4 marks**.*

Candidates must make direct comparisons of the two sources, either overall or in detail. A simple comparison will indicate what points of detail or overall viewpoint they agree or disagree about and should be given **1 mark**.

A developed comparison of the points of detail or overall viewpoint should be given **2 marks**. Candidates may achieve full marks by making four simple comparisons, two developed comparisons or by a combination of these.
Possible points of comparison may include:

Source A	Source B
Overall:	
The sources agree that Darnley and a group of nobles entered Mary's chamber uninvited/ killed Riccio	
Suddenly, Darnley forced his way into the chamber with a large group of followers	Darnley unexpectedly appeared with a group of armed nobles, including Lord Ruthven, and burst into Mary's chamber
One of the intruders held Mary back and a pistol was pointed towards her pregnant belly	Mary, who was pregnant, could not do anything because she had been seized and had a gun pointed to her stomach
He was then dragged from the room and stabbed many times	Riccio was then pulled out of the room and stabbed over 50 times

7. *Candidates can be credited in a number of ways **up to a maximum of 5 marks**.*

Candidates must show a causal relationship between events.

Up to a **maximum of 5 marks in total, 1 mark** should be given for each accurate, relevant reason, and a **second mark** should be given for reasons that are developed. Candidates may achieve full marks by providing five straightforward reasons, three developed reasons, or a combination of these.

Possible reasons may include:
1. Mary was implicated in the murder of her husband, Lord Darnley which put pressure on her to abdicate
2. her marriage to Bothwell cast further suspicion on Mary
3. Mary allowed Bothwell to prevent a fair investigation into the death of Darnley which angered many
4. Mary was forced to abdicate because Protestant Lords wanted her infant son on the throne
5. her half-brother Moray forced Mary to abdicate so he could become regent
6. Mary was unpopular as some objected to being ruled by a female monarch
7. military defeats forced Mary to abdicate eg Carberry Hill

8. *Candidates can be credited in a number of ways **up to a maximum of 6 marks**.*

Candidates must make an overall judgement about how fully the source explains the events. **1 mark** may be given for each valid point interpreted from the source or each valid point of significant omission provided. The candidate can achieve **up to 3 marks** for their interpretation of the parts of the source they consider are relevant in terms of the proposed question where there is also at least one point of significant omission identified to imply a judgement has been made about the limitations of the source. For full marks to be given each point needs to be discretely mentioned in terms of the question.

A maximum of 2 marks may be given for answers which refer only to the source.

Possible points which may be identified in the source include:
1. she learned that the trial would be held even in her absence
2. Mary defended herself/not allowed to call witnesses
3. Mary was not even allowed to consult any documents during her trial
4. she knew she would be found guilty because it was too great a risk to let her live

Possible points of significant omission may include:
1. Mary was arrested in September 1586 and held at Fotheringay Castle until her trial
2. Mary was implicated in a number of plots against Elizabeth eg Babington Plot, 1586
3. Mary was charged with treason
4. Mary was denied legal counsel
5. Mary claimed that she could not be accused of treason because she was not an English subject
6. Mary was convicted on 25 October 1586 and sentenced to death
7. Mary was beheaded on 8 February 1587 at Fotheringay Castle

Section 1, Part C, The Treaty of Union, 1689-1715

9. *Candidates can be credited in a number of ways up to a maximum of 5 marks.*

Candidates must show a causal relationship between events.

Up to a **maximum of 5 marks in total, 1 mark** should be given for each accurate, relevant reason, and a second mark should be given for reasons that are developed. Candidates may achieve full marks by providing five straightforward reasons, three developed reasons, or a combination of these.

Possible reasons may include:
1. many in Scotland were angry that the Navigation Acts prevented Scotland trading with English colonies
2. there was a feeling that the English had not done enough to help Scotland during the Ill Years of the 1690s
3. Scots were angry as they felt the Darien scheme had been sabotaged by William as it went against English interests
4. Scots' loyalties were considered suspect by the English after the Jacobite rebellion of 1689
5. Scots were angry that the English Parliament passed the succession to Sophia of Hanover without consulting the Scottish Parliament
6. the English were angry at Scottish legislation such as the Act of Security/Act Anent Peace and War
7. the English were angry over the execution of Captain Green of the Worcester

10. *Candidates can be credited in a number of ways up to a maximum of 6 marks.*

Candidates must make an overall judgement about how fully the source explains the events. **1 mark** may be given for each valid point interpreted from the source or each valid point of significant omission provided. The candidate can achieve **up to 3 marks** for their interpretation of the parts of the source they consider are relevant in terms of the proposed question where there is also at least one point of significant omission identified to imply a judgement has been made about the limitations of the source. For full marks to be given each point needs to be discretely mentioned in terms of the question.

A maximum of 2 marks may be given for answers which refer only to the source.

Possible points which may be identified in the source include:
1. the supporters of Union were clear that it would help Scotland to become richer in the future

2. many Protestants argued that the main advantage of Union would be securing the Protestant Succession
3. they also pointed out that the English had made it clear they would respect the independence of the Church of Scotland
4. it was also pointed out that if Union was rejected England might simply invade and take over anyway

Possible points of significant omission may include:
1. Union would guarantee the Scots access to trade with English colonies
2. Union would guarantee security against Catholic France
3. Union would see Darien investors compensated through the Equivalent
4. Union would end English piracy

11. *Candidates can be credited in a number of ways up to a maximum of 4 marks.*

Candidates must make direct comparisons of the two sources, either overall or in detail. A simple comparison will indicate what points of detail or overall viewpoint they agree or disagree about and should be given **1 mark.**

A developed comparison of the points of detail or overall viewpoint should be given **2 marks.** Candidates may achieve full marks by making four simple comparisons, two developed comparisons or by a combination of these.

Possible points of comparison may include:

Source B	Source C
Overall: Both sources agree that most Scots opposed the Union	
Many feared that the proposed Union would lead to a rise in taxes	It was claimed that after the Union higher taxes would hit all Scots in the pocket
They argued that England was the far bigger country and so would control Scotland	Many Scots felt that the Union would not be a partnership but a takeover
Some feared for the independence of the Church of Scotland	Religion was very important to many Scots and they did not want the English to interfere in their Church

12. *Candidates can be credited in a number of ways up to a maximum of 5 marks.*

They may take different perspectives on the events and may describe a variety of different aspects of the events.

1 mark should be given for each accurate relevant key point of knowledge. **A second mark** should be given for each point that is developed, up to a maximum of **5 marks.** Candidates may achieve full marks by providing five straightforward points, by making three developed points, or a combination of these.

Possible points of knowledge may include:
1. there was a growth in smuggling
2. increased taxes (led to attacks on excisemen eg at Ayr in 1714)
3. the Scottish linen industry suffered because of increased taxes
4. the Scottish Privy Council was abolished in 1708
5. led to the Jacobite rebellions of 1708 and 1715
6. led to the 1712 Toleration Act which granted Episcopalians the right to worship freely in Scotland

Section 1, Part D, Migration and Empire, 1830–1939

13. *Candidates can be credited in a number of ways up to a maximum of 6 marks.*

Candidates must make an overall judgement about how fully the source explains the events. **1 mark** may be given for each valid point interpreted from the source or each valid point of significant omission provided. The candidate can achieve **up to 3 marks** for their interpretation of the parts of the source they consider are relevant in terms of the proposed question where there is also at least one point of significant omission identified to imply a judgement has been made about the limitations of the source. For full marks to be given each point needs to be discretely mentioned in terms of the question.

A maximum of 2 marks may be given for answers which refer only to the source.

Possible points which may be identified in the source include:
1. many Scots invested money in the Empire and reinvested their profits in Scotland, adding to Scotland's wealth
2. profits were spent in other ways on luxury houses and impressive public buildings which changed the appearance of Scottish cities
3. profits from trade with the Empire were also used to develop chemical industries and textiles, creating even more jobs
4. the Empire provided markets for Scottish coal/employed thousands of miners

Possible points of significant omission may include:
1. Clyde shipyards produced much of the shipping needed to trade goods and carry passengers to the Empire
2. thousands of railway locomotives were produced in Scotland and exported to India, Canada, New Zealand etc
3. raw materials produced in the Empire were brought to Scotland for processing eg jute to Dundee, sugar to Greenock, cotton to Paisley
4. cheap food imports from the Empire eg wheat/Canada, lamb/Australia affected Scots farmers
5. Glasgow thought of itself as the Second City of the Empire/Scotland was known as the 'Workshop of the Empire'
6. provided Scots with jobs abroad as administrators, diplomats, soldiers etc.
7. provided Scots with the opportunity to emigrate abroad to the Empire e.g. Canada, Australia etc.

14. *Candidates can be credited in a number of ways up to a maximum of 5 marks.*

Candidates must show a causal relationship between events.

Up to a **maximum of 5 marks in total, 1 mark** should be given for each accurate, relevant reason, and a **second mark** should be given for reasons that are developed. Candidates may achieve full marks by providing five straightforward reasons, three developed reasons, or a combination of these.

Possible reasons may include:
1. many small farms/smallholdings disappeared as landowners created large farms, leaving tenants without a livelihood
2. new larger farms were too expensive for most tenant farmers to rent/buy
3. increased mechanisation in agriculture meant fewer workers were needed
4. skilled craftsmen such as weavers lost their livelihoods when more factories were built
5. trade depressions put many out of work and encouraged them to seek work abroad
6. family, relations wrote letters home telling of better wages, living standards etc.
7. wages in Scotland were low/wages in USA and Canada were higher
8. living conditions in Scottish cities were poor with much overcrowding
9. faster Atlantic crossings on steamships enabled more temporary emigration especially for skilled workers
10. skilled Scottish workers eg engineers/fishermen/ stonemasons were in great demand in the colonies
11. countries such as Australia and Canada advertised heavily for Scottish immigrants/sent agents to give talks on emigration
12. cheap or free land was offered in Canada, Australia and New Zealand
13. government schemes encouraged emigration with cheap fares to boost numbers of British settlers in Empire countries

15. *Candidates can be credited in a number of ways up to a maximum of 5 marks.*

They may take different perspectives on the events and may describe a variety of different aspects of the events.

1 mark should be given for each accurate relevant key point of knowledge. **A second mark** should be given for each point that is developed, up to a maximum of **5 marks.** Candidates may achieve full marks by providing five straightforward points, by making three developed points, or a combination of these.

Possible points of knowledge may include:
1. gave new settlements/towns Scottish names eg Hamilton, Glendale
2. settled in groups together/helped other Scots immigrants to settle
3. built churches and continued to worship in their traditional ways eg Presbyterian Churches in Australia
4. continued to place emphasis on education/built schools and founded universities
5. continued to speak Gaelic/taught Gaelic to their children
6. formed Caledonian societies/St Andrews societies/ Masonic Lodges
7. organised Burns Suppers/ate traditional foods (e.g. haggis)
8. played bagpipes/sang Scottish songs/taught Highland dancing/organised ceilidhs
9. celebrated Tartan Day (Australia)/wore tartan/created new local tartans
10. established Highland Games eg Grandfather Mountain, Maryborough
11. founded golf clubs
12. kept traditions such as Hogmanay/New year's Day holiday
13. researched their ancestry
14. produced magazines with Scottish content
15. Heritage retained Scots martial traditions eg Canadian Scots regiments in WW1

16. *Candidates can be credited in a number of ways up to a maximum of 4 marks.*

Candidates must make direct comparisons of the two sources, either overall or in detail. A simple comparison will indicate what points of detail or overall viewpoint they agree or disagree about and should be given **1 mark.**

A developed comparison of the points of detail or overall viewpoint should be given **2 marks**. Candidates may achieve full marks by making four simple comparisons, two developed comparisons or by a combination of these.

Possible points of comparison may include:

Source A	Source B
Overall: The sources agree that Scots made a positive contribution to the development of Australia	
Thomas Mitchell from Stirling was the first European to explore the rich lands of Victoria for new settlement	The Scottish explorer John McDouall Stuart was the first European to cross Australia
Scottish Australia Company was formed in Aberdeen to encourage Scottish investment to businesses in Australia	Glasgow investors formed the influential New Zealand and Australian Land Company to encourage the wool export trade
Fife-born Sir Peter Russell gave £100,000 to the University of Sydney to develop the study of engineering	Francis Ormond from Aberdeen gave large sums for setting up the Working Men's Technical College in Melbourne to support education

Section 1, Part E, The Era of the Great War, 1910-1928

17. *Candidates can be credited in a number of ways* ***up to a maximum of 6 marks.***

Candidates must make an overall judgement about how fully the source explains the events. **1 mark** may be given for each valid point interpreted from the source or each valid point of significant omission provided. The candidate can achieve **up to 3 marks** for their interpretation of the parts of the source they consider are relevant in terms of the proposed question where there is also at least one point of significant omission identified to imply a judgement has been made about the limitations of the source. For full marks to be given each point needs to be discretely mentioned in terms of the question.

A maximum of 2 marks may be given for answers which refer only to the source.

Possible points which may be identified in the source include:
1. the sudden appearance of the new weapon stunned their German opponents
2. early tanks were very slow moving.
3. they often broke down
4. tanks often became stuck in the heavy mud of no man's land.

Possible points of significant omission may include:
1. they destroyed enemy machine guns/enemy pill boxes (concrete emplacements)
2. were a great life-saver of infantry/gave protection to advancing troops crossing no-man's land
3. raised British morale at crucial period in war.
4. were more effective than an artillery bombardment/ allowed element of surprise/short bombardment
5. cross-country mobility allowed them to go over rough ground/no-man's land
6. smashed gaps in the barbed-wire
7. able to cross enemy trenches

8. their 6 pounder guns and machine-guns could clear enemy troops out of their trenches
9. their armour meant bullets couldn't stop them
10. could only be stopped by a direct shell hit
11. some initial success at Cambrai
12. their advance was blocked by wide ditches, rivers, canals etc
13. land captured by tanks often lost when Germans counterattacked/tanks could capture land but not hold it.
14. massed tank attacks in 1917 & 1918 helped break German morale and win war

18. *Candidates can be credited in a number of ways* ***up to a maximum of 4 marks.***

Candidates must make direct comparisons of the two sources, either overall or in detail. A simple comparison will indicate what points of detail or overall viewpoint they agree or disagree about and should be given **1 mark**.

A developed comparison of the points of detail or overall viewpoint should be given **2 marks**. Candidates may achieve full marks by making four simple comparisons, two developed comparisons or by a combination of these.

Possible points of comparison may include:

Source B	Source C
Overall: The sources agree the conditions in the trenches were terrible.	
poor men in trenches standing in very deep mud	soldiers had to make their way sometimes through very heavy mud
water is often up to their waists	thirty yards of waterlogged trench/ chest-deep in water in some places
shells burst all round and shook the place	the duckboard track was constantly shelled, and in places a hundred yards of it had been blown to smithereens

19. *Candidates can be credited in a number of ways* ***up to a maximum of 5 marks.***

Candidates must show a causal relationship between events.

Up to a **maximum of 5 marks in total, 1 mark** should be given for each accurate, relevant reason, and a **second mark** should be given for reasons that are developed. Candidates may achieve full marks by providing five straightforward reasons, three developed reasons, or a combination of these.

Possible reasons may include:
1. people were unhappy that they could not strike for better working conditions/pay
2. people were upset with censorship of the press/the censorship of private correspondence related to the war
3. people disliked the treatment of/restriction of movement of foreign nationals/many were interned
4. pub owners were unhappy with restrictions on alcohol/ limitation of pub opening hours/watering down of alcohol/the effect on their ability to make a living
5. blackouts made it dangerous to get around at night
6. pigeon fanciers resented the complication of having to have a licence to keep their birds/other seemingly trivial restrictions annoyed people (e. g. not being able to fly kites/buy binoculars)

7. people could be fined/arrested/imprisoned for breaking the terms of DORA
8. some resented the restrictions of their civil liberties
9. government took control of land to turn it over to food production, which landowners
10. people resented restrictions on movement around railways and docks
11. other government restrictions were resented (redirection of labour, leaving certificates, conscription, rationing)

20. *Candidates can be credited in a number of ways **up to a maximum of 5 marks.***

They may take different perspectives on the events and may describe a variety of different aspects of the events.

1 mark should be given for each accurate relevant key point of knowledge. **A second mark** should be given for each point that is developed, up to a maximum of **5 marks.** Candidates may achieve full marks by providing five straightforward points, by making three developed points, or a combination of these.

Possible points of knowledge may include:
1. foreign competition affected industries (such as coal, iron, steel, jute and shipbuilding)
2. downturn in demand affected industries (such as shipbuilding, iron, steel and jute)
3. poor industrial relations was a difficulty
4. High unemployment in certain industries/areas
5. shortages of skilled manpower/materials also led to problems
6. the collapse of foreign markets for herring greatly affected the industry
7. much of the fishing fleet needed to be replaced/compensation was inadequate
8. the price of goods collapsed (the government removed the guaranteed price for herring in 1920/food prices fell)
9. coal industry in decline due to competition from electricity
10. Lack of government investment
11. Technology was outdated and needed to be improved

Section 2, Part A, The Creation of the Medieval Kingdoms, 1066-1406

21. *Candidates can be credited in a number of ways **up to a maximum of 5 marks.***

They may take different perspectives on the events and may describe a variety of different aspects of the events.

1 mark should be given for each accurate relevant key point of knowledge. **A second mark** should be given for each point that is developed, up to a maximum of **5 marks.** Candidates may achieve full marks by providing five straightforward points, by making three developed points, or a combination of these.

Possible points of knowledge may include:
1. barons took an oath of fealty/promised to be loyal and serve the king
2. barons provided knights for the king's army
3. barons were an important part of the feudal system eg gave land to knights/peasants
4. barons protected those who lived on their land
5. barons were members of the king's council/helped him govern the country
6. barons helped enforce law and order at local level
7. trusted barons became sheriffs and collected fines and taxes for the king
8. barons paid extra tax during times of war

22. *Candidates can be credited in a number of ways **up to a maximum of 5 marks.***

Candidates must show a causal relationship between events.

Up to a **maximum of 5 marks in total, 1 mark** should be given for each accurate, relevant reason, and a **second mark** should be given for reasons that are developed. Candidates may achieve full marks by providing five straightforward reasons, three developed reasons, or a combination of these.

Possible reasons may include:
1. Henry felt betrayed by the behaviour of his former close friend eg Becket resigned as chancellor
2. Becket disagreed with Henry over the issue of Criminous Clerks
3. Becket refused to sign the Constitution of Clarendon
4. Henry kept Becket imprisoned for 3 days until the document was signed
5. Becket failed to appear at the Northampton Trial
6. Henry charged Becket with contempt of court
7. Henry humiliated Becket and confiscated his lands/Henry accused him of fraud
8. Becket fled to France without the King's permission
9. Becket appealed to the Pope/continued to defend the rights of the Church
10. Henry refused to give Becket the royal kiss when they met in France
11. Henry asked the Archbishop of York, instead of Becket, to crown his son
12. Becket excommunicated the Archbishop of York and the bishops involved in the coronation

23. *Candidates can be credited in a number of ways **up to a maximum of 5 marks.***

Candidates must make an overall judgement about how fully the source explains the events. **1 mark** may be given for each valid point interpreted from the source or each valid point of significant omission provided. The candidate can achieve **up to 3 marks** for their interpretation of the parts of the source they consider are relevant in terms of the proposed question where there is also at least one point of significant omission identified to imply a judgement has been made about the limitations of the source. For full marks to be given each point needs to be discretely mentioned in terms of the question.

A maximum of 2 marks may be given for answers which refer only to the source.

Possible points which may be identified in the source include:
1. monks were expected to carry out hard physical labour in the field or herb garden
2. well-educated monks studied the bible/spent hours copying and illuminating books
3. monks supported their local community by collecting alms and caring for the poor
4. monks provided the only medical help available at the time, looking after the sick in the monastery's infirmary.

Possible points of significant omission may include:
1. monks prayed for the souls of the dead
2. monks educated boys/prepared them for a career in the Church
3. monks looked after pilgrims who stayed at the monastery
4. monks were involved in politics eg wrote charters
5. monks ran monastic farms/reared sheep
6. monks were involved in the fishing industry eg built harbour at Arbroath

24. *Candidates can be credited in a number of ways **up to a maximum of 5 marks**.*

Candidates must make a judgement about the usefulness of the source and support this by making evaluative comments on identified aspects of the source.

1 mark should be given for each relevant comment made, up to a **maximum of 5 marks in total**.
- A maximum of 4 marks can be given for evaluative comments relating to the author, type of source, purpose and timing.
- A maximum of 2 marks may be given for comments relating to the content of the source.
- A maximum of 2 marks may be given for comments relating to points of significant omission.

Examples of aspects of the source and relevant comments:

Aspect of the source	Possible comment
Author: Doctor	Useful because he was an eyewitness/expert to the symptoms of the Black Death
Type of Source: Book	Useful because it will have been well researched
Purpose: To inform	Useful because it gives a detailed description of how terrible the symptoms of the Black Death were
Timing: 1350	Useful because it was written at the time of the Black Death

Content	Possible comment
The first sign of death was a swelling called a buboe under the armpit or in the groin	Useful because it gives accurate details of the symptoms of the Black Death
Soon after, the victim began to vomit and developed a fever	Useful because it gives accurate details of the symptoms of the Black Death
This was followed by the appearance of black and purple spots on the arms or thighs	Useful because it provides accurate information on what happened next

Possible points of significant omission may include:
1. victims suffered terrible headaches
2. victims suffered spasms

Section 2, Part B, War of the Three Kingdoms, 1603–1651

25. *Candidates can be credited in a number of ways **up to a maximum of 5 marks**.*

They may take different perspectives on the events and may describe a variety of different aspects of the events.

1 mark should be given for each accurate relevant key point of knowledge. **A second mark** should be given for each point that is developed, up to a maximum of **5 marks**. Candidates may achieve full marks by providing five straightforward points, by making three developed points, or a combination of these.

Possible points of knowledge may include:
1. no new institutions or government structures were put in place (except that, when parliament met, a royal 'commissioner' represented the King)

2. a postal service was established between Edinburgh and London to keep the King in touch with his government in Edinburgh (the origins of the Royal Mail)
3. James declared himself to be 'King of Great Britain', although for legal reasons, the separate kingdoms of Scotland and England continued to exist
4. King was based in London so rarely visited Scotland after his coronation
5. Scotland was to be ruled by a Privy Council
6. Privy Council ensured the King's will was followed in Scotland
7. Parliament was brought under strict royal control
8. Parliament was run by a small committee called the Committee of Articles (Lords of the Articles)
9. Committee/Lords of the Articles could only suggest new laws for Scotland
10. the King chose the Lords and bishops to become part of the Committee/Lords of the Articles

26. *Candidates can be credited in a number of ways **up to a maximum of 5 marks**.*

Candidates must make a judgement about the usefulness of the source and support this by making evaluative comments on identified aspects of the source.

1 mark should be given for each relevant comment made, up to a **maximum of 5 marks in total**.
- A maximum of **4 marks** can be given for evaluative comments relating to the author, type of source, purpose and timing.
- A maximum of **2 marks** may be given for comments relating to the content of the source.
- A maximum of **2 marks** may be given for comments relating to points of significant omission.

Examples of aspects of the source and relevant comments:

Aspect of the source	Possible comment
Author: King James VI and I	Useful because it is written by King James himself who had a strong personal belief in the Divine Right of Kings/eyewitness
Type of Source: Book	Useful because it has been researched (written specifically to outline the King's beliefs in Divine Right)
Purpose: To inform	Less useful because it is a biased view
Timing: 1598	Useful because it is written at the time when the King was asserting his belief in the Divine Right of Kings

Content	Possible comment
The power of the monarchy is the supreme authority on Earth	Useful because it accurately outlines the power of the King as being the highest power on earth
it is treason for a King's subjects to challenge what a King may or may not do	Useful because it accurately states that the King's authority cannot be challenged
King is not obliged to follow that law unless he sees fit to do so	Useful because it accurately illustrates the belief that the King is above earthly law

Possible points of significant omission may include:

1. Even if a king behaved badly no one could criticise him, only God could punish him
2. God bestows on a king the right to rule
3. The king is not subject to the will of his people, the aristocracy, or any other estate of the realm, including (in the view of some, especially in Protestant countries) the Church

27. *Candidates can be credited in a number of ways **up to a maximum of 5 marks.***

Candidates must show a causal relationship between events.

Up to a **maximum of 5 marks in total, 1 mark** should be given for each accurate, relevant reason, and a **second mark** should be given for reasons that are developed. Candidates may achieve full marks by providing five straightforward reasons, three developed reasons, or a combination of these.

Possible reasons may include:

1. the General Assembly was not allowed to meet which caused resentment
2. resentment at Charles' money raising methods (e.g. Ship Money)
3. Scottish nobles resented Charles' Act of Revocation whereby church lands which had been alienated since 1540 had to be returned to the Crown
4. Charles' coronation in Edinburgh was a High Church ceremony based on Anglican forms and Scottish Presbyterians were suspicious of Anglican ideas
5. Charles demanded that Scottish Ministers accept and use the new English Prayer Book which caused a great deal of resentment and some riots in Edinburgh
6. Scottish clergy opposed Laud's Canons and their requirement to wear gowns and surplices because it seemed too Catholic
7. Bishops were to be introduced into the Scottish Church which was resented by the Scots
8. rejection of the Canons was included in the National Covenant for the Defence of True Religion in 1638 and was signed by thousands because they wanted to protect Scottish religious practices

28. *Candidates can be credited in a number of ways **up to a maximum of 5 marks.***

Candidates must make an overall judgement about how fully the source explains the events. **1 mark** may be given for each valid point interpreted from the source or each valid point of significant omission provided. The candidate can achieve **up to 3 marks** for their interpretation of the parts of the source they consider are relevant in terms of the proposed question where there is also at least one point of significant omission identified to imply a judgement has been made about the limitations of the source. For full marks to be given each point needs to be discretely mentioned in terms of the question.

A maximum of 2 marks may be given for answers which refer only to the source.

Possible points which may be identified in the source include:

1. the demands in the Nineteen Proposals divided Parliament (between those who supported the Nineteen Proposals and those who thought Parliament had gone too far)
2. Parliament and Charles then began to raise their own armies
3. People were then forced to choose sides

Possible points of significant omission may include:

1. the King dissolved the parliament in 1640 (Short Parliament) after only 3 weeks
2. activities of the Long Parliament angered the King (e.g. arrest and imprisonment of Archbishop Laud/arrest and imprisonment of Strafford)
3. The Grand Remonstrance in November 1641 divided the House of Commons
4. rumours over the causes of the Irish rebellion in November 1641 angered Protestants who thought the King was behind it
5. attempted arrest of 5 Members of Parliament in January 1642 angered Parliament
6. Parliaments decision to throw Bishops out of the House of Lords in February 1642 divided the House of Commons
7. Parliament took control of the army in March 1642 without the Kings consent

Section 2, Part C, The Atlantic Slave Trade, 1770-1807

29. *Candidates can be credited in a number of ways **up to a maximum of 5 marks.***

They may take different perspectives on the events and may describe a variety of different aspects of the events.

1 mark should be given for each accurate relevant key point of knowledge. **A second mark** should be given for each point that is developed, up to a maximum of **5 marks.** Candidates may achieve full marks by providing five straightforward points, by making three developed points, or a combination of these.

Possible points of knowledge may include:

1. ships sailed from Europe to Africa carrying manufactured goods.
2. ships often departed from/arrived at British ports such as Bristol, Liverpool, occasionally Glasgow.
3. manufactured goods eg guns, alcohol, glass beads, pots and pans were exchanged for slaves.
4. slaves were held in slave factories on the west coast of Africa.
5. slave ships left West Africa carrying slaves to West Indies and the Americas (the Middle Passage).
6. slaves were packed on to ships to maximise profits.
7. conditions on the middle passage were very poor and slaves often died from disease or mistreatment.
8. slaves were usually sold by auction upon arrival in West Indies/America.
9. profits from slave auctions were then invested in sugar, coffee, cotton, tobacco.
10. ships carrying tobacco, sugar, molasses, cotton would sail back across the Atlantic (the Home Run).
11. cotton, tobacco, sugar, coffee could be sold on return to Britain for a large profit.

30. *Candidates can be credited in a number of ways **up to a maximum of 5 marks.***

Candidates must make an overall judgement about how fully the source explains the events. **1 mark** may be given for each valid point interpreted from the source or each valid point of significant omission provided. The candidate can achieve **up to 3 marks** for their interpretation of the parts of the source they consider are relevant in terms of the proposed question where there is also at least one point of significant omission identified to imply a judgement has been made about the limitations of the source. For full marks to be given each point needs to be discretely mentioned in terms of the question.

A maximum of 2 marks may be given for answers which refer only to the source.

Possible points which may be identified in the source include:

1. the slave trade had raised Liverpool from a struggling port to one of the richest and most prosperous trading centres in the world
2. the slave trade provided work in almost every industry in the town
3. slave cotton provided work for the mills of Lancashire
4. merchants made huge profits importing sugar from the Caribbean

Possible points of significant omission may include:

1. the importation of tobacco was a big part of Glasgow's economy
2. the economy of Glasgow later shifted to the processing of sugar imported from the West Indies
3. jobs were provided in many industries: shipbuilding, rope making, dock work, banking, finance, sailors
4. profits from the slave trade were invested in British Industry
5. wealthy colonial families built huge mansions in many British cities.
6. the profits from the slave trade were invested in the development of British towns and cities
7. many important civic buildings in British cities were constructed using the profits of the slave trade

31. *Candidates can be credited in a number of ways* **up to a maximum of 5 marks.**

Candidates must make a judgement about the usefulness of the source and support this by making evaluative comments on identified aspects of the source.

1 mark should be given for each relevant comment made, **up to a maximum of 5 marks in total.**

A maximum of **4 marks** can be given for evaluative comments relating to the author, type of source, purpose and timing.

A maximum of **2 marks** may be given for comments relating to the content of the source.

A maximum of **2 marks** may be given for comments relating to points of significant omission.

Examples of aspects of the source and relevant comments:

Aspect of the source	Possible comment
Author: Written by a modern historian	Useful because he would have carried out research/ studied the topic
Type of Source: a history book	Useful as it is likely to contain relevant and accurate information
Purpose: to inform people about the impact of the slave trade on the Caribbean island of Barbados	Less useful as it only informs us about one of the Caribbean islands.
Timing: 1987	Useful because it is a secondary source, written a long time after the end of the slave trade/slavery in the Caribbean with the benefit of hindsight.

Content	Possible comment
the Caribbean island of Barbados was transformed by slave trade/ small farms replaced by large plantations	Useful because it accurately describes the changes brought to Barbados by the slave trade
The beautiful wilderness was slowly but surely cleared of its native people and its vegetation	Useful because it accurately shows the damage to the island and its native people
Plantations were the work place and final resting place of armies of African slaves	Useful because it accurately shows the scale of the suffering involved in the slave trade

Possible points of significant omission may include:

1. many other Caribbean islands such as Jamaica were also affected in a similar way
2. many of the native people were killed by the white settlers, or died from disease
3. as well as plantations, factories were also set up on the islands to refine the sugar

32. *Candidates can be credited in a number of ways* **up to a maximum of 5 marks.**

Candidates must show a causal relationship between events.

Up to a **maximum of 5 marks in total, 1 mark** should be given for each accurate, relevant reason, and a **second mark** should be given for reasons that are developed. Candidates may achieve full marks by providing five straightforward reasons, three developed reasons, or a combination of these.

Possible reasons may include:

1. life on the plantations was controlled by very strict laws or codes
2. many of the islands were small and there was little hope of fleeing the island
3. it was difficult for slaves with basic weapons to fight back against plantation owners who had guns
4. the brutal treatment of captured slaves acted as a powerful deterrent to other slaves
5. captured slaves would often be put to death/subject to horrific punishments/mutilation
6. plantation owners offered large rewards for the capture of escaped slaves
7. escaped slaves could easily be identified by brandings or lack of legal papers
8. plantation owners used bounty hunters/bloodhounds to track down runaway slaves

Section 2, Part D, Changing Britain, 1760-1900

33. *Candidates can be credited in a number of ways* **up to a maximum of 5 marks.**

Candidates must make an overall judgement about how fully the source explains the events. **1 mark** may be given for each valid point interpreted from the source or each valid point of significant omission provided. The candidate can achieve **up to 3 marks** for their interpretation of the parts of the source they consider are relevant in terms of the proposed question where there is also at least one point of significant omission identified to imply a judgement has been made about the limitations of the source. For full marks to be given each point needs to be discretely mentioned in terms of the question.

A maximum of 2 marks may be given for answers which refer only to the source.

Possible points which may be identified in the source include:

1. spinning improved by the invention of the Spinning Jenny/could spin eight threads at once
2. Arkwright's Water Frame used water power and made much better thread than the Spinning Jenny
3. steam engine was easy to use in factories
4. steam engine meant that factories did not have to be built near fast-running water for power supply

Possible points of significant omission may include:

1. Crompton's Mule combined ideas of Spinning Jenny and Water Frame/made high quality thread
2. Arkwright developed Carding Engine in 1770s
3. flax spinner developed in 1780s
4. weaving greatly improved by invention of the Power Loom (in 1785)
5. Power Loom now meant that weaving as well as spinning could be done in factories.
6. many handloom weavers were made unemployed when weaving was mechanised/wages of workers fell
7. machine/cylinder printing used to print patterns on to finished cloth
8. technological inventions meant that one person or even a child could now do the work of many people
9. technology meant that there were huge numbers of textile mills built in Britain

34. *Candidates can be credited in a number of ways **up to a maximum of 5 marks.***

They may take different perspectives on the events and may describe a variety of different aspects of the events.

1 mark should be given for each accurate relevant key point of knowledge. **A second mark** should be given for each point that is developed, up to a maximum of **5 marks.** Candidates may achieve full marks by providing five straightforward points, by making three developed points, or a combination of these.

Possible points of knowledge may include:

1. young children worked as trappers/opening and closing trap doors (to help circulate air around the mine)
2. women and teenagers worked as putters/drawers/pushing or pulling carts of coal along
3. dangerous as carts could run over fingers/toes/knock workers over
4. women worked as bearers/carried coal to the surface in baskets on their backs
5. dangerous as ladders slippery/coal could fall out of baskets/baskets very heavy
6. men worked as hewers cutting coal by hand with picks and shovels
7. danger of cave-ins
8. danger of flooding
9. danger of explosions (explosive gasses/fire damp)
10. danger of suffocation (suffocating gasses/choke damp)
11. lack of adequate ventilation
12. risks of falls down the shaft
13. safety lamps were available, but lighting was poor
14. long working hours
15. it was very hot in the mines

35. *Candidates can be credited in a number of ways **up to a maximum of 5 marks.***

Candidates must make a judgement about the usefulness of the source and support this by making evaluative comments on identified aspects of the source.

1 mark should be given for each relevant comment made, **up to a maximum of 5 marks in total.**

A maximum of 4 marks can be given for evaluative comments relating to the author, type of source, purpose and timing.

A maximum of 2 marks may be given for comments relating to the content of the source.

A maximum of 2 marks may be given for comments relating to points of significant omission.

Examples of aspects of the source and relevant comments:

Aspect of the source	Possible comment
Author: Railway inspector	Useful as eyewitness experience of working on the railways
Type of Source: Book	Useful because it will have been well researched/based on expert knowledge
Purpose: To inform readers of changes in railway travel	Useful as it is balanced/an honest personal reflection
Timing: 1870	Useful because it was written at the time of improvements in railway travel

Content	Possible comment
Third-class carriages were often little different from basic cattle trucks	Useful as it is accurate, third class carriages were little more than boxes.
For a considerable time they were completely open and had no seats	Useful as it is accurate/third-class carriages were open/had no roof
First and second class carriages were covered and had seating/the luggage of the passengers was packed on top of the carriages	Useful as it is accurate/second and first-class carriages did have roofs/luggage was stored on top

Possible points of significant omission may include:

1. carriages modelled on stage-coaches
2. third-class carriages were covered by law after the 1844 Railway Act
3. parliamentary trains/cheap fares introduced after the 1844 Railway Act
4. later corridors added to trains
5. later additions included sleeping and buffet cars
6. railway travel considerably cheaper/more comfortable than road travel
7. platforms made train travel safer
8. continuous brakes/brakes on carriages made train travel safer
9. improved signalling made train travel safer
10. as railway network developed it was possible to travel to nearly every town or city by train/made leisure trips/holidays easier
11. rail travel faster than other forms of transport

36. *Candidates can be credited in a number of ways **up to a maximum of 5 marks.***

Candidates must show a causal relationship between events.

Up to a **maximum of 5 marks in total, 1 mark** should be given for each accurate, relevant reason, and a **second mark** should be given for reasons that are developed. Candidates may achieve full marks by providing five straightforward reasons, three developed reasons, or a combination of these.

Possible reasons may include:
1. immunisation and vaccination campaigns led to decline of killer diseases such as smallpox/made compulsory 1853
2. anaesthetics improved surgical survival rates
3. antiseptics reduced deaths from infection
4. more fresh food was available due to railways so diet improved/ people more resistant to disease
5. improved working conditions led to fewer accidents
6. Public Health Acts gave local authorities the powers to improve social conditions
7. clean water supplies meant the eradication of water borne diseases e.g. Cholera
8. new reservoirs built in the countryside to supply large towns/cities meant improved hygiene
9. town councils took responsibility for piping fresh water supplies which enabled people to keep clean
10. cleaner streets reduced the spread of vermin
11. improved sewerage systems/proper drainage reduced spread of germs/diseases
12. impact of Housing Acts/destruction of slum properties provided better standards of housing so reducing overcrowding and the spread of disease
13. flushing toilets improved sanitation
14. more hospitals helped to treat more people/reduce spread of disease
15. wash houses and public baths introduced in 1878 which improved personal hygiene
16. cheaper soap available improving hygiene
17. cheap cotton clothing was easier to wash which improved personal hygiene
18. improved food standards reduced illness caused by adulterated food
19. by 1900 milk could be sterilised which reduced risk of illness caused by contaminated milk

Section 2, Part E, The Making of Modern Britain, 1880-1951

37. *Candidates can be credited in a number of ways up to a maximum of 5 marks.*

They may take different perspectives on the events and may describe a variety of different aspects of the events.

1 mark should be given for each accurate relevant key point of knowledge. **A second** mark should be given for each point that is developed, up to a maximum of **5 marks.** Candidates may achieve full marks by providing five straightforward points, by making three developed points, or a combination of these.

Possible points of knowledge may include:
1. School Medical Inspections were introduced in 1907
2. local councils received grants to provide medical treatment for the poor (school clinics were introduced in 1912)
3. Liberals introduced national insurance for sickness/ National Insurance Act (Part 1)
4. contributory scheme/workers, employers and state paid into the scheme
5. government tried to sell the scheme with the slogan '9d for 4d'
6. compulsory for all workers who earned under £160 per year
7. contributions were recorded by stamps on cards

8. insured workers received benefits when they were off sick (10 shillings per week for 26 weeks/5 shillings a week after that until fit to return to work)
9. free medical treatment and medicine for insured workers
10. sanatorium treatment for those suffering from TB
11. National Insurance covered wage-earners, but not their families
12. (Workmen's Compensation Act) provided compensation for workers injured or made ill through work
13. workers entitled to half of their salary until they were fit to return to work

38. *Candidates can be credited in a number of ways **up to a maximum of 5 marks**.*

Candidates must make a judgement about the usefulness of the source and support this by making evaluative comments on identified aspects of the source.

1 mark should be given for each relevant comment made, up to a **maximum of 5 marks in total.**

A maximum of **4 marks** can be given for evaluative comments relating to the author, type of source, purpose and timing.

A maximum of **2 marks** may be given for comments relating to the content of the source.

A maximum of **2 marks** may be given for comments relating to points of significant omission.

Examples of aspects of the source and relevant comments:

Aspect of the source	Possible comment
Author: Book based on author's own life/autobiographical	Useful as eyewitness account
Type of Source: Book	Useful because it will have been well researched/based on personal experience
Purpose: To inform readers of the benefits of pensions	Useful as it is an honest personal reflection
Timing: Published in 1939, over 30 years after the events it describes	Less useful as details may have been forgotten/author may selectively remember the facts or useful because it has the benefit of hindsight

Content	Possible comment
Pensions transformed the life of the old	Useful as it is accurate that pensions did make a real difference to many/Less useful as an exaggeration. Pensions helped those who were entitled, but limited.
Pensioners were relieved of anxiety and were suddenly rich	Useful as it is accurate that pensions did relieve anxiety for many of the elderly poor/ Less useful as exaggeration Pension amount was very small.
Pensioners were grateful/ tears of gratitude/God bless that Lord George	Useful as it is accurate that pensioners were grateful/ pensions helped to keep some of the elderly poor out of the workhouse

Possible points of significant omission may include:

1. amount of pensions – between 1s and 5s on a sliding scale/7s 6d for a married couple
2. who was entitled to pensions – over 70s
3. pensions were non-contributory
4. collection at the Post Office removed the stigma of Poor Relief
5. exemptions – those who had been in prison within last ten years/those who had habitually failed to work
6. pensions were not intended to provide subsistence
7. pensions did keep many of the elderly poor out of the workhouse

39. *Candidates can be credited in a number of ways up to a maximum of 5 marks.*

Candidates must make an overall judgement about how fully the source explains the events. **1 mark** may be given for each valid point interpreted from the source or each valid point of significant omission provided. The candidate can achieve **up to 3 marks** for their interpretation of the parts of the source they consider are relevant in terms of the proposed question where there is also at least one point of significant omission identified to imply a judgement has been made about the limitations of the source. For full marks to be given each point needs to be discretely mentioned in terms of the question.

A maximum of 2 marks may be given for answers which refer only to the source.

Possible points which may be identified in the source include:

1. tackling one of the five giants wouldn't do much good; the government would have to tackle them all
2. there should be a welfare system that would look after people from the 'cradle to the grave'
3. there should be a comprehensive social security system, providing benefits for the unemployed, the sick, the elderly and widows
4. advised the government to adopt a policy of full employment

Possible points of significant omission may include:

1. explanation of what the 'five giants' were
2. National Health Service to tackle disease
3. family allowances to tackle poverty/want
4. System of national insurance to tackle want
5. standard weekly national insurance payments were to be made by all workers
6. payments to be made at a standard rate, without a means test
7. unemployment benefit to be paid for an indefinite period
8. Reform of the education system/raising of school leaving age to tackle ignorance
9. House-building/slum clearance to tackle squalor

40. *Candidates can be credited in a number of ways up to a maximum of 5 marks.*

Candidates must show a causal relationship between events.

Up to a **maximum of 5 marks in total, 1 mark** should be given for each accurate, relevant reason, and a second mark should be given for reasons that are developed. Candidates may achieve full marks by providing five straightforward reasons, three developed reasons, or a combination of these.

Possible reasons may include:

1. by time of 1951 election still a shortage of (750,000) homes/(750,000) fewer houses than households

2. massive destruction/bombing of Second World War had created a huge housing shortage
3. great deal of slum housing still existed
4. post-war marriage and baby boom added to pressure for housing
5. shortage of building materials
6. shortage of skilled labour
7. Bevan given Ministry of Health and Housing – too much/should have been a separate Ministry of Housing
8. Bevan emphasised quality over quantity/insisted on a high standard for council houses
9. government faced financial restraints/had to prioritise
10. government faced many social problems/scale of problem meant that it would take more than one term to tackle
11. provision of prefab houses as a temporary solution to the housing shortage
12. New towns planned but not built by 1951 (12 planned in Scotland, only 4 built)
13. New towns isolated/lacked proper amenities/destroyed previous communities

Section 3, Part A, The Cross and the Crescent; the Crusades, 1071-1192

41. *Candidates can be credited in a number of ways up to a maximum of 8 marks.*

Candidates must use knowledge to present a balanced assessment of the influence of different possible factors and come to a reasoned conclusion. Up to 5 marks are allocated for relevant points of knowledge used to address the question. **1 mark** should be given for each relevant, factual key point of knowledge used to support a factor. **If only one factor is presented, a maximum of 3 marks should be given for relevant points of knowledge.**

Possible factors may include:	Relevant, factual, key points of knowledge to support this factor may include:
Religious	1. the Pope stated that it was the duty of every Christian to help their brothers in the east 2. wanted to protect Christian churches and shrines which had been damaged or destroyed 3. wanted to re-open pilgrim routes to Jerusalem
Political	4. wanted to heal the schism/unite the Christian Churches 5. wanted to increase his own power/ become head of a united Church 6. wanted to demonstrate power of the Church to European rulers eg Dispute with the Holy Roman Emperor
Economic	7. wanted to re-open trade routes with the east 8. wanted to make money from pilgrims again

| Threat of Islam | 9. wanted to stop the spread of Islam in Europe eg Muslims had already conquered part of Spain |
| Other factors | 10. Any other valid point |

Up to 3 marks should be given for presenting the answer in a structured way, leading to a conclusion which addresses the question, as follows:

1 mark for the answer being presented in a structured way, with knowledge being organised in support of different factors.

1 mark given for a conclusion with a valid judgement or overall summary.

1 mark given for a reason being provided in support of the judgement.

42. *Candidates can be credited in a number of ways* **up to a maximum of 6 marks**.

Candidates must show a causal relationship between events.

Up to a **maximum of 6 marks in total, 1 mark** should be given for each accurate, relevant reason, and a **second mark** should be given for reasons that are developed. Candidates may achieve full marks by providing six straightforward reasons, three developed reasons, or a combination of these.

Possible reasons may include:
1. Crusaders were divided eg Guy de Lusignan and Reynald of Chatillon hated each other
2. Crusaders had different ideologies towards the Muslims eg the Hawks and the Doves
3. death of Baldwin IV meant that Jerusalem did not have a strong ruler
4. King Guy made a tactical error by leaving Jerusalem with the Crusader army
5. Crusaders were defeated at the Battle of Hattin
6. Crusaders lacked resources to defend Jerusalem once army defeated
7. Muslims were united under Saladin's leadership making them stronger
8. Saladin's army outnumbered the Crusaders.

43. *Candidates can be credited in a number of ways* **up to a maximum of 6 marks**.

Candidates must make a judgement about the usefulness of the source and support this by making evaluative comments on identified aspects of the source.

1 mark should be given for each relevant comment made, up to a **maximum of 6 marks in total.**
- A maximum of 4 marks can be given for evaluative comments relating to the author, type of source, purpose and timing.
- A maximum of 2 marks may be given for comments relating to the content of the source.
- A maximum of 2 marks may be given for comments relating to points of significant omission.

Examples of aspects of the source and relevant comments:

Aspect of the source	Possible comment
Author: Crusader	Useful because he was an eyewitness to events
Type of Source: Chronicle	Useful because it was a well-researched record of events

| **Purpose:** To persuade people that Richard's actions were justifiable | Less useful as clearly biased/author may have exaggerated when describing Saladin's behaviour |
| **Timing:** 1191 | Useful because it was at the time of the Third Crusade |

Content	Possible comment
Saladin did not pay the ransom agreed for the Muslim hostages/did not return the True Cross to the Crusaders	Useful because it provides accurate details of the negotiations between Richard and Saladin
Saladin attempted to trick King Richard, sending him gifts and treasures/he hoped that Richard would release the Muslims for free	Less useful because it may have exaggerated Saladin's responsibility for the massacre
The next morning the king ordered the Muslims to be led out of the city and beheaded	Useful because it provides accurate details of the massacre

Possible points of significant omission may include:
1. nearly 3,000 Muslim men, women and children were killed
2. some Muslims were beaten
3. some Muslims were killed with an axe or a lance

Section 3, Part B, "Tea and Freedom": the American Revolution, 1774-83

44. *Candidates can be credited in a number of ways* **up to a maximum of 6 marks**.

Candidates must show a causal relationship between events.

Up to a **maximum of 6 marks in total, 1 mark** should be given for each accurate, relevant reason, and a **second mark** should be given for reasons that are developed. Candidates may achieve full marks by providing five straightforward reasons, three developed reasons, or a combination of these.

Possible reasons may include:
1. the colonists were unhappy with the imposition of laws and taxes which were seen as unjust
2. the passing of the Stamp Act and Townshend Act in 1760s had been very unpopular measures
3. the colonists resented being taxed without representation
4. events such as the Boston Massacre and the Boston Tea Party led to an increase in anti-British feeling among colonists
5. boycott of British goods added to tension
6. the continuing presence of British soldiers in the colonies had caused tension
7. the colonists were further angered by the passing of The Quartering Act
8. some colonists were frustrated that the British were stopping them from moving west
9. some colonists felt that the policies of the British government were damaging trade
10. the First Continental Congress in 1774 had created a feeling of anti – British unity among the leaders of the colonies

11. the colonists started to establish their own armed forces following the First Continental Congress in 1774/ Continental Congress declared to be traitors by British Crown meant no going back

12. clashes between British forces and colonists at Lexington and Concord in 1775 led to the outbreak of war

45. *Candidates can be credited in a number of ways up to a maximum of 6 marks.*

Candidates must make a judgement about the usefulness of the source and support this by making evaluative comments on identified aspects of the source.

1 mark should be given for each relevant comment made, up to a **maximum of 6 marks in total.**

A maximum of **4 marks** can be given for evaluative comments relating to the author, type of source, purpose and timing.

A maximum of **2 marks** may be given for comments relating to the content of the source.

A maximum of **2 marks** may be given for comments relating to points of significant omission.

Examples of aspects of the source and relevant comments:

Aspect of the source	Possible comment
Author: Army surgeon	Useful as he is an eyewitness
Type of Source: A diary	Useful as it is likely to give an honest/ accurate description of the condition of the American army/less useful as it only gives information about the American army.
Purpose: To record the difficulties being faced by the soldiers during the winter of 1777	Useful because it provides a detailed/ balanced description of the conditions
Timing: 1777	Useful as it is taken from 1777, during the course of the war

Content	Possible comment
The army now begins to grow tired of the continued difficulties they have faced in this winter campaign.	Useful as it gives an accurate and detailed insight into difficulties faced by the colonial army
Poor food, tough living conditions, cold weather, sickness, fatigue, nasty clothes, nasty cookery, the Devil's in it!	Useful as it gives accurate and detailed information on the conditions faced by the American army.
Our men still show a great spirit and morale that is unexpected from such young soldiers.	Useful as it gives an accurate insight into why the Americans were eventually able to win the war.

Possible points of significant omission may include:

1. the American army had suffered a series of setbacks during the winter of 1777 – 1778

2. the Americans had difficulty holding on to their recruits and many would return home after a short period of service

3. conditions were also very difficult for the British as it was difficult to supply an army that was fighting so far from home

4. American soldiers were acclimatised, British found climate difficult

46. *Candidates can be credited in a number of ways up to a maximum of 8 marks.*

Candidates must use knowledge to present a balanced assessment of the influence of different possible factors and come to a reasoned conclusion. **Up to 5 marks** are allocated for relevant points of knowledge used to address the question. **1 mark** should be given for each relevant, factual key point of knowledge used to support a factor. **If only one factor is presented, a maximum of 3 marks should be given for relevant points of knowledge.**

Possible factors may include:	Relevant, factual, key points of knowledge to support this factor may include:
Foreign intervention	1. France provided the colonists with finance 2. France provided the colonists with military assistance – soldiers, gunpowder etc 3. the French attacked British colonies in the Caribbean and elsewhere 4. the French harassed British shipping in the Atlantic 5. Foreign intervention caused Britain to lose its control of the seas 6. Foreign intervention made it more difficult for Britain to reinforce and supply its forces in America 7. Spain distracted Britain by attacking Gibraltar 8. a Franco-Spanish force threatened Britain with invasion in 1779
American strengths:	9. George Washington held the American army together and emerged as a great leader 10. the colonists had greater forces/ American colonies were relatively wealthy and could support an army 11. the colonists were able to call on minutemen when required 12. the colonists knew the terrain better/used to the climate 13. the colonists often used guerrilla tactics against the British

British weakness:	14. the British were poorly led
	15. the British made tactical errors eg Yorktown, Saratoga
	16. the British army was small in number/ British army had a large empire to protect as well as fight the colonists and had to rely on mercenary forces
	17. the British soldiers were not properly trained/ equipped to cope with terrain and conditions
	18. diseases like smallpox affected British much more than Americans.
	19. the British never had a clear strategy for winning the war
	20. the British were weakened by their reliance on supplies from overseas
	21. the British Parliament was not united behind the war effort
	22. unlike Americans British had no allies to assist them
Other factors	23. Any other valid point

Up to 3 marks should be given for presenting the answer in a structured way, leading to a conclusion which addresses the question, as follows:

1 mark for the answer being presented in a structured way, with knowledge being organised in support of different factors.

1 mark given for a conclusion with a valid judgement or overall summary.

1 mark given for a reason being provided in support of the judgement.

Section 3, Part C, USA 1850-1880

47. *Candidates can be credited in a number of ways* **up to a maximum of 6 marks.**

Candidates must show a causal relationship between events.

Up to a **maximum of 6 marks in total**, **1 mark** should be given for each accurate, relevant reason, and a **second mark** should be given for reasons that are developed. Candidates may achieve full marks by providing six straightforward reasons, three developed reasons, or a combination of these.

Possible reasons may include:
1. the migration of the buffalo was disturbed (homesteaders/railways)
2. settlers were killing the buffalo
3. settlers spread disease such as cholera among tribes
4. Native Americans were being forced off their traditional/sacred lands

5. Native Americans were signing treaties with the US Government (such as Laramie and Medicine Creek) which were broken
6. Native Americans felt lied to by the US Government
7. Native Americans felt cheated – food was of poor quality or money promised was not paid
8. army attacks such as Sand Creek or Washita River continued to cause resentment
9. Native Americans were being forced to live on reservations which they resented

48. *Candidates can be credited in a number of ways* **up to a maximum of 8 marks.**

Candidates must use knowledge to present a balanced assessment of the influence of different possible factors and come to a reasoned conclusion. **Up to 5 marks** are allocated for relevant points of knowledge used to address the question. **1 mark** should be given for each relevant, factual key point of knowledge used to support a factor. **If only one factor is presented, a maximum of 3 marks should be given for relevant points of knowledge.**

Possible factors may include:	Relevant, factual, key points of knowledge to support this factor may include:
Lincoln's election	1. southerners feared he would abolish slavery
	2. some Southern States had not carried his name on ballot papers which angered Republican supporters in the North
	3. south Carolina seceded from Union as a result of Lincoln's election/other states followed
	4. rise of the Republican party seen as representing Northern interests which upset the South
Issue of Slavery	5. South feared economic impact of abolition e.g. loss of cheap labour
	6. abolitionist activities caused tension between North and South ('Uncle Tom's Cabin'/ Underground Railroad)
	7. compromise of 1850 had allowed California to be a free state/it also saw the introduction of Fugitive Slave Law – this caused more hostility in the North
	8. raid on Harpers Ferry by John Brown had worried Southern States
	9. Dred Scott case concerned many anti-slavery supporters, it allowed the existence of slavery in the Northern States
	10. Kansas Nebraska Act allowed popular sovereignty. This led to violence between pro and anti-slavery supporters which heightened tension

Attack on Fort Sumter	11. the fort was besieged by Confederate troops
	12. food supply to the fort was cut off
	13. the commander of the fort was warned of an attack
	14. the fort was attacked by Confederate troops
Other factors	15. Any other valid point

49. *Candidates can be credited in a number of ways up to a maximum of 6 marks.*

Candidates must make a judgement about the usefulness of the source and support this by making evaluative comments on identified aspects of the source.

1 mark should be given for each relevant comment made, up to a **maximum of 6 marks in total.**

A maximum of **4 marks** can be given for evaluative comments relating to the author, type of source, purpose and timing.

A maximum of **2 marks** may be given for comments relating to the content of the source.

A maximum of **2 marks** may be given for comments relating to points of significant omission.

Examples of aspects of the source and relevant comments:

Aspect of the source	Possible comment
Author: Officer of the Freedman's Bureau	Useful because he was an eyewitness/expertise
Type of Source: Report	Useful because reports have usually been well researched
Purpose: To inform	Useful because it provides a detailed account of the effects of Reconstruction/less useful because it is one-sided
Timing: 1866.	Useful because it was written shortly after the end of the Civil War

Content	Possible comment
The freed slaves in Texas have been terrorised by attacks from the desperate men of the local area.	Useful as it is accurate because many attacks did take place on freed slaves after 1865
The murderers dislike the fact that they no longer have control over their former slaves.	Useful as it is accurate because attacks by Southern Whites were an attempt to keep control over the freed slaves
Many of the freedmen are unhappy with their freedom and would prefer to be slaves as it offered them some protection	Useful as it is accurate because some freed slaves did not see a major improvement in their lives after 1865

Possible points of significant omission may include:
1. no mention of the work of the Freedman's Bureau – education/advice
2. no mention of the changes that took place involving freed slaves eg ability to vote
3. led to other ways to keep control over freed slaves e.g. Jim Crow Laws

4. the violence of the Ku Klux Klan towards the freed slaves e.g. lynchings
5. sharecropping was disadvantageous to blacks in the South

Section 3, Part D, Hitler and Nazi Germany, 1919–1939

50. *Candidates can be credited in a number of ways up to a maximum of 6 marks.*

Candidates must show a causal relationship between events.

Up to a **maximum of 6 marks in total, 1 mark** should be given for each accurate, relevant reason, and a **second mark** should be given for reasons that are developed. Candidates may achieve full marks by providing six straightforward reasons, three developed reasons, or a combination of these.

Possible reasons may include:
1. some people felt coalition governments were weak/parties seemed too busy arguing to solve the country's problems
2. many Germans didn't like democracy/longed for the return of the strong leadership of the Kaiser
3. frequent changes of government made it difficult to follow consistent policies
4. appeared to be unable to solve the country's economic problems such as war debt/hyper-inflation
5. six governments in six years in the mid-1920s created an appearance of a weak government
6. it seemed incapable of maintaining order/stopping frequent outbreaks of violence/political assassinations
7. criticised by nationalists for giving in to foreign powers
8. criticised for allowing the French invasion of the Ruhr
9. associated with Germany's defeat in the First World War
10. blamed the Weimar Government for accepting the Treaty of Versailles

51. *Candidates can be credited in a number of ways up to a maximum of 8 marks.*

Candidates must use knowledge to present a balanced assessment of the influence of different possible factors and come to a reasoned conclusion. **Up to 5 marks** are allocated for relevant points of knowledge used to address the question. **1 mark** should be given for each relevant, factual key point of knowledge used to support a factor. **If only one factor is presented, a maximum of 3 marks should be given for relevant points of knowledge.**

Possible factors may include:	Relevant, factual, key points of knowledge to support this factor may include:
Social policies	1. Nazi youth policy encouraged loyalty 2. Nazi education policy brainwashed the young 3. Nazi policy towards the Jews – first isolate, then persecute and finally destroy created a fear of similar treatment 4. Nazi family policy – Kinder, Kirche, Kuche won support/ from tranditionalists 5. subsidised holidays/leisure activities of the Kraft durch Freude programme were popular 6. a Concordat with the Catholic Church was reached/a Reichsbishop was appointed as head of the Protestant churches which limited possible opposition from the churches 7. creation of the national community (*Volksgemeinschaft*) created a sense of national purpose
Economic policies	8. Nazi economic policy/ German labour Front attempted to deal with economic ills affecting Germany, especially unemployment and won support 9. Nazis began a massive programme of public works; work of Hjalmar Schacht providing jobs, which won support
Propaganda	10. use of Nuremburg Rallies inspired loyalty 11. use of radio ensued that the Nazi message was widely spread 12. Cult of the Leader: the Hitler Myth ensured that Hitler remained personally very popular 13. use of the Cinema: Triumph of the Will etc spread the Nazi message widely 14. Nazi propaganda effectively spread the Nazi message

Establishment of totalitarian state	15. political parties outlawed; non-Nazi members of the civil service were dismissed, crushing possible opposition 16. Nazis never quite able to silence opposition to the regime 17. speed of takeover of power and ruthlessness of the regime made opposition largely ineffective 18. anti-Nazi judges were dismissed and replaced with those favourable to the Nazis ensuring the support of the legal system 19. Acts Hostile to the National Community (1935) – all-embracing law which allowed the Nazis to persecute opponents in a 'legal' way
Fear and state terrorism	20. the use of fear/terror through the Nazi police state; role of the Gestapo made opposition unlikely/ impossible 21. the use of the SS created a climate of fear and enforced loyalty 22. a) concentration camps were set up
Crushing of opposition	22. b) opponents liable to severe penalties, as were their families which added to the climate of fear and enforced loyalty 23. opponents never able to establish a single organisation to channel their resistance – role of the Gestapo, paid informers 24. opposition lacked cohesion and a national leader; also lacked armed supporters 25. lack of cooperation between socialists and communists
Other factors	26. any other relevant points

Up to 3 marks should be given for presenting the answer in a structured way, leading to a conclusion which addresses the question, as follows:

1 mark for the answer being presented in a structured way, with knowledge being organised in support of different factors.

1 mark given for a conclusion with a valid judgement or overall summary.

1 mark given for a reason being provided in support of the judgement.

52. *Candidates can be credited in a number of ways up to a maximum of 6 marks.*

Candidates must make a judgement about the usefulness of the source and support this by making evaluative comments on identified aspects of the source.

1 mark should be given for each relevant comment made, up to a **maximum of 6 marks in total**.
- A maximum of **4 marks** can be given for evaluative comments relating to the author, type of source, purpose and timing.
- A maximum of **2 marks** may be given for comments relating to the content of the source.
- A maximum of **2 marks** may be given for comments relating to points of significant omission.

Examples of aspects of the source and relevant comments:

Aspect of the source	Possible comment
Author Historian	Useful because author is an expert who will have researched the topic
Type of Source Textbook	Useful because the information would be informative/factual
Purpose To inform	Useful because the historian provides a detailed account of the discrimination faced by Jews in Nazi Germany
Timing 2013	Useful because it is a secondary source with the benefit of hindsight

Content	Possible comment
On buses and park benches, Jews had to sit on seats marked for them.	Useful because it gives accurate and relevant examples of how Jews were segregated
Jewish children were ridiculed by teachers	Useful because it gives accurate and relevant examples of how Jewish children were discriminated against in schools
Bullying of Jews in the playground by other pupils went unpunished.	Useful because it gives accurate and relevant examples of how Jewish children were intimidated in schools

Possible points of significant omission may include:
1. violence against Jews (eg Kristallnacht)
2. from 1933 Anti-Jewish Laws/boycott of Jewish shops/doctors/lawyers/ lecturers dismissed
3. Law for the Restoration of the Professional Civil Service banned Jews from government jobs
4. 1935: Jews forbidden to join the Army; restrictions on opportunities for employment/education; Civil Liberties restricted; Anti-Jewish signs displayed in shops/restaurants/cafes
5. 1935 Nuremburg Laws for the Protection of German Blood and Honour: ban on marriage between Jews and non-Jews
6. sexual relations between Jews and non-Jews outside marriage – criminal/prison offence
7. 1935 National Law of Citizenship meant Jews lost citizenship – no vote/ rights
8. 1938 only Aryan doctors were allowed to treat Aryan patients

Section 3, Part E, Red Flag: Lenin and the Russian Revolution, 1894-1921

53. *Candidates can be credited in a number of ways up to a maximum of 6 marks.*

Candidates must show a causal relationship between events.

Up to a **maximum of 6 marks in total, 1 mark** should be given for each accurate, relevant reason, and a **second mark** should be given for reasons that are developed. Candidates may achieve full marks by providing six straightforward reasons, three developed reasons, or a combination of these.

Possible reasons may include:
1. the Fundamental Laws gave the Tsar autocratic power
2. the nobility controlled the peasants on their estates
3. Civil Service enforced the Tsar's decisions
4. the Secret Police (Okhrana) arrested opponents and exiled them to Siberia
5. the Okhrana had spies everywhere listening for criticism of the Tsar
6. censorship used to restrict opposition
7. army used to crush opponents
8. Orthodox Church taught people to obey Tsar
9. Government Minister was put in charge of church and he passed on the Tsar's instructions to the Bishops

54. *Candidates can be credited in a number of ways up to a maximum of 8 marks.*

Candidates must use knowledge to present a balanced assessment of the influence of different possible factors and come to a reasoned conclusion. **Up to 5 marks** are allocated for relevant points of knowledge used to address the question. **1 mark** should be given for each relevant, factual key point of knowledge used to support a factor. **If only one factor is presented, a maximum of 3 marks should be given for relevant points of knowledge.**

Possible factors may include:	Relevant, factual, key points of knowledge to support this factor may include:
Problems caused by the First World War	1. defeats in 1914 at Tannenburg/Masurian Lakes reduced public confidence 2. Tsar became Commander in Chief so could now be blamed for defeats 3. Tsar blamed for the shortages of weapons 4. high casualty rates made the Tsar even more unpopular 5. shortages of food/fuel in Petrograd led to widespread discontent 6. rising prices due to inflation/food prices were rising faster than wages and this upset the Russian people 7. growing political opposition/due to the continuation of the war

Dislike of the Royal Family	8. Tsarina was seen as a German spy who could not be trusted 9. she replaced ministers regularly who disagreed with her which caused confusion – "Ministerial Leapfrog"
Rasputin	10. people resented his sinister influence over the Tsarina 11. brought his friends into important positions which was not popular 12. seen as drunkard and people disapproved of his corrupt influence
Other factors	13. Any other relevant point

Up to 3 marks should be given for presenting the answer in a structured way, leading to a conclusion which addresses the question, as follows:

1 mark for the answer being presented in a structured way, with knowledge being organised in support of different factors.

1 mark given for a conclusion with a valid judgement or overall summary.

1 mark given for a reason being provided in support of the judgement.

55. *Candidates can be credited in a number of ways* **up to a maximum of 6 marks.**

Candidates must make a judgement about the usefulness of the source and support this by making evaluative comments on identified aspects of the source.

1 mark should be given for each relevant comment made, up to a **maximum of 6 marks in total.**

- A maximum of **4 marks** can be given for evaluative comments relating to the author, type of source, purpose and timing.
- A maximum of **2 marks** may be given for comments relating to the content of the source.
- A maximum of **2 marks** may be given for comments relating to points of significant omission.

Examples of aspects of the source and relevant comments:

Aspect of the source	Possible comment
Author: British Ambassador	Useful because he was an eyewitness
Type of Source: Diary	Useful because it will usually give an honest opinion
Purpose: To record	Less useful because it gives his biased opinions on the Russian Government
Timing: 24 October 1917	Useful because it is from the time of the Bolshevik seizure of power

Content	Possible comment
I heard this morning that the Bolsheviks would overthrow the Government in the course of the next few days because they had captured enough weapons	Useful because it accurately shows the Bolsheviks were well armed
I was not convinced that the Government had enough force behind them to deal with the situation	Useful because it accurately shows how weak the Government was
I told him that I could not understand how the Government could allow Trotsky to go on encouraging the population to murder and steal	Useful because it accurately shows that the Government had little control of Petrograd

Possible points of significant omission may include:
1. no mention of the reasons why Provisional Government was unpopular eg continuing the war, land problem, high food price and shortages
2. Bolshevik promises of peace, bread and land gained support
3. no mention of Military Revolutionary Council or its influence over army units
4. Red Guards provided Bolsheviks with a disciplined army
5. no mention of the lack of military support for the Government

Section 3, Part F, Mussolini and Fascist Italy, 1919-1939

56. *Candidates can be credited in a number of ways* **up to a maximum of 8 marks.**

Candidates must use knowledge to present a balanced assessment of the influence of different possible factors and come to a reasoned conclusion. **Up to 5 marks** are allocated for relevant points of knowledge used to address the question. **1 mark** should be given for each relevant, factual key point of knowledge used to support a factor. **If only one factor is presented, a maximum of 3 marks should be given for relevant points of knowledge.**

Possible factors may include:	Relevant, factual, key points of knowledge to support this factor may include:
Widespread appeal	1. by 1921 fascism was anti-communist/ anti-trade union/ anti-socialist/ nationalist and thus became attractive to the middle and upper classes 2. Fascism became conservative/appealed to family values/supported church/ monarchy 3. the Fascists were able to exploit the anger of various different sections of Italian society at the post war peace settlement eg the failure to give Fiume to the Italians
The personal appeal of Mussolini	4. Mussolini attracted many with his oratory 5. Fascist propaganda presented Mussolini as a strong man who could save Italy 6. Mussolini was able to exploit his own humble background to present himself as a man of the people

Fascist opponents were weak	7. parliamentary government was weak – informal 'liberal' coalitions 8. Mussolini's political opponents were divided and this weakened them 9. the King gave in to Fascist pressure during the March on Rome/he failed to call Mussolini's bluff
Use of violence	10. Mussolini's Blackshirts terrorised the cities and provinces 11. destruction of opposition press severely weakened them 12. the murder of Matteotti intimidated potential opponents
Other factors	13. Any other valid reason

Up to 3 marks should be given for presenting the answer in a structured way, leading to a conclusion which addresses the question, as follows:

1 mark for the answer being presented in a structured way, with knowledge being organised in support of different factors.

1 mark given for a conclusion with a valid judgement or overall summary.

1 mark given for a reason being provided in support of the judgement.

57. *Candidates can be credited in a number of ways **up to a maximum of 6 marks.***

Candidates must make a judgement about the usefulness of the source and support this by making evaluative comments on identified aspects of the source.

1 mark should be given for each relevant comment made, up to **a maximum of 6 marks in total.**
- A maximum of **4 marks** can be given for evaluative comments relating to the author, type of source, purpose and timing.
- A maximum of **2 marks** may be given for comments relating to the content of the source.
- A maximum of **2 marks** may be given for comments relating to points of significant omission.

Examples of aspects of the source and relevant comments:

Aspect of the source	Possible comment
Author: Historian	Useful because he is well informed/an expert
Type of Source: Book	Useful because it will have been well researched
Purpose: To inform	Useful because it contains details of aspects of life in Fascist Italy
Timing: 2006	Useful because it will have been written with the benefit of hindsight

Content	Possible comment
The Battle for Grain began in 1925 and was a major attempt to promote Fascist power and national self-sufficiency	Useful because it is accurate, the Fascist regime constantly sought propaganda opportunities
The government tried to boost grain production by giving farmers grants so that they could buy tractors, fertiliser and any other machinery necessary for wheat production	Useful because it is accurate, the Fascists were willing to intervene directly in the economy when they felt this was necessary
Farmers were also guaranteed a high price for the grain they produced	Useful because it is accurate, the Fascists were willing to intervene directly in the economy when they felt this was necessary

Possible points of significant omission may include:
1. initially, under de Stefani, economic policy limited spending in order to control inflation.
2. the currency was revalued in the "battle for the lira."
3. tariffs were placed on many foreign imports.
4. corporations composed of workers, bosses and Fascist trade unions were set up in each sector of the economy.
5. public works schemes were used to build motorways.

58. *Candidates can be credited in a number of ways **up to a maximum of 6 marks.***

Candidates must show a causal relationship between events.

Up to a **maximum of 6 marks in total, 1 mark** should be given for each accurate, relevant reason, and a **second mark** should be given for reasons that are developed. Candidates may achieve full marks by providing six straightforward reasons, three developed reasons, or a combination of these.

Possible reasons may include:
1. many opponents of the regime were murdered which removed potential rivals
2. some opponents were sent to concentration camps which scared people
3. opponents were denied a platform for their views as political activity outside of the Fascist Party was banned
4. censorship made it difficult to oppose Mussolini
5. the banning of trade unions removed another potential source of opposition
6. opponents were spied upon by the Secret Police
7. the rewards given to loyal journalists and academics discouraged opposition
8. the Lateran Agreements neutralised opposition from the Catholic Church

Section 3, Context G, Free at Last? Civil Rights in the USA, 1918-1968

59. *Candidates can be credited in a number of ways **up to a maximum of 8 marks.***

Candidates must use knowledge to present a balanced assessment of the influence of different possible factors and come to a reasoned conclusion. **Up to 5 marks** are allocated for relevant points of knowledge used to address the question. **1 mark** should be given for each relevant, factual key point of knowledge used to support a factor. **If only one factor is presented, a maximum of 3 marks should be given for relevant points of knowledge.**

Possible factors may include:	Relevant, factual, key points of knowledge to support this factor may include:
Fear of white violence	1. lynching of black Americans was commonplace in the South 2. black Americans were beaten/crippled to punish them and to intimidate others 3. the Ku Klux Klan bombed churches, schools and other meeting places /burned crosses to intimidate black Americans 4. masked Klansmen marched through the streets of towns and cities carrying posters threatening black Americans with punishment and warning others to leave town 5. black American businesses were destroyed to ensure black Americans would not prosper
Segregation	6. Southern states enforced segregation of the races through Jim Crow laws 7. the Jim Crow laws affected all areas of life – education, entertainment, housing, travel, health, leisure, marriage, work 8. typically, facilities for blacks were far inferior to those for whites
Political Disenfranchisement	9. Southern states had restricted voting rights for blacks through literacy tests, poll taxes and Grandfather Clauses
Sharecropping	10. many blacks were poor sharecroppers heavily in debt to white landowners for farming equipment and seeds for planting 11. the boll weevil damaged crops throughout the South between 1910 and 1920 - as a result, there was less demand for agricultural workers, leaving many blacks unemployed

Employment Opportunities	12. in the South blacks suffered from discrimination in jobs and were only employed in low paid unskilled work. 13. during the First World War workers were in great demand in Northern factories and steel works. 14. agents from various industrial sectors arrived in the South, enticing black men and women to migrate North by paying their travel expenses. 15. wages in the Northern factories were typically double those received by most black workers in the South.
Other pull factors	16. publications (such as the Chicago Defender) published train schedules and lists of jobs to persuade Southern blacks to migrate North. 17. other publications (such as the Pittsburgh Courier and the Amsterdam News) published editorials and cartoons showing the promise of moving from the South to the North. 18. these promises included better education for children, the right to vote, access to various types of employment and improved housing conditions
Other factors	19. any other relevant points

Up to 3 marks should be given for presenting the answer in a structured way, leading to a conclusion which addresses the question, as follows:

1 mark for the answer being presented in a structured way, with knowledge being organised in support of different factors.

1 mark given for a conclusion with a valid judgement or overall summary.

1 mark given for a reason being provided in support of the judgement.

60. *Candidates can be credited in a number of ways **up to a maximum of 6 marks**.*

Candidates must show a causal relationship between events.

Up to a **maximum of 6 marks in total, 1 mark** should be given for each accurate, relevant reason, and a **second mark** should be given for reasons that are developed. Candidates may achieve full marks by providing six straightforward reasons, three developed reasons, or a combination of these.

Possible reasons may include:
1. it proved that blacks had economic power and could use it to end segregation/the bus company had no choice but to desegregate the buses as they were losing so much money
2. it gave other blacks the confidence and determination to campaign for civil rights/proved that non-violent protest could work (other bus boycotts followed in over 20 of the Southern states)
3. non-violence became a useful and popular tactic in the civil rights campaign
4. it generated a lot of publicity and support/funding for the Civil Rights Movement, particularly in the North
5. it led to a district court ruling that segregation on the buses in Montgomery was unconstitutional /this was later supported by the Supreme Court
6. it brought Martin Luther King to the forefront of the Civil Rights Movement
7. it led to the setting up of the Southern Christian Leadership Conference (SCLC) – which was to become involved in many of the most famous protests of the 1960s

61. *Candidates can be credited in a number of ways* **up to a maximum of 6 marks.**

Candidates must make a judgement about the usefulness of the source and support this by making evaluative comments on identified aspects of the source.

1 mark should be given for each relevant comment made, up to a **maximum of 6 marks in total.**
- A maximum of **4 marks** can be given for evaluative comments relating to the author, type of source, purpose and timing.
- A maximum of **2 marks** may be given for comments relating to the content of the source.
- A maximum of **2 marks** may be given for comments relating to points of significant omission.

Examples of aspects of the source and relevant comments:

Aspect of the source	Possible comment
Author: Malcolm X	More useful as it will give an insight to the beliefs of Malcom X at first hand
Type of Source: Speech	May be less useful as it may not include all of his beliefs/could be tailored to a particular audience
Purpose: To persuade	More useful as it will explain the beliefs of Malcolm X/ gives several reasons to support the Nation of Islam
Timing: December 1962	More useful as by this time Malcolm X had emerged as a leading public figure in the Black Power movement/less useful as does not reflect his later beliefs

Content	Possible comment
The teaching of the Honourable Elijah Muhammad is making our people, for the first time, proud to be black, and that is most important	More useful as it accurately reflects Malcom X's support for the Nation of Islam/ belief in the need for black Americans to celebrate their black heritage and culture
I just wanted to point out that whites are a race of devils	More useful as it accurately reflects Malcolm X's belief that whites were evil
If we separate then we have a chance for salvation	More useful as it accurately reflects Malcom X's belief in the need for black Americans to separate themselves from white Americans

Possible points of significant omission may include:
1. Malcolm X also disagreed with the methods of Martin Luther King - he criticised his non-violent tactics and argued that for black Americans "non-violence is another word for defenceless."
2. Malcolm X later renounced his support for Elijah Muhammad and the Nation of Islam
3. Malcolm X later adopted a more moderate view of white Americans

Section 3, Part H, Appeasement and the Road to War, 1918-1939

62. *Candidates can be credited in a number of ways* **up to a maximum of 6 marks.**

Candidates must show a causal relationship between events.

Up to a **maximum of 6 marks in total, 1 mark** should be given for each accurate, relevant reason, and a **second mark** should be given for reasons that are developed. Candidates may achieve full marks by providing six straightforward reasons, three developed reasons, or a combination of these.

Possible reasons may include:
1. Hitler wanted to restore German national pride
2. Hitler hated the Treaty of Versailles and was determined to break the military restrictions it imposed on Germany
3. the Treaty of Versailles was loathed by most Germans and Hitler believed that by rearming he could strengthen his support amongst the German people
4. Hitler was a militarist and believed in a country having strong armed forces
5. Hitler also knew that recruiting men into the army would reduce unemployment, further increasing his popularity amongst the German people
6. Hitler believed it was Germany's right to have an army of equal size to the other major powers in Europe
7. Hitler believed that Germany would have to rearm to achieve lebensraum - the policy required land to be taken from other countries and armed conflict was likely
8. Hitler believed that a stronger army was required to resist the Communist threat from Soviet Russia
9. Hitler was encouraged by the lack of firm action against him by Britain and France

63. *Candidates can be credited in a number of ways* **up to a maximum of 8 marks.**

Candidates must use knowledge to present a balanced assessment of the influence of different possible factors and come to a reasoned conclusion. **Up to 5 marks** are allocated for relevant points of knowledge used to address the question. **1 mark** should be given for each relevant, factual key point of knowledge used to support a factor. **If only one factor is presented, a maximum of 3 marks should be given for relevant points of knowledge.**

Possible factors may include:	Relevant, factual, key points of knowledge to support this factor may include:
Public opinion	1. majority of the public were still fearful of war after the huge losses suffered during World War One 2. public fears of war were further heightened by novels and films giving terrifying portrayals of the devastation that bombers would bring in any modern war/ these fears were further heightened by newsreel footage of the Nazi bombing of Guernica in the Spanish Civil War 3. public concerns over the cost of rearmament (welfare vs warfare) 4. there was a significant pacifist movement in the 1930s which was strongly against war 5. the problems of Czechoslovakia seemed remote to the majority of the public who cared little about a problem in a country far away inhabited by 'people of whom we know nothing'
German demands	6. Chamberlain believed that Hitler had a genuine grievance over the Sudetenland/Versailles was unjust and Germans should have some form of self-determination 7. Chamberlain felt Hitler had only limited demands/was a man he could do business with
Military reasons	8. Britain's air preparations were inadequate, with insufficient fighter planes, radar systems or anti-aircraft artillery 9. Britain's military chiefs stressed Britain's military weakness and the need to avoid a major war with Germany, Italy and Japan at the same time 10. the Munich agreement allowed Chamberlain to 'buy time' to rearm 11. ten year rule to avoid conflict
Lack of allies	12. France was unwilling to support conflict over the Sudetenland 13. USA was isolationist 14. Chamberlain did not trust Soviet Russia
Concerns over Empire	15. Australia, Canada and South Africa would not be easily convinced to support conflict over Czechoslovakia. 16. Empire was unwilling to fight eg disturbances in India
Other factors	17. Any other valid point

Up to 3 marks should be given for presenting the answer in a structured way, leading to a conclusion which addresses the question, as follows:

1 mark for the answer being presented in a structured way, with knowledge being organised in support of different factors.

1 mark given for a conclusion with a valid judgement or overall summary.

1 mark given for a reason being provided in support of the judgement.

64. *Candidates can be credited in a number of ways **up to a maximum of 6 marks.***

Candidates must make a judgement about the usefulness of the source and support this by making evaluative comments on identified aspects of the source.

1 mark should be given for each relevant comment made, up to a **maximum of 6 marks in total.**

- A maximum of **4 marks** can be given for evaluative comments relating to the author, type of source, purpose and timing.
- A maximum of **2 marks** may be given for comments relating to the content of the source.
- A maximum of **2 marks** may be given for comments relating to points of significant omission.

Examples of aspects of the source and relevant comments:

Aspect of the source	Possible comment
Author: Historian	More useful as he is well informed/expert
Type of Source: Book	More useful as it will have been well-researched
Purpose: To inform	More useful as it is likely to be a balanced/ comprehensive account of the events leading up to the outbreak of war in 1939
Timing: Published in 1989	More useful as written with the benefit of hindsight

Content	Possible comment
On 15th March 1939, German troops marched in to Prague and within two days Czechoslovakia ceased to exist.	More useful as accurately reflects the destruction of Czechoslovakia as a nation state.

On 29th March the British government gave Poland a guarantee to protect it against any threat to its independence.	More useful as accurately reflects Britain's issue of the 'Polish Guarantee'.
On 22nd May Hitler and Mussolini strengthened the ties between their two countries by signing an agreement which required them to help each other in time of war.	More useful as accurately reflects the signing of the 'Pact of Steel' between Germany and Italy.

Possible points of significant omission may include:
1. the day after entering Prague, Hitler declared Bohemia and Moravia as a 'Protectorate' of Germany
2. Slovakia remained independent but had to sign a treaty accepting German protection
3. Ruthenia was given to Hungary
4. France joined Britain in the 'Polish Guarantee'
5. just days following the 'Polish Guarantee', Hitler gave secret orders for the German army to be ready to invade Poland by 1st September
6. in August, Germany and the Soviet Union signed the Nazi-Soviet Pact whereby they agreed not to attack each other and to divide Poland
7. on 1st September, German forces attacked Poland
8. both Britain and France issued ultimatums to Hitler to withdraw German forces from Poland or face war
9. Hitler did not respond to the ultimatums and on 3rd September Britain and France declared war on Germany

Section 3, Part I, World War II, 1939-1945

65. *Candidates can be credited in a number of ways **up to a maximum of 6 marks.***

Candidates must make a judgement about the usefulness of the source and support this by making evaluative comments on identified aspects of the source.

1 mark should be given for each relevant comment made, up to a **maximum of 6 marks in total.**
- A maximum of **4 marks** can be given for evaluative comments relating to the author, type of source, purpose and timing.
- A maximum of **2 marks** may be given for comments relating to the content of the source.
- A maximum of **2 marks** may be given for comments relating to points of significant omission.

Examples of aspects of the source and relevant comments:

Aspect of the source	Possible comment
Author: Sailor	Useful because the sailor was an eyewitness
Type of Source: Interview	Useful because it provides honest personal opinions
Purpose: To inform	Useful because it gives a balanced account of the events
Timing: May 1940	Useful because it is from the time of the evacuation from Dunkirk

Content	Possible comment
Soldiers coming back without equipment	Useful because it is accurate - the army at Dunkirk had to leave a lot of equipment behind
Began to think it was the end of our way of life	Useful because it is accurate that many people did see it as a defeat
We knew we had the Navy, and that we could fight/ however we didn't know what our soldiers would be able to do if Jerry invaded, because they had nothing	Useful because although it is accurate that some people wanted to fight, others were worried that they could not continue the war

Possible points of significant omission may include:
1. British military had been pushed back to the beaches of Dunkirk by the advancing German army
2. British government requested all available civilian boats to travel across the Channel to evacuate the stranded British army
3. over 300,000 British and French soldiers rescued

66. *Candidates can be credited in a number of ways **up to a maximum of 6 marks.***

Candidates must show a causal relationship between events.

Up to a **maximum of 6 marks in total, 1 mark** should be given for each accurate, relevant reason, and a **second mark** should be given for reasons that are developed. Candidates may achieve full marks by providing six straightforward reasons, three developed reasons, or a combination of these.

Possible reasons may include:
1. Japanese were angered at the US economic restrictions placed on them after their expansion into French Indochina/Chinese mainland
2. Japanese were confident in their military superiority over the US
3. Pearl Harbour was chosen because the entire US fleet was based there
4. Japanese wanted to extend their influence into South East Asia/needed to knock out the US Pacific fleet in order to gain control of the Pacific
5. Japanese hoped to crush US morale by destroying its prestigious naval fleet
6. Japan hoped to destroy the US naval fleet in order to gain breathing space – aircraft carriers were a particular target
7. Japanese confident of the support of Hitler/Pact with Germany

67. *Candidates can be credited in a number of ways **up to a maximum of 8 marks.***

Candidates must use knowledge to present a balanced assessment of the influence of different possible factors and come to a reasoned conclusion. **Up to 5 marks** are allocated for relevant points of knowledge used to address the question. **1 mark** should be given for each relevant, factual key point of knowledge used to support a factor. **If only one factor is presented, a maximum of 3 marks should be given for relevant points of knowledge.**

Possible factors may include:	Relevant, factual, key points of knowledge to support this factor may include:
Effective Allied planning	1. deception plans led German intelligence to believe an attack would target Calais 2. use of dummy staging areas in Dover fooled the Germans 3. lessons learned after the failure of Dieppe invasion in 1942 4. Allies took advantage of bad weather to surprise the Germans
Allied resources	5. Allied superiority in men and equipment 6. use of Mulberry harbours 7. use of Pluto – pipeline transporting fuel across the Channel 8. gaining of naval and air superiority during the invasion 9. paratroopers landed the night before to secure bridges and roads near Normandy landing sites
Failure of German counter-attack	10. Communication problems caused German commanders to fail to react to the assault 11. German High Command remained fixated on the Calais area even after the attack on Normandy had started 12. German troops of poorer quality
Other factors	13. Any other valid point

Up to 3 marks should be given for presenting the answer in a structured way, leading to a conclusion which addresses the question, as follows:

1 mark for the answer being presented in a structured way, with knowledge being organised in support of different factors.

1 mark given for a conclusion with a valid judgement or overall summary.

1 mark given for a reason being provided in support of the judgement.

Section 3, Part J, The Cold War, 1945–1989

68. *Candidates can be credited in a number of ways up to a maximum of 8 marks.*

Candidates must use knowledge to present a balanced assessment of the influence of different possible factors and come to a reasoned conclusion. **Up to 5 marks** are allocated for relevant points of knowledge used to address the question. **1 mark** should be given for each relevant, factual key point of knowledge used to support a factor. **If only one factor is presented, a maximum of 3 marks should be given for relevant points of knowledge.**

Possible factors may include:	Relevant, factual, key points of knowledge to support this factor may include:
Difference in political beliefs	1. a clash of political beliefs led to division – Capitalism v Communism 2. a multi-party system operated in the West, while the Soviet Union and its satellites were one party states which led to tension 3. the Soviets claimed that Western societies were run by the rich, while the Americans claimed the Eastern bloc countries were totalitarian dictatorships which led to mistrust
Military reasons	4. the Soviets were angry that the Americans had not shared nuclear technology with them 5. the Soviets believed the atom bomb was used against Japan so that America could bully other countries 6. suspicions were raised as each side raced to develop new technology, eg the H Bomb 7. NATO vs Warsaw Pact
The Berlin Blockade	8. tensions rose in Berlin as the wartime alliance between the Americans and the Soviets broke down 9. the Soviets closed routes into West Berlin in an attempt to force the Western powers to leave which upset the West 10. the Berlin airlift showed the determination of the Western powers to keep hold of West Berlin which annoyed the Soviets 11. the Blockade cemented division by leading to the creation of West and East Germany
Soviet actions in Eastern Europe	12. Soviet troops occupied most of Eastern Europe and this caused tension 13. the Americans believed the Soviets had violated the Yalta agreement which annoyed the US 14. the Soviets claimed control of Eastern Europe was vital to stop future attacks on their homeland and resented Western interference
Other factors	15. Any other valid point

Up to 3 marks should be given for presenting the answer in a structured way, leading to a conclusion which addresses the question, as follows:

1 mark for the answer being presented in a structured way, with knowledge being organised in support of different factors.

1 mark given for a conclusion with a valid judgement or overall summary.

1 mark given for a reason being provided in support of the judgement.

69. *Candidates can be credited in a number of ways **up to a maximum of 6 marks.***

Candidates must make a judgement about the usefulness of the source and support this by making evaluative comments on identified aspects of the source.

1 mark should be given for each relevant comment made, up to a **maximum of 6 marks in total.**
- A maximum of **4 marks** can be given for evaluative comments relating to the author, type of source, purpose and timing.
- A maximum of **2 marks** may be given for comments relating to the content of the source.
- A maximum of **2 marks** may be given for comments relating to points of significant omission.

Examples of aspects of the source and relevant comments:

Aspect of the source	Possible comment
Author: Journalist	useful because he was an eyewitness
Type of Source: Newspaper	more useful as it should accurately reflect opinion at the time/less useful because it only gives British view
Purpose: To inform/persuade	More useful as it gives a detailed account of events during the Hungarian revolution in 1956/ less useful as he may exaggerate the level of support for the revolution
Timing: 23 October 1956	useful because it dates from the time of the Hungarian revolution

Content	Possible comment
Rebellion against their Soviet masters/Send the Red Army home	more useful as it is accurate, Soviet occupation was deeply unpopular
We want free and secret elections	more useful as it is accurate, people were tired of Communist/ one party rule
Demanding the sacking of the present government	more useful as it is accurate, the old regime was associated with corruption

Possible points of significant omission may include:
1. the Hungarian secret police were hated
2. many wanted repression of the Catholic Church to end
3. central control had stifled economic growth
4. Krushchev's move away from Stalinism led Hungarians to believe the Soviets would allow them to exercise more independence
5. many in Hungary believed the Americans would give support to their revolution

70. *Candidates can be credited in a number of ways **up to a maximum of 6 marks.***

Candidates must show a causal relationship between events.

Up to a **maximum of 6 marks in total, 1 mark** should be given for each accurate, relevant reason, and a **second mark** should be given for reasons that are developed. Candidates may achieve full marks by providing six straightforward reasons, three developed reasons, or a combination of these.

Possible reasons may include:
1. America was trying to supply a war 8,000 miles from home which made it very difficult for them
2. the Vietcong were able to make use of local knowledge/ familiarity with the terrain which gave them a clear advantage
3. many Vietnamese gave shelter to the Vietcong/it was very difficult for the Americans to identify the enemy
4. the Vietcong were highly motivated as they were fighting to drive out invaders from their country
5. the morale of US soldiers was very low and this reduced their combat effectiveness
6. most Vietnamese wanted to see the defeat of the US and the corrupt South Vietnamese regime
7. the brutality of the Americans (eg My Lai Massacre) alienated the Vietnamese

Acknowledgements

Permission has been sought from all relevant copyright holders and Hodder Gibson is grateful for the use of the following:

Source A: An extract from 'History of the Reformation in Scotland' by John Knox (public domain) (Model Paper 1 page 4);

Source A: An extract from 'History of the Union' by Daniel Defoe, 1709 (public domain) (Model Paper 1 page 5);

Source A: An extract from 'The Glasgow Reporter', 4 March 1846 (public domain) (Model Paper 1 page 6);

Source B: An extract from 'Modern World History' by Ben Walsh, published by John Murray 1996 © Hodder Education (Model Paper 1 page 7);

Source A: An extract from 'The History of Mary, Queen of Scots' by F. Mignet (public domain) (Model Paper 2 page 4);

Source B: An extract from 'The Emperor's New Kilt' by Jan-Andrew Henderson, published by Mainstream, 2000 © The Random House Group Ltd. (Model Paper 2 page 6);

Source A: An extract from 'Scotland: A New History' by Michael Lynch, published by Pimlico, 1992 © The Random House Group Ltd. (Model Paper 2 page 7);

Source B: An extract from 'Women's Suffrage: A Short History of a Great Movement' by Millicent Fawcett, 1912 (public domain) (Model Paper 2 page 7);

Source A: An extract from 'Waterloo to the Great Exhibition' by Colin McNab and Robert MacKenzie, published by Longman, 1982 © Pearson Education (Model Paper 2 page 9);

Source C: An extract from 'Race Relations in the USA 1863–1980' by Vivienne Sanders, published by Hodder Murray, 2006 © Hodder Education (Model Paper 2 page 12);

Source A: An extract from 'Inside The Third Reich' by Albert Speer, 1970 © The Macmillan Company, New York (Model Paper 2 page 13);

Source B: An extract from 'Turning Points in History – The Abolition of Slavery 1863' by Janet Riehecky, published by Heinemann, 2002 © Capstone Global Library Ltd. (Model Paper 3 page 12);

Source A: An extract from 'People and Power: Germany' by Ian Matheson, published by Hodder & Stoughton, 1999 © Hodder Education (Model Paper 3 page 13);

Source B: An extract from 'Weimar Germany and the Third Reich' by J.F. Corkery and R.C.F. Stone, published by Heinemann, 1982 © J.F. Corkery and R.C.F. Stone (Model Paper 3 page 13);

Source A: An extract from 'History of the Russian Revolution' by Leon Trotsky, published by Pathfinder Press, 1932 (public domain) (Model Paper 3 page 14);

Source B: An extract from 'Dear Francesca' by Mary Contini, published by Ebury Press © The Random House Group Ltd. 2003 (2014 page 6);

Source A: 'The War Memoirs of David Lloyd George', 1938, published by Odhams (public domain) (2014 page 7);

Source A: An extract from 'Black Peoples of the Americas', by Nigel Smith published by Oxford University Press, 1995 (2014 page 10);

Source A: An extract from a report on housing in Manchester, written by a doctor in 1832. Taken from 'The Report from the Poor Law Commissioners on an Inquiry into the Sanitary Conditions of the Labouring Population of Great Britain, London, 1842' by Edwin Chadwick (2014 page 11);

Source A: An extract from 'From the Cradle to the Grave: Social Welfare in Britain 1890s–1951' by Simon Wood & Claire Wood, published by Hodder Gibson 2002 (2014 page 12);

Source B: An extract from 'Leaves from an Inspector's Logbook', by John Kerr. Published by Thomas Nelson (2015 page 17);

Source A: An extract from 'Lark Rise to Candleford' by Flora Thompson, published by Oxford University Press, 1939 (2015 page 18);

Source A: An extract from 'Roads to War: The Origins of the Second World War, 1924-1941' by Josh Brooman, published by Longman, 1989 © Pearson Education (2015 page 26).

Hodder Gibson would like to thank SQA for use of any past exam questions that may have been used in model papers, whether amended or in original form.